WAITING *for the* KICK

WAITING
for the KICK

A Midwife's Grief *and* Rebirth in Africa

SHEILA KIMBLE-HAAS

SHE WRITES PRESS

Content Warning

This book includes depictions of attempted suicide as part of a character's journey through grief and trauma. These scenes may be distressing for some readers. Please prioritize your well-being as you engage with this story.

DEDICATED TO:

Dr. Richard Charles Haas II and to all the avian melodies that grace my most vulnerable days, their calls resounding with screeches, chirps, or hoots—a reminder, as he once mused, "I shall return to greet you as a bird."

CONTENTS

PART 3: RUNNING INTO MYSELF

Give me my Romeo; and, when he shall die,
Take him and cut him out in little stars,
And he will make the face of heaven so fine
That all the world will be in love with night
And pay no worship to the garish sun.
—SHAKESPEARE

PROLOGUE

September 2010

Everything smelled like dust in Sudan.

Despite seeking refuge beneath the canopy of what I believed was an acacia tree, the heat still churned around my bare ankles. I lobbed the three-strand cotton rope of the baby sling over the highest reachable branch. A simple canvas tool, with two cutouts for their legs, allowed us to weigh children. It hung on a circular-faced dial with a long sticklike needle that bounced with each puff of wind. The sounds I now identified as African encased the surroundings: lively chatter of mothers in various dialects, an occasional bleat from a goat, and the wails of children longing to be elsewhere.

No matter how often I blew my nose, dry earth settled in my nasal cavities and crowded my passageway with dust boogers. I was over the embarrassment of inserting my index finger and retracting the uncomfortable foreign body. All the locals did it. Of the two seasons in Sudan, the rainy and the dry, the second was the most wicked. Each season divvied up its balance of blessings and burdens, but they still shared a commonality: oppressive heat and persistent flies.

When I first arrived in Sudan, I moaned about the flies. They appeared at mealtime, perched on my arms when I was in the middle of delivering a baby, and mocked me by landing on the rim of my coffee cup each morning. They taunted me at every turn, leaving me powerless to stop them.

My exasperation with the flies and their relentless buzzing was like the grief that drove me to join a medical humanitarian mission in Sudan. In my harebrained search for relief, I sought an alternative to help me forget "Pete," the moniker we gave to the uninvited disease that swooped in and ended the life of Ric, my young spouse, and my idyllic world. Since the evening Ric took his last breath, grief was a constant drone in my head. And just like the flies, when I told myself, "I can't take another nanosecond," the sound petered out. The buzzing vanished, and I falsely presumed it was gone. Then, an unexpected sweet memory resurfaced, enticing the grief to return, which forced a rerun of gut-wrenching memories that seemed to land on every exposed part of my body. This forced me into a never-ending cycle of trying to swat it away, making me feel utterly hopeless.

Ric's passing had gobbled me up and hurled me out into the world as a *relicta*. Death had transformed me into an odd, widowed character. I could still trace a fine outline of the old Sheila, but Sudan had not yet sketched my footpath.

So I remained.

Our medical team of expatriates and national staff traveled three bumpy hours to reach this village. My primary role in the mission was to teach the national staff how to practice obstetrics with limited resources, ensuring better outcomes when our organization was no longer there. Mothers and babies surrounded me, and on some days, we aimed to investigate cases of malnutrition when locals reported a community had been suffering from food scarcity.

No roads existed, no Google Maps—just Tut, our hired local driver, who drove like he had a built-in compass in his head. He also had a heavy foot and goosed the gas when the Land Cruiser approached a rough patch of ground. It put air under the butts of the national staff sitting in the back, encouraging them to egg Tut on when we approached the next rugged section. They were a beautiful group of humans who did not dwell on the "what ifs" or "the tomorrows" but let the moments of today's laughter lead the way.

We passed cattle camps, emaciated dogs, clusters of *tukuls* with inky smoke rising from their fires, and naked kids running about. I noticed deerlike creatures camouflaged in the scruffy bushes and peculiar scavenger storks dressed in feathers resembling tuxedos waddling around, looking for sustenance. Some remarkable sights, reminders of all there was to see when I stayed present.

"Hey, Sheilee, there are lots of mamas and babies here for evaluation," yelled Moses over the commotion. His straight white teeth flashed between his upturned dimples.

The national staff had already organized the group and formed a queue before me, a sea of mothers and babies. *How many of these babies "kicked their way out" in our delivery room?* I laughed. Unexpectedly, the intensity of the wind and the group's voices surged. The mothers scurried to turn their backs to shield their children from the encroaching dust devil barreling in from the North. I flicked the persistent fly from my cheek, covered my face with the end of my gauze scarf, and followed suit. Sudanese mothers were steadfast guardians of their creations. *Would my mother have done that for me?*

I coughed, flicked my scarf, and replied to Moses, "We will do our best to get to as many as possible."

The country's insecurity limited our time away from the base and set our curfew for returning to our village.

Like a well-oiled machine we began, a testament to our dreaded regularity of events like these. We used another simple colored tool, a MUAC tape measure, which stood for the middle upper arm circumference, placed around each child's arm. Measurement of green or yellow, we praised the mother in the Nuer language, "*Gat goa long*" ("Your child is good"), gave them a new mosquito net, and they went on their way. It was the red or orange that troubled us.

The temperature rose as I placed naked baby after naked baby in the cloth sling that dangled in front of me. Women had lots of babies here because the chance of a child surviving past the age of five was slim, making each birth a hopeful gamble at life against the odds.

Each mother, in turn, relinquished her baby to me, whether from a swaddle, her arms, or a head basket. Sweaty babies screamed for their lives and dug their tiny nails into their protectors as they tried to escape, screeching, peeing, and pooping from their fright. *It's going to be a long day.*

Then reality punched through.

It felt like the chaos of wrangling, squirming kids gave way to a new page where resistance dissolved under the degrees of the midday heat—no more tears, no more battles. Mothers began to tenderly hand over their babies, too sick to whimper—tiny, floppy bodies with only enough energy to force a mew-like sound. *Like a wounded kitten.* Babies so ill they could not support the weight of their heads as the glazed eyes of their mothers stared at a problem for which they had no solution.

The reality of Sudan.

My father told me when I was young and fussed over not wanting to eat the beef stew put before me, "Clean your plate, Sheila. You know there are starving kids in Africa."

He never lied, and his words floated through my mind as I lifted the next weightless child in my arms.

PART 1:
RUNNING AMOK

CHAPTER 1: SOON

December 2008

The iridescent Christmas garland strung over the doorframe in a perfect *U* swayed as the oncologist ducked under it and entered the exam room, but the message he carried, "Ric, you will die soon," knocked us sideways.

"I am sorry, there is nothing more we can do."

"Soon? What the fuck does that mean?" We exchanged glances across the exam room and spoke the words in unison.

"Soon," the doctor said. "Less than two weeks."

For eleven months, we had been holding our breaths ever since Ric's crushing diagnosis in late 2007. We knew how the end of the game would play out, but the timing of the final whistle felt like a cruel mystery.

I looked at Ric, sitting on the exam table, absorbing the news. At that moment, it felt like the walls of the clinic room exhaled, and then there was a suffocating silence. *He really is going to die.* His now-skinny arms sported a farmer's tan and an overflowing hospital gown, evidence that he still buzzed around on his John Deere tractor on his good days.

Chemotherapy had left its mark, like a dart trying to hit a flickering target, ravaging more than it could heal. By trade, Ric treated feet; but in his heart, he dreamed of dirt between his fingers, of being a farmer. Squashed dreams.

After thanking the oncologist for his help, Ric said, "This is really sad." The doctor nodded in agreement, looking at his shoes; no doubt something he did a lot in his line of work. Ric dropped his chin, sobbing, trying to comprehend and accept his destiny: You will die soon. A sharp, high-pitched whine buzzed in my ears, like a malfunctioning device that had taken up residence in my head, bouncing off the walls of my skull. I shook my head to stop it, but only my guttural cry remained. This pancreatic trespasser robbed him of his life.

Doctors told him along the way that "most patients with this diagnosis don't last this long." I didn't know how to react to that, grateful or mournful for those who passed sooner. Maybe Ric's "living longer than most" was thanks to a lifetime of staying fit. Ric now recognized there was no miracle in sight. His fight terminated, like the toxic treatments, the needles, the pretreatment optimism, and the posttreatment side effects. Not later, but *soon*, swirled in my mind.

There was a light tap on the door, and a nurse stepped into the room, explaining how she facilitated hospice services to come to our house. As she elaborated, her words became an incoherent, noisy conversation. My mind drifted to Ric's final wishes, the ones he shared with me days after his diagnosis in the fall of 2007.

His request came before he received any treatment, before the surgeon sutured a port into his chest wall, and before the chemotherapy set a fire on the nerves of his feet, keeping him awake at night and off-balance during the day.

"Sheil, I have four wishes," he said.

"Okay, tell me," I said.

I do not want to have this conversation.

I felt his hand tighten around mine as we moved closer to each other on the couch.

"First, I want to die at home, on my homemade couch, under a quilt," he said.

I nodded. "Okay."

"Second, please never bring a hospital bed into the living room and let people prance around me."

I nodded again.

"Third, I want to move closer to your dad and spend more time with him."

My father and Ric shared a relationship as close as that of a father and son, and this wish uprooted us from South Dakota to Upstate New York.

"And lastly, help me with the pain because I'm afraid of that."

"I will," I promised.

At that moment, his request somehow flipped a switch in my emotions.

To off.

Instinctively, I shifted into full Mama Bear mode to protect him like a cub. I promised myself I would fulfill his last wishes, to bite the bullet until the end, because I had the rest of my life to sort this out.

I quit my day job and plunged into the unknown. Over the past months, I reminded myself daily, *This is not about you. This is about Ric.* I wasn't trying to be a martyr; it was simply about rolling up my sleeves and helping my soulmate to the other side. In a way, it was an honor that he entrusted me with such a request.

I still didn't know if that was the "right" way to deal with death and dying, but at that time, it felt right. I pushed through it, held my shit together, carried out my *job*, and, dammit, I was determined to see it through.

But it wasn't finished, and I dreaded what was coming.

The doctor stood, said nothing, hugged Ric, and followed the nurse out of the room. What could he say? Goodbye? See ya later? Good luck? I bet on days like that he hated his job. I fumbled with the pamphlets the nurse gave us about hospice, knowing we would contact them as soon as we got home. Leaving the medical office, the staff questioned if we needed another appointment, not knowing what happened in the exam room. They were likely used to seeing the red eyes of the patients coming and going in their weekly sessions for a needle here, a lab there, a typical routine of trying to die later. We did not need one. "Soon"—our next appointment, our future.

As we passed into the hallway, we held each other, our soggy faces pressed together. We were oblivious to the other patients coming and going, those still trying to hold on to their hope. Our anchor to hope was severed as we drifted out to sea. No GPS.

Until now, we charted blocks of time like the rest of the world. We bantered with each other as we crossed paths in the hospital, with me making my way toward the delivery room and Ric headed to his clinic filled with feet needing attention. "One month until the next three-day weekend" and "five more patients, and you're done for the day" gave us something to anticipate. And now this unusual time-table—"soon"—a prediction for the time left on the earth, was unsettling. The end was inevitable, but we still clung to the hope that the doctor was a poor math student.

Two consonants sandwiched around double Os quantified Ric's trajectory. Upon Ric's diagnosis, we spoke of Ric's trip to somewhere unknown and untouchable, and my journey into the world as we know it. Together, we imagined the exciting and mysterious parts of our separate lives. There was no need to rehash our past narrative.

We huddled together as we passed through the revolving hospital doors, the doors Ric had passed through for the past months, trying to hold on. We sidestepped the walkway and made diagonal passes through the frozen yellow grass to our car. Together, we kept pace with a rhythmic crunch under our boots, avoiding the KEEP OFF THE GRASS sign.

Driving home, Ric, in the passenger seat, said, "You know, I have a simple job, dying . . . you are the one with the tough job." I continued to listen without comment. He added, "Don't change your ways, spirit, or sense of adventure." He ended it with, "You are the strongest person I know." The blurriness of my eyes distorted the lines on the road and forced me to pull the car to the berm.

Seatbelts still attached, we embraced; we were already missing each other.

When we finally unlocked, Ric looked at me with a wide-mouthed grin.

"Now, take me to McDonald's," he demanded.

"What?" I asked. "You are a vegetarian and haven't eaten meat for over twenty years."

"I don't think it matters now, do you?" he laughed.

For a second, our grief was untethered, and we laughed at the ridiculousness of our conversation.

"Big Mac, here we come," I said.

I made a quick U-turn on the gravel and pointed the VW toward the closest Golden Arches.

We scooted around the drive-through and collected our order from the takeaway window. The frigid winter day in Upstate New York forced us to park in a vacant lot and picnic in the car with the heat on full blast. Bite by bite, I listened to Ric's admiration for the beef he once loved.

"Oh my God, this is so damn good!" he said, wiping the ketchup from his chin.

Each french fry formed a ball of dread in the back of my throat.

He rapidly exhausted all his energy trying to eat a burger and said, "I'm ready. Can we go?" His fatigue was more potent than his hunger.

"Sure," I replied.

The scent of McDonald's filled the interior of our car. As I headed home, concentrating on the winding roads, my peripheral vision hinted that his satiety and the car's heat were enough to rock him to sleep. Deep breaths escaped his open mouth as his head, in a relaxed, prayerlike position, bounced softly on the passenger window. A few yellow, wrinkly fries lay scattered on his lap, while a grease-stained McDonald's bag holding a partially eaten burger teetered on the dashboard—a clear sign of his fast-food craving. I reached for his hand, trying to rid myself of this unrelenting terror. He looked so peaceful.

I glanced into the rearview mirror. *Ric may be right about the survivors having the most challenging job. My appearance proves that theory, and he is still alive.* I was long overdue for a haircut, with twin plums under each eye and a sclera injected with red webs. *What a hot mess.*

How can this be?

Less than a year ago, we pedaled our way across the USA via the Southern route—3,092 miles of hysterical conversations and dreams of our future fueled by a gazillion Snickers and liters of Coke. One of Ric's best virtues was his humor. When we passed through Mississippi, we came upon a white triple-D bra on the side of the road—an unusual hitchhiker still held its worth. Ric snatched it from the asphalt and positioned the underwire over his helmet. It flapped in the breeze for a few miles until the force of a passing semi whisked it away. Even mentioning a bra after that threw us into a fit of laughter. And the stories we invented about its origin were even more comical.

Arriving in Florida, we celebrated with a pint and fries at a local eatery. That night, we soaked in the tub and discarded our biking clothes. "My butt will be sore forever," I said.

"My calves will never look the same," Ric laughed as he chimed in—the fastest biker I knew, with the skinniest legs around.

When we crawled out of bed late the following day, Ric said, "I have this pain right here," pointing to his left side.

"Food will improve it; let's go find some," I said. But it didn't. The invader was already predicting our future, and the presumed innocent indigestion turned out to be evil.

I eased off the accelerator, flicked on my turn signal, and veered off Route 13 onto the county road leading to our farm.

Ric lifted his head and asked, "Hey, are we home?"

"Almost." Part of me didn't want to get home; the other part wanted to get it over with. I wanted Ric's suffering to stop. He faded back into a slumber for the remaining miles home.

Pulling into the driveway, I softly said, "We are home, baby."

"Oh good!" he said, yawning, unbuckling his seatbelt and smiling. *Always smiling.*

The following days after Ric's last oncology appointment and after the indigestion of McDonald's eased, we watched for clues. *Is that edema in his feet a sign?* I wondered.

"Do you think it's because I am peeing more?" or "What about this rash?" Ric asked. We waited and secretly waited for a rescue. Like the rhyme, *"Row, row, row your boat. Gently down the stream."* The song where you pretend you are in a boat, fake paddling through the currents of life. A jingle that teaches you if you paddle like hell and never give up, you can control the direction of your life. That brouhaha kind of stuff. *"Merrily, merrily, merrily, merrily. Life is but a dream."* Neither of us could find the oars.

The days ticked by, and it seemed his battery was losing charge. Everything slowed down. He curled up on the couch and idled between somnolence and a few spoken words. When he spoke, I tried to understand what he was saying, and when he slept, I watched. And then, one morning, the final blast of air strummed his vocal cords.

"Hey hey hey," he cleared his throat, pulling himself up to sit. "I love you, Sheila. I always have and always will." He returned to his side and pulled his Colorado quilt over his shoulders. Peaceful without a struggle, he slept his life away. Perhaps this was the beautiful side of death, sleep being a humane progression in which to part from the world. A motionless moment that only mocked sleep, without pain or struggle, just a well-deserved rest.

For the rest of his hushed days, I read to him from his favorite book: *Miles from Nowhere: A Round-the-World Bicycle Adventure* by Barbara Savage. His favorite piano pieces played in the background. Someone told me once hearing was the last sense to give up the ghost. I hoped. As George Winston tickled the ivories, the clock hands crawled methodically forward.

Why would the world discard such a beautiful human? I now wondered alone. Numbness was my shield, so I focused on logging each medication I gave to him, noting his reactions—my order within the chaos. I had a job to finish: to help him leave this earth pain-free, on his couch, under his quilt. In hindsight, it was my way of steering clear of the harsh reality that was coming very fast.

Forty-eight hours later, from his serene state, he took a few labored breaths, like the start of a meditation session— a release. I held my breath.

Is this it?

The noiselessness of the room made it clear he had no other breaths in the queue. The victor emerged, having triumphed with no need for a final battle. Precisely fifteen days after the word "soon" plummeted into our lives, I wrapped my arms around his still-warm body.

It arrived.

CHAPTER 2: RELIEF

March 2009

*H*ello, *beautiful Black Hills.*

I sat in a sagging-bottom canvas lawn chair smack-dab in the middle of a weathered deck perched on the mountainside of our golden years' property. Momentarily, I felt at ease surrounded by the usual neighbors: ponderosa pines, elk, coyotes, and a welcoming nighttime sky peppered with stars.

I want to remember this.

Will I?

Can I trust the everlasting allure of a magical world on the other side, as described by those who have never set foot there? The promised existence of cumulus clouds, tantalizing flute music, joyful reunions with lost loved ones, perpetual gaiety, and no pain?

The blustery wind with a low-pitched whistle carried me around the distant hills. *How can it feel both eerie and soothing?* It was creepy because tonight's destination was unknown to me, but soothing because I knew my pain would finally be gone. As I repositioned my hand deep into the pockets of my coveralls, a tiny plastic bottle rattled as my relief tapped the sides of the container.

These hills were sacred to but no longer owned by the Lakota Sioux, who named them He Sapa, or Black Ridge. Black now, but in the daylight, the tall, swaying silhouettes of the ponderosa pine that blanketed this area flaunted their elegance. And then, when the light withered, it accentuated their form and decolorized their deep green, turning the forest into a charcoal sketch. Those who lived here first gave it a perfect name: the Black Hills.

Just as those people were gone, so was my beloved. It had been ninety days since I slept beside his warm body, heard him slurp his tea and laugh, or wondered if he was still breathing.

The nocturnal breeze picked up speed and strength. Force-fully, I drew the frigid air into my nose. *Ah, the smell of damp pine, almost minty-like.* It was a bountiful fragrance that ricocheted amongst a cluster of trees, arcade-like, until it escaped and delivered its essence to those paying attention.

This place, our place, enlivened my senses.

I despised how grief wielded its power, dragging up all my unresolved issues and electrifying my already overwhelmed body. Perhaps the emotion felt inadequate on its own, needing to pull in other dastardly acts to add to the havoc, stripping me naked and stirring up the dust of unresolved insecurities and past traumas. I had no idea at that time it could act as a form of healing, nudging you to examine the broader perspective. Because at that moment, I only felt the burden of it all. The fresh pain of my present reopened old scars—ugly reminders from the dark past. The pain of her beatings was gone, but the unjustified labels I carried from my childhood remained. Insults given to me by her: Barb.

The woman who brought me into this world. It was clear to me that each of the acts of giving birth and nurturing a child required unique strengths.

Amid my whirlwind of emotions, thoughts of Barb kept resurfacing. She always made me feel like an encroaching vine entangled my feet, like I was a failed gardener, with her titanium spindles growing around my calves, tethering me to surrender. I couldn't help but remember the names she called me. *What would she be calling me, sitting here in my struggle?* Would she taunt me on the sidelines with a sly grin, saying, "I told you so, you will never amount to anything"?

A flood of indelible memories pushed their way into my mind.

I was a gangly beanpole of a teen when I noticed trouble brewing between my parents. It seemed like the family was on a collision course as the harshness of their night-time fights intensified. If I wasn't eavesdropping through the register in the second-floor hallway, I buried my head under my pillow to escape the noise and the feeling. The odd curiosity of children trying to decipher their parents' fights, perhaps wondering if they caused them.

When their shouting started, I felt culpable, believing that if I were a better-behaved daughter, their frustration wouldn't escalate. Now, I understand that children often incorrectly connect the dots in these situations. Still, in my innocence, I convinced myself their anger was entirely my doing, unwarranted self-blame for the turmoil that unfolded most nights.

When they hammered the FOR SALE sign into the ground by our mailbox, it was clear the big D was in their future.

Like a crafty business deal, they divided the proceeds from the farm equally. Dad got the truck; Mom got the car. My little sister and I got her. Preoccupied with her childish imagination, my young sister couldn't grasp the bigger picture. My older brother and older sister had already beat feet. Both were trying to prove something to the world: My brother was trying to impersonate Jacques Cousteau, and my older sister was performing duties as a wife. Dad escaped to a four-wheeled home and a job in the coal mines.

Mom got her new fancy house in the suburbs, away from the dairy cows and the drone of insects from the farm. She didn't wear white as she swore her vows for the third time. Perhaps this would be the charm. Her order of marriages went like this: Her first union brought my older sister into the world. She then married my father, with whom she had three children—my brother, my younger sister, and me. In her third and current marriage, her husband often worked, leading us to stay out of each other's hair. I wasn't sure what kind of bond I would form with the new step-father, but I couldn't help but wonder what would change with no dad around. And sooner than expected, concealed inside the walls of our new brick suburban house, my new schooling began.

Sweet sixteen.

Weeks after being forced to change zip codes, my bedroom door flew open and collided with the wall behind it. The echo of the noise made my heart pound; I threw off the covers and turned to look. *It must be night because the face on my Barbie light is still illuminated.* Earsplitting "Goddamn you, you rotten kid" bounced around the room like a pinball.

I rubbed my eyes as the obnoxious overhead light added to my confusion. Next to me stood a middle-aged woman with bottle-blond hair and piercing eyes gathered at the corners. Her dimpled thighs, below her cut-off shorts, looked like a thousand eyes staring at me. Wide-eyed and with a clenched lower jaw, her hands trembled at her side, not wanting to listen, as she told them just to be on standby. Exhaling, I wondered if tonight's storm might be mild because she did not hold her usual "teaching tools"—a wooden spoon, a bar of soap, a stick, a flyswatter, or another inanimate object. *Just her palms tonight.*

Years of familiarity with her unhinged behavior taught me the receiver was often not the instigator of the storm. Yet the move to the new house in the burbs somehow amplified her inner mayhem. A simple internal sparkle, unrelated to me, caused it. It could be as simple as a peanut on the floor, an overflowing laundry basket, or the telephone bill in the mail: a minuscule irritation that ignited her bonfire. I wanted her to love me, to adore me, to be proud of me, but one slap or another vile name turned me into a wooden soldier of "fuck you."

That night, one of many I wished I could forget, felt different. The atmosphere charged with a strange, unsettling energy. I couldn't put my finger on it. And then she began.

"How many times do I have to tell you to do things right?" she said as she wiggled her index finger before my nose.

My comforter still protected my body. I raised my voice and asked, "What did I do?"

"You know what you didn't do!"

Her skinny fingers blanched the skin on my upper arm as she steered me to a sitting position. Her face flushed, and her neck veins were blue and full. She filled her hand with my messy blond hair—a sizeable, greedy handful on the crown of my head. I rummaged through my sleepy mind to figure out which of her laws I broke. My head throbbed, but my follicles recognized this reused weapon. *I must gently comb my hair when I get ready for school tomorrow.*

I choked back my worthless tears, convinced Barb was an impersonator of a mother, a fraud to the role. Her behavior clashed with what I witnessed at my friends' homes. My reality was Mommy, Mother, Mom, Ma—evil destructor and destroyer of innocent souls.

"Get your ass out of bed," she bellowed.

Unable to comply quickly enough, I fell to her feet.

"Get up, you loser," she barked.

Her knotted knuckles returned to my head, but this time, it was not just a yank to get my attention but a full-on tug. My hair served as a tow bar, a way for her to pull me to her destination, to get me to where she believed the alleged crime transpired. The house was on fire with reactions—reactions to old triggers and old wounds the family never discussed or mended. So, secretly, in a big house, in the middle of the night, out of view of others' eyes, the innocent became the medium to absorb their assailant's hidden anger and loneliness.

The closed doors to the bathroom and her bedroom whizzed past me as she dragged me down the hallway to the kitchen. The speed and friction of the movement made me feel like there was a fire between my pajamas and the oak floors.

"Ouch," I said as my hip struck the corner of the baseboard and slowed my trajectory.

"You Goddamn kid," she shrieked.

Then silence, the vibration of molecules under me no longer felt on fire. Rolling over, I sat and saw my reflection in the oven's glass door. The faint smell of cooked onions from last night's supper remained. Gazing back at me was a skinny, blond-haired teen massaging her head, wearing flannel PJs with a tiny purple flower print. *Lilacs*, I thought.

She stood with her hands on her hips, sweat dripping from her neck wattles. Her open mouth exaggerated the vibrations of her staccato breathing. I cracked the door to my invented safe house and repeated my silent mantra: *You will not destroy me.* The outside could not touch me—abandoning reality for survival—no title to the screenplay inside my mind. This film was my foxhole, and I have watched it dozens of times without boredom.

So it began: A leafy oak tree surrounded by blooming daffodils that swayed in the sunshine, a bluebird sky with cotton-shaped animals, metallic butterflies searching for a landing pad, bees struggling to take off with their pollen-like socks, and the fresh scent of grass. I laid my words, anger, tears, and wishful thinking to rest there.

I must look dead from the outside. I unplugged all that circuitry for now. My dreamy, robot-like state to ignore, imagine, and endure—my go-to strategy.

It was unsettling to witness unfounded rage: frantic gestures, physical attacks, and verbal insults—razor-edged arrows crying out for a target. *Does a person in her state of mind hear, feel, or see what is before her eyes? Or does she possess a switch that gets flipped, identical to mine?* Only mine took me to a safe, magical place and blocked the ugliness of her dark one.

Interrupted by her voice, "Get your ass in that chair," I pulled myself up and sat on the floral cushion of the kitchen chair. She typically kept the chair in the dining room with five others, but moved one for the night's showcase. I was on the stand, and the cross-examination began.

"I asked you to clean the refrigerator, but you didn't."

Like a factory worker in an assembly line, she punched in and began her repetitive job. She grabbed one Tupperware after another. She removed each lid and threw it on the

Formica countertop. The food was her acrylics, a medium to artistically imprint her rage inside the lit, cold box. Her masterpiece adhered to the metal racks, the light, and the drawers: every nook and cranny. Smelly leftover meatloaf, moldy applesauce, a new container of sour cream, hamburger casserole from yesterday, and pickled eggs all transposed—a mishmash of fury. She finished painting the countertops and sink with the last plastic tub.

How could she have so much anger in the middle of the night? We should all be sleeping.

"It's your fault. Now do it right. You will clean everything, even if it takes until midnight."

She stomped down the hall, slamming the door of her bedroom. The storm was over, and being alone in this house guaranteed no demoralization. Parents can teach self-regulation skills to their children, but first, they need to learn them themselves. Without that know-how, the toxic cycle mutates. But then, the question that consumed me was how to unravel the mystery of why. *Why did I ignite her rage?*

I raised my hand and touched the crown of my head. "Oh, that hurts," I mumbled to myself. Repugnant odors filled the room, so I stood on my tippy toes and cracked the kitchen window. The perfume of the outdoors drifted by as the cool night breeze coerced the stench into the dining room. Stars carried out their twinkling dances while the fat moon observed. Night-loving insects sent messages to the world to continue to sleep. I rolled my sleeves past my sticklike elbows. A janitor for the outburst. Grotesque, but no more than the spectacle I had just witnessed.

After all these years, I found the answer to Barb's why. It had nothing to do with being a good or a bad kid. Her behavior stemmed from a hodgepodge of past regrets, unfulfilled hopes, a missing element of nurturing, and perhaps remembered errors. It was when the warm air met the cold air, and the unpredictable spinning tunnel wiped out the neighbor's barn. I used to think I would always feel responsible for her rage and carry the label of "loser" to my grave.

In the distance, the coyotes' yipping, barking, childlike screams grew louder, dragging me from one misery to another. A sound to alert those living in the forest that night had come. *What are they talking about?* Ric used to wear this cherry-red, long underwear union suit thingy to bed when we stayed here. It was usually chilly inside the camper. I teased him and called it his boy unitard. At the first sounds of the coyotes' nightly serenade, his six-foot, lanky frame, wearing his button-up nighttime uniform and his faithful Mountain Hardwear beanie, bolted outside onto the deck of the Rambler and stood right where I sat now and howled with them. Mocking them until they quieted and then returned to the bed, laughing that they did.

We built this deck five summers ago, making a porch for our two-tone tan 1970s camper, which now rested on wooden blocks, anchored firmly to the earth with zero probability of ever seeing double yellow lines. The pressure-treated wood was now gray and cracked from the elements—a short-term solution to extend our living space while we masterminded our retirement strawbale home. This RV was our temporary weekend shelter. Indecipherable markings on the rear of the RV—the *H*, and the *R*, were missing, leaving only a faint "oliday ambler." Otherwise sturdy, she stood the test of time, nicknamed the Rambler.

During the week, our jobs held us two hours south of the Rambler. We began our quips most Friday afternoons, passing each other hurriedly in the hospital corridor.

"Want to hook up for the weekend, Madame?" Ric flashed his big, toothy grin.

Me forcing a deadpan expression and slowly walking away, I turned around and teased, "I am off to the Rambler. Want to join me, Big Daddy?"

He shot back, "Oh yeah!", lifting himself into the air, like the luck of the leprechaun, tapping both heels together. As his white lab coat swirled behind him, he hurried down the hall to finish his day. The faster we finished, the quicker we would be on the road.

"Ready to go?" Ric would ask as I climbed into the SUV.

The Great Danes were first in the vehicle and settled in their designated seats. On the drive to or from, Ric would remark, "I can't wait until we live there full time, Sheila. Can you imagine how neat it will be to use the sun, wind, and earth to support our existence?"

But until that came to fruition, it served as our weekend and holiday go-to place—a dream in progress.

Most days on the mountain, we built fences or monkeyed around with other tasks. But at the first hint of sunset, we grabbed our beat-up lawn chairs and two cold beers to watch the kaleidoscope of fading colors of the day—a non-negotiable moment. After our nightly appreciation for the beauty of this area, the cool nighttime air pushed us inside the RV. Inside, we filled the hours creating less-than-impressive canned meals on the tiny gas burner, played cards, read books aloud, and tried to catch a few radio waves from Rambo Jo on a clear night. Then, poised like two interlocking puzzle pieces, we snuggled on our knobbly futon until the sun positioned itself above and told us we needed to start our new day. We had our never-burdensome routine for weekends and holidays, grateful for our luck and the life we built together.

But that little tap on our door out of nowhere changed our luck and lives in late 2007. It wasn't until we returned home a week after the biking vacation that the second faint "knock, knock" arrived at Ric's door.

The second sign was when Ric approached me in the kitchen and asked, "Hey, Sheil, do my eyes look yellow?"

"Holy crap," I replied.

We nervously laughed. "I guess I shouldn't wear green today, it will clash with my new eye color." We faked laughter again, but our matching grimaces lingered—dark sarcasm from medical professionals.

"Do you feel okay?" I raised my hand to touch his forehead.

"I feel fine. Just a little indigestion," he responded. This tall, wiry guy could devour an entire sixteen-inch pizza, burp twice, and ask, "Do you mind if I eat the leftovers from last night?"

"I am calling your doctor today," I said, picking up the phone while I ran through a handful of differential diagnoses. *I bet it's a stone in his common bile duct causing the jaundice.*

Forty-eight hours later, after a doctor's visit, a CAT scan, a slew of labs, and the dreadful news, his nausea, vomiting, and uncontrollable abdominal pain amplified the "knock, knock," wiping out the "I feel fine." The malady we dubbed "Pete" invaded our sanctuary with brute force and vengeance. This noiseless parasite planned his demise for years. Soundlessly and with precision, extending its sinister appendages outward from Ric's pancreas.

"Hi there, Mr. Liver. Do you mind if I move in?"

"I need just a little space."

Before any outward symptoms showed their face, Pete, this slimmest of slime, bartered for just a little more elbow room here and there—one organ after another.

Peritoneum. Colon. Liver.

"Excuse me, a little more room, please"—with an underlying intent to evict all normal functioning. We both understood Pete's Machiavellian maneuvers would eventually make him the victorious landlord a year later.

Another shrill cry of the coyote and a flash of bitter wind hit my wet cheeks. *I can't believe this happened.* I zipped the front of my black-insulated Carhartts, trapping as much heat as possible. Typically, two lawn chairs occupied this space, but now, just one. Twins, currently separated. Its mate under the trailer, crammed next to an old red gas container. No doubt, it was its final resting place.

I pulled my misfitting hand-knit beanie down over my ears. It was too big—one of my first failed knitting projects—but I liked the mix of purples and greens, so I wore it. The cold chilled my bones, and I felt a sharp prickling in my hands from the elements.

Over the past few months, my growing baggy clothes made me more susceptible to the frigid air. I reached toward the dirt-stained cooler and wrestled to open the lid. Beer bobbed on the ice, and I plunged my hand into the cold water for another. I reached into my right-hand jacket pocket, and my fingers traveled over the cylindrical bottle, feeling the distinct ridges of the childproof cap.

Not yet. A cigarette first.

Pushing the container aside, I removed my pack of smokes deep in my pocket. *Habits never die.* With a click of the lighter, I inhaled the familiar fumes of a Marlboro Light. Several years ago, I quit smoking, but the desire to smoke just one pack returned with a vengeance. *Who fucking cares?* This cigarette asked the same question as Ric's Big Mac: Does it matter now? Alone, I didn't laugh at this dark humor.

I used to love the click of the lighter, pulling outside air through the cigarette, causing the end to spark and snap. Mainstream smoke filled my lungs, and I tilted my head, shooting the fumes toward the stars. My head spun, identical to my virgin childhood lungs behind the barn—experimentation then, now comfort. The odd friend in times of need, the one who was always there, reminisced like an ex-lover.

Once, I was counseling a patient about the risks of nicotine. *It feels a bit ironic to think about that right now, holding a cigarette.* She told me, "Smoking is the most intimate relationship I have ever had with an inanimate object." Words I never forgot. The ingenuity of Philip Morris. The power of less than four inches tightly rolled around the body craving nicotine. That seductive crackling crimson end, urging us to take another toke.

Yep, and just like that, my right index and middle fingers, ruddy from the cold, pinched together my old addiction. Trickles of water escaped the corners of my eyes again. The constant leak, which no plumber could repair, obscured the moon's outline. Alone with the coyotes. *Fucking alone.* I swallowed more liquid courage. The fizz of the cold drink burned the back of my throat.

Over the past few months, friends tried to smooth the bumps since Ric's death.

"What doesn't kill you will make you stronger," some said. Turning my head, I'd roll my eyes.

"Yeah, right," I murmured.

Family members said, "The sun will come out someday." I puffed away their words.

Colleagues told me, "Soon, you will be able to remember Ric without tears." *Sure*, I silently doubted. Now, I know they all just wanted me to feel better and move on.

Not all the opinions ruffled my feathers. Lisa, my BFF, gave me the best advice after Ric died.

None.

She had this uncanny ability to listen to my same recycled storylines, inundated with my unpredictable emotions. Whether over the phone or in person, she was resolute. She was a reversible goodness. Once, I sent her a card depicting our friendship. It went something like this: A messy-haired woman knocks on the door of her friend, and as the friend opens the door, she says, "I killed the bastard." The friend who opened the door replied, "Let me get the shovel." Lisa had my shovel.

After Ric's death, my initial phone call was to her. Separated by thousands of miles, we shared an intimate silence, our tears weaving a tapestry of collective sorrow. Weeks after his death, when others offered generic assurances in phone calls and emails—"Sheila, call me if you need anything"—she courageously appeared at my doorstep. A beacon of solidarity. She stood knocking on the door with a small backpack slung over her shoulder, offering to help and embody it. She brought strength to face whatever came next, a willingness to sit over strong coffee and put her fear and grief aside as we navigated the uncharted waters.

Everyone else tried to help, but their words felt shallow, overused, and abused. Proof that nothing could help this pissed-off, slightly bitter widow. I willed him to live, and it failed. Desperate, I even prayed to God, vowing I would check in more often if he helped me out just this once.

Both of us failed to keep our word.

My head spun from the deep inhalation of the burning nicotine. A few yards from the deck, I saw my half-frozen SUV tracks in the mud next to the circle of rocks holding the dying fire. Part of me wanted to put another log on it, but I refused to walk behind the camper to dislodge another frozen log from the pile. The deep tracks looked like they came from one of those monster trucks. I pictured myself sitting in a similarly oversized beast grinding the gears while mud slapped the windshield and the scratchy radio played my same song, "No Traction, No Help in Sight." And that same Goddamn line, Ric is dead, "blip," Ric is dead, "blip." *Where did the rest of our story go?* "Blip."

Unfixable blips.

The last "blip" I fixed was during my childhood.

Growing up, we had a record player inside a waist-high cabinet in the same room as the piano. I loved our Alvin and the Chipmunks Christmas vinyl. But right at the part when Theodore, Simon, and Alvin took to the microphone, a *blip, blip, blip* started. The needle jumped over the hidden obstacle. I discovered that taping a penny on the player's tonearm would encourage the stylus to find the correct grooves on the disc. It worked and was such an easy fix—then.

The racing thoughts in my mind slowed down, and the overwhelming shadow returned, *Release me, Goddamn it, please.* I had no fear of complete darkness, but I was scared shitless of the future. The angst of living felt unbearable. Others have told me, "Well, at least you don't have kids; that would be much worse." I initially thought, *Wow, that was heartless,* but maybe they were on the mark. It did simplify this moment. Little did they know my real reason for being childless: "You would never be a good mother" was already imprinted into my amygdala. More baseless words from Barb.

As the years have blurred most events, I can't recall the specifics of what precipitated her comments. I probably messed up; Barb got triggered and exploded in a physical and verbal tizzy. The welts she delivered faded, but her words stuck in my core. I learned that tossing your fears at someone else will never free you from your suffering.

I stamped out my cigarette and chucked it in the fire pit. Removing my glove, I reached into my pocket and emptied the contents of the orange opaque bottle into my hand. A pyramid of colorful chemicals, pilfered from every cabinet, stared back. All gathered for this moment, holding freedom. A sardonic copy, resulting from Ric's pain-relieving leftovers. Looking back, it felt like eons had floated by as if a different version of myself embodied the role of "Sheila." At that instant, fear eluded me. Yet, with hindsight, I quivered at the precipice on which I stood.

Once after Ric died, while commenting on a neighbor who ended their life, a female relative told me in her overconfident voice, "You know, suicide is a selfish act." Recalling her words at this moment caused a proliferating heaviness that constricted me like a boa, emptying each of my alveolar sacs of the invisible life-giving gas. Tighter and tighter, it made me lightheaded and cyanotic. I now grasp the intricate and misunderstood nature of this unimaginably lonely, tragic moment. Even more, I wondered if it was greedy to want to slough off the layer that imprisoned me in an endless, painful loop. I didn't think so; I called it relief.

I am so tired. I just want to sleep.

CHAPTER 3: WET TISSUES

June 2009

Sitting at the picnic table in the backyard of my Upstate NY home, I unrolled the sleeves of my denim shirt, shielding myself from the briskness of the early morning air. When I pulled up to the Rambler three months ago and parked my SUV—what seemed like a lifetime ago—I was walking a confident path toward freeing myself from the ache of my loss. That failure plunged me deeper into defeat, more profoundly than ever before—loser with a capital *L*. I was on the brink of success but fell short of my goal.

Twelve weeks after my failed attempt to leave this planet, I went through the motions, like coming outside to try to enjoy the morning.

It was just something I did.

As the buds of the surrounding trees burst forth into a canopy of lime green and the crocuses nudged through the clay, I knew June had arrived. Flashy dragonflies gracefully skimmed the pond's periphery outside the house, intermittently dive-bombing its center to quench their thirsts.

I have always loved bugs. They are fascinating creatures with an artistic mix of extraordinary craftsmanship. Some have golden beady eyes, dazzling wings in shades of the rainbow, flittering telescopic antennas, and long, spiny legs. Many, when threatened, show a different side, like the Red Man's spittle from a defenseless grasshopper or the acrid smell of a stink bug. Those without this superpower blend into the wallpaper—a facade to project strength and resilience when confronted with uncertainty.

Growing up on a farm in North Central Pennsylvania exposed me to a cornucopia of insects. Manure and overgrown foliage provided the perfect milieu. For me, childhood summers meant a quest to find a new species. With a screw-top quart jar under my arm, I ran from rock piles to cow patties to stacks of mildewed lumber behind the barn. I flipped things over, rooted in the newly exposed moist dirt, and searched for bug after bug. After my catch, I tracked down my father, a curious creature himself.

"Dad, what do ya think it is? Does it bite?"

"Let's look," he'd say, placing his hammer on the workbench, allowing me to dump the bug into his thick, fleshy palm.

After briefly discussing its funny-colored belly, the three pairs of wings, or the dangerous-looking mouth, he'd remark, "I think we should let this guy go. We don't want him to die. What do you think?" I loaded him back into the jar and dumped the contents on the grass before the shed, sprinting off for another round.

Whenever I had the chance, I eagerly caught, examined, and released any bugs I stumbled upon, following my dad's advice to set them free before they died. That was, until my curiosity—and a kid's dare—pushed me in another direction. I must have been in grade school when a brassy boy told me at recess, with a challenging smirk, "I bet you can't put a fly on a leash."

"What?" I rolled my eyes and gave him a knuckle bump on the shoulder.

"Yeah, pull a hair out of your head and tie it gently around its neck."

"Yeah, right," I responded, wondering if it was true, and walked away to join the others at the monkey bars.

Once I got home from school, I grabbed my quart jar, captured a few innocent flies, and headed to the shed next to the house. I yanked a few hairs out of my head. After making a tiny loop, I placed it around the neck of the first fly—my first attempt, Marie Antoinette–like. On the second try, I tied it tight enough to keep the fly from taking flight, leaving his head intact. It kept trying to soar, a very bizarre walking-the-fly game, as I held the end of my hair. I chuckled in a strange, cringey way and quickly let the harmless insect free. As a kid, I saw it as a dark and cruel act.

Now, looking back with a bit of embarrassment, I wonder what drove me to do it. I never repeated it and dismissed the boy who later asked if I had tried the "fly trick." The dare piqued my curiosity back then, but I now understand it was about more than that. It was my early need to try to control something. Anything. Years later, I tried the same way to control my grief, yet it clung to me like a stubborn pest. No matter where I went or what I did, it refused to be subdued, resisting my every attempt to rein it in. No lasso was big enough to hogtie the grief, make it behave, or walk the line. It was beyond my control.

When I wasn't filling my jar, I spent hours sitting on the cold concrete of the machine shed next to a raised tractor or a vehicle. Dad's two stocky legs poked out from under the three-ton problem above him, and the toes of his muddy boots pointed toward the sky. I was the scrub tech, anticipating the needs of the surgeon.

"Hand me the three-eighths-inch crescent wrench, Sheila. . . . Now, the small torque wrench," he asked.

Afterward, while he wiped his greasy hands on the T-shirt rag laden with past projects, his quick nod of approval made digging through the greasy, smelly tools worth it. We talked a lot about things, things that did not include feelings. It felt mostly okay. I wondered later if his avoidance of the apparent issues allowed his mind to roam freely, affording him the mental space to devise his means of a getaway.

At night, with his backside in his chair, a pair of shiny Brylcreem comb tracks swooped back from his temples, and a clean white T-shirt signaled work was over for the day. I remember brushing past him in his overstuffed chair, waiting for his sausage-like fingers to pick me up and place me next to him. The pat on my knobby knees was my life buoy—a sacred moment from the scary waters of Barb, the vine with fewer pickers and gentler thorns.

But it wasn't always peachy with him either. I hated the times growing up when he marched me into the cellar and beat me because Barb told him to do it. Like a whipped soldier getting orders from the captain, he got up from his chair, directed me down the cellar steps, and obeyed his duty. His burly hands left their mark on the backsides of those who shared his DNA. But somehow, I always gave him a get-out-of-jail card. Receiving his love and attention half the time was preferable to not receiving any.

When we spoke about this in my thirties, I asked him

why he beat me when Barb told him, but loved me when she wasn't looking. He gave me love, but it came at a price. Why did he not stand up to her and protect me? He never really answered the questions. I got the impression he was ashamed. Each time I broached the subject, he paused, looked at the sky, and commented on whether it seemed like rain. I doubt he knew which direction to take, but being married to her likely pushed him to follow the path of least resistance. Plus, I always perceived he saw me as more forgiving than her. Ric, on the other hand, independent of Barb, chose the right path—me. Two men I loved each took a different route, shaped by the circumstances they faced.

I always wondered how my parents became one. Once, I asked Dad how they met. "On my first date with your mother, we saw *Gone with the Wind*." Then he paused, laughed, and said, "I should have been." I never got more than that and thought it was his typical humor reacting to his disappointment from unfulfilled aspirations. But the end game was how we process that remorse, bitterly or gently. Dad was the latter.

The humidity rose as the sun conquered the sky, and I shoved my long sleeves back beyond my elbows. I tilted my coffee cup and realized it was empty, but I was too lazy to walk into the kitchen for more. Looking at the pond, the intense light illuminated one half while the other half shimmered with ripples that crashed against the lily pads. I spotted the dancing dimples of the six-legged water striders skating on the surface. *Hunting for mosquito larvae or searching for a mate.* Their long, spindly legs, covered with thousands of tiny hairs and lined with grooves that trapped air, allowed them to do the Jesus walk. I was aware of what lay in the bleached-out space of the pond, having just seen it, but now it was concealed from my view. This image created a striking contrast between the hidden and the obvious, a reminder of the mysteries lurking just out of sight.

Anticipation of my future washed waves of uneasiness over me. I wondered how my life would unfold. I had once mapped out detailed plans for my hopes and expectations. But as I reflected on those dreams, I couldn't help but feel a sense of loss, recognizing how many would remain unfulfilled without Ric by my side. No more shared sunsets at the Rambler, indulging in pizza, or those contagious belly laughs. Irreplaceable. Our anniversary was in June; now it was just another day, like the other 364 hanging on the calendar in the kitchen. In the past foggy months, I found myself searching but unable to pinpoint the triggers that caused my angst. Was it the month itself? Was it his bottle of cologne sitting next to the bathroom sink? Was it a framed tapestry we bought in China that hung in the kitchen? Was it looking at a half-filled, bear-shaped honey jar he used daily? Was it his fading smell on his pillow?

Actually, it was everything.

Without exception, every fucking single thing.

I understood why I wanted to take my life and why, in that first year without Ric, my singular conviction was a solitary pathway, a place free of torment. However, with time, that overarching wish to cease living slowly waned, resurfacing intermittently, still unpredictable, but now triggered by poignant reminders. That scary moment at the Rambler was just another failed attempt to calm my demons. Years later, I learned there was no shortcut, because the metaphorical monkey had a fierce grip.

So there I was, trying to find an alternative route forward

while simultaneously grappling with grief and the sting of defeat. Oddly, friends and family had returned to their daily routines, which made me feel like they had already moved on from Ric. It was as if I were the sole bearer of this burden, left to carry the weight of his memory alone.

My phone rang from somewhere in the house, and I felt a twinge of apprehension as I rose from the picnic table and made my way indoors. I became oddly obsessed with this newfound ambivalence toward my phone. Each ring was a double-edged sword: I wanted people to call, but I also wanted them to leave me alone. My iPhone's nonstop ringing since Ric's death taught me there were two types of callers, each requiring a different approach.

I named the first type Fiction. These were the ones I could fake: "I'm fine, yep, things are good," leading the conversation down the path of their further questions and, yes, to my additional lies. It was a get-in-and-get-out. And with them, before my last lie had zeroed in on their tympanic membrane, I was already fumbling for the "End Call" button.

"Help, I Need Somebody," the Beatles song blasted from my phone, an appropriate new ringtone I downloaded last week. My index finger was ready to turn it off when I saw the caller, Greg. He was in the other group, the hardcore Nonfiction group—those who knew me intimately and still loved me through madness and goodness. Plus, they filtered my bullshit and served as my pressure-release valve. For each conversation, I needed to weigh my neediness with the possibility of choking them with the same old story. I had ample sadness in my warehouse; I realized no one deserved all of it every time we spoke. The rules of gardening reminded me that an even thickness of nitrates fertilized the grass and allowed it to grow, but too much in one spot would burn the roots and turn the grass yellow.

So, I tried to spread my breakdowns, keeping track of who I last broke.

I quickly answered the call.

"How are you?" Greg asked.

Silence. That familiar bile taste.

"I am losing my mind."

There was more silence, and I wondered if he hung up.

Hopelessness leaked from my pores and paralyzed my vocal cords. For months I have heard, "It won't be long until you can think of him and smile"—bullshit advice sermons.

He listened to my sniveling, the tones of juicy nose blowing, and loud gulps while never offering false promises or interruptions. Greg listened without interruption as I tried to get it all out.

"I am so tired of this, Greg." One last honk into the tissue. "I feel like my feet are in concrete."

"I can't imagine how hard this is for you."

Silence. Gladys, the brindle Dane, appeared for a scratch on the head. I reached down and delivered one.

"Have you ever thought about going to counseling?"

Silence.

"Maybe it would be a good idea?" Greg gently offered.

Silence. *Who me? Me? I can't believe he thinks I need counseling.* I shook my head from side to side, knowing he couldn't see me. *Did he just say that?*

I was a kickass, in-charge kind of gal. Day after day in my profession, when the patients' dams overflowed, I was the one who offered options and solutions to their struggles. I was the master at solving other people's problems, a glass full of practiced solutions and propositions for others. The tables had turned; at forty-five years old, I found myself sitting there, my hair unkempt, nose dripping on my lap with a wrecking ball zipping past my temples. Earplugs jammed into my canals prevented incoming sound waves from trampolining off my eardrums. Stone-deaf to my advice. I should be strong enough to figure this out. I should be able to pick myself up by the bootstraps. I should possess enough life skills to escape this mess. But there has been a heist, and someone ran off with the shoulds.

"I will think about it," I told him, hanging up and stepping away from my device.

I lay on the rug; Esther, the ebony Great Dane, yawned from her rug in the kitchen's corner. Gladys followed my lead and snuggled beside me. Her head pressed on my belly.

A few weeks later, grâce á Google, I found a slew of therapists in Ithaca, New York—the closest town with generous options. I looked at their profile pictures, rosy pledges, and promises to sort me out. *Who would I be willing to cry in front of? Who could I trust to tell my deepest secrets to?* It was bizarre that my vanity and my vulnerability still sat on the top rung of my ladder of depression.

I chewed on my criteria as I scrolled through the psychological forum. Not too young (*could be inexperienced*), not too smiley (*could be lackadaisical*), not too old (*could be preachy*), not talking about metaphysical elements in their profile (*I never understood that*), and it had to be a woman. *Why a woman?* That was the same reason I chose a woman to do my Pap smear. *Because.* Reading through Amazon product-like reviews, I sifted out a woman with a solid portfolio. I shuddered to think my method trusted the advice of total strangers.

Finding her phone number, I unlocked my phone and dialed the 4.5 stars—the one who might be able to save my ass.

The following week, I arrived ten minutes before my appointment. I took a swig from my sticker-covered Nalgene
bottle. *I can't do this.* I glanced at my makeup-free face. My
crow's feet were more prominent than usual. *When was the
last time I curled my eyelashes? Let's go, Sheila.*

Marigolds lined the walkway and welcomed me to her
front door. Seconds after ringing the doorbell, a delicate
Caucasian woman appeared at the door. She dressed like
she was meeting an old friend, with a dainty, flowery scarf
around her neck. She smiled. "Come in. I am happy to
meet you."

She motioned me to the couch.

"I'll get us some water," she said, departing for the kitchen.

I took in the space—hordes of plants hanging in the windows, collecting the sun's rays. None of the leaves had that
spreading rust stain like mine at home. That warning sign on
the leaves just before they turned yellowish, shrunk into nothing, and fell on the floor. No Ouija board, dream catchers, or
incense swirling its magic in the room; she must be legitimate.

Oh, crap. I spied the white, fan-shaped "ultra soft"
waving at me from its rectangular cardboard box on a stand
next to me—this tissue box—the Walmart door greeter for
a psychologist.

She placed the small water bottle on the table closest to
me and sat on the same couch.

Her knees pressed tight together in a pencillike posture,
and she said, "I am so glad you are here." She seemed all prim
and proper, but her soft voice permitted my chin to quiver.

"What's happening with you?" she asked.

*Can't I get through the first ten minutes of this session
without a meltdown? Damn you, Greg.*

Her eyes tried to hold my gaze, but I took a deep dive
and looked at my toes poking through my sandals, my

weak attempt to take my mind for a walk. *I share those fat Kimble toes like my dad's.* He called it the fat-toe syndrome, stemming from our family genes. My mind chuckled, and then I refocused on her question.

Resting my hands on my damp forehead, I paused momentarily and squeaked out, "I feel so hopeless and powerless." Then it began.

I grabbed one tissue at a time, sometimes two, landing one after the other into the rapidly filling receptacle below the coffee table. One big old fat tear after another, I told my story.

A couple of weeks into the therapy, my counselor urged me to take on something Ric and I planned to do together. Her encouragement felt forced, but she had her reasons for suggesting it.

"You mean like our bucket list?" I asked.

"Exactly," she said.

I nodded and agreed to think about it.

Every session with my therapist left my burning question unanswered: How and why did certain individuals excel at the art of survival? Why did some sail and exceed all expectations, and others flopped on the couch with a bottle of gin, stinking to high heaven, wearing lint-covered sweats, and binge-watch *Breaking Bad*? Too often, the daily news highlighted the divide between the haves and the have-nots facing tragedy. Occasionally, we hear stories about some poor soul who rises to do something fantastic despite being down and out. Lacking money, support, and education, they single-handedly slipped into home base after hitting a home run. More often than not, they remain unnoticed. Silent survivors, strong as hell, are not seeking publicity; instead, they rely on their strength to find solutions. Rising from nothing, flicking off the residue of despair, knowing today is enough, and tomorrow is just tomorrow.

How do they do it?

Can I learn to anchor myself to the ground beneath my feet, inhale the air, feel the fabric in my pockets, and run my tongue over my teeth, savoring the last hint of mint toothpaste? Be in the now? To quietly observe my hands— the scars and wrinkles that log my journey? To embrace the present, overwhelmed by its beauty, not by my past disappointments? I have to find the keys that allow me to be bombarded by the richness of the present moment rather than by regrets about what could have been.

When I asked my therapist why most people are never satisfied with their lives, she answered my undying curiosity: "Humans are complicated." The other issue that surfaced during those months on her couch was how my shattered expectations disrupted my life. Expectations: Ric would still be alive, and we would build our straw-bale home at the Rambler while planning our next international adventure. My failing assumption. My all-knowing belief about my future, what I have earned, and what I deserve. A rigid sense of entitlement far from reality.

We all expect life to be rosy. We expect our kids to go to Yale, our husbands to grow old and eventually stop snoring, and a CEO in our future title. Then, we handcuff our expectations to our identity and hit the "Control" button. Now, they become more than just a future hope; they become part of our fiber. Kevlar. Clinging to the idea that if we just hold on tight enough, everything will fall into place as intended. Yet when it doesn't, we find ourselves disheartened as the world we tried to control slips away. I had not yet grasped the beauty of hope that lies in a perspective filled with gratitude, adaptability, authenticity, and optimism for the future.

It hadn't dawned on me that a crucial element of survival was rooted in one's internal fire. We discussed this during my counseling sessions, and the therapist underscored how my past choices and experiences would serve as building blocks for shaping my future.

She said, "You have always harbored an internal fire. It is still there even after Ric's death. Merely on hold for a moment."

The spark that pushes us forward, even as we see the danger on the horizon? That innate ability to gather our kindling while others, without the flame, peer through a narrow, cracked window, waiting for the cords of wood to be delivered? Those who look at life as a puzzle, their job to solve. That dig-in, smoke-billowing-from-the-ears, nothing-will-knock-me-out attitude. The same people who get up repeatedly, with the avidity of conquering each day, while laughing at the mud stuck on the soles of our shoes. An outlook that keeps tomorrow off today's agenda. No blame for parents, society, or misfortune. An ability to storm their own castle. I wasn't sure I believed my counselor, but secretly, I hoped she was right.

If this fire was an across-the-board trait, I wondered if outsiders could also impact these flames. Do we all have destroyers and caretakers of these fires? Could another stomp on one's internal fire and leave them with a smoldering pile of no gumption?

Annihilate it? For sure, Barb tried.

Moreover, was it possible to stumble upon someone who becomes a custodian of our blaze? *Indeed, that was Ric.* He knew when to "put another log on the fire" because he instinctively recognized my dying embers. He possessed the keen ability to spot my orange, pulsating searchlights begging for more fuel as the edges of each hot coal emitted gray, drifting ash. The one always on the lookout. A watchman who silently fed my crackling, hissing, and spitting coals, giving oxygen to the golden and blue flames as they licked the wounds of the past.

Before meeting Ric, it felt like my fire was nearly extinguished. After his death, it was similar, but I held on to the belief that I still had lingering embers—glowing coals waiting for more fuel, ones I needed to rekindle tenderly but did not know how.

I wondered how long it would be before my waning fire sizzled and roared into a grand bonfire, casting ginger sparks into the dark sky to join the dance with the fireflies.

CHAPTER 4: POLE, POLE

Beginning of December 2009

A month after that bucket-list conversation with my therapist, I woke up tired, attempting to lick my lips but unable to find any moisture. *Where am I?* I shuffled through the first thoughts that came to mind, allowing the rest of my body to wake. Then I had a whirlwind body scan, feet toasty in my new wool socks, a little bitty caffeine-withdrawal headache, my mouth parched, and yes, I had to pee again. I stretched my legs and thrust my toes to the end of my sleeping bag. *Ouch.* My burning thighs and right big toe broadcasted my whereabouts.

Five other climbers and I would test our fortitude in grappling to the top of Mount Kilimanjaro, 19,341 feet tall. She's perched alone with no other mountains to lean on—no shifting of tectonic plates to form her beauty, just a massive hibernating stratovolcano. Alone, that strange similarity we share. And her cherry on top: the few remaining glaciers, struggling to stick around on this warming planet. She carried the accolades of being the highest freestanding mountain in the world and the highest peak in Africa. Little did I know then that getting to this peak wouldn't be the most challenging mountain I would climb on this continent.

It took seven—or was it eight?—days of hiking to get there: Barafu High Camp at 15,790 feet, our last camp before the peak. I persuaded my eyes to open; they preferred to remain shut, still tired and dry from the climb the day before. *Rise and shine, little darling. Our bucket-list day, Ric,* I thought, grinning. I tried to hold on to the smile, but the muscles returned to a familiar position.

It was also December.

One year after Ric's death. The anniversary of a terrible day.

Naturally, I anticipated the month's arrival. Yet, I had wished it wouldn't resurface sorrow alongside its coming. So, I dared myself to climb the highest peak in Africa, hoping to push it aside. The thought of his death awakened a dormant injury. Ric and I planned to fulfill another adventure on our bucket list by traveling to Africa and conquering that peak. Still, in an instant, unwelcome memories took me back to revisit the gut-wrenching sentiments. I did not plan for it; I did not anticipate it, nor did I want it. It just came knocking, time and time again—phantom pain.

Would it always arrive unexpectedly, like stinging on your lower lip, before a cold sore breaks out? The memory deliberately and meticulously lifted the periphery of the scab, stinging a bit and forming tiny drops of serous fluid around the edges, just when I believed this past wound was partially mended. As in the past, the scabs of this wound had become partially unroofed, and it made me wonder if I should rip them off or leave them alone. *Will there be less of a scar if I let it alone?* Then, with no need to help it along, the protection was gone, and under that lost layer of dermal protection lies the ruddy, raw tissue, stinging with exposure to the new air and soliciting to be covered.

I tried to draw comfort from the laughter echoing outside my tent, needing to be cheered up. Sighing, I closed my eyes and opened them again. A gentle rubbing, a nylon-on-nylon noise, startled me. Clues that someone was outside. The sunlight peeked through the tent, then a silky, sweet *"Habari za asubuhi"* ("Good morning"). My senses were spot-on. Bundled mummy-like in my warm sleeping bag, the tip of my nose jutted out. I unzipped my bag's side zipper, squirmed to free my arms, and lugged myself into a sitting position. Sliding beside the door, I was reluctant to remove the fitted head portion of the sleeping bag, which had become my warm hoody. More melodic Swahili words floated in: *"Jambo,* Sheila."

"Yes?" I said after clearing my throat.

Snatching the tent's front-door zipper pull, it made a high-pitched *zziippp* as I glided it quickly to the ground. The tent door flapped as the biting, dehydrated air sprinted in. I quickly shoved my warm, filled-to-the-brim pee bottle off to the side, away from my visitor's eyesight. *It's almost transparent, a good sign.*

All climbers use pee bottles, but it is not so pleasant to visualize some others' waste products first thing in the morning. At high altitudes, we produce excessive amounts of bicarbonates. To rid us of this surplus, our kidneys work overtime to steer us clear of respiratory alkalosis. Simply put, we pee out the problem. Our phenomenal body—a big hunk of flesh and fluids. A fine machine, with unseen organs squirting this and that, and a heart bulldozing blood to places that demand oxygen. Recycling centers working nonstop; exit ramps prepared to shoulder any task—all with the same MO: homeostasis. The stupendous human body, avoiding death at all costs.

This bottle enables you to stay in your warm tent at night. On top of that, it adds a safety feature. It prevents the dreaded twisting of an ankle or tumbling over the ledge while you search for a private place to relieve yourself on an unlit mountainside at midnight. A mountain climber's best-concealed tool, never to be confused with your drinking bottle.

Squatting in front of my open tent door, Anthony, a Tanzanian mountain guide, greeted me. Blessed with big brown eyes, curly lashes, and a gentle smile, he held a thermos of hot chai, cup in hand, ready to pour. Silently, he handed me the empty cup. Hurricane-shaped swirls of steam escaped the thermos as he poured the tea. Notes of cardamom and cinnamon squeezed the fresh air out of my tent.

"*Asante sana* (thank you very much), Anthony," I whispered in my newly memorized Swahili.

"*Karibu sana* (very welcome)," he replied with a grin, expertly retightening the thermos lid.

As quickly as he came into view, he retreated to his other duties. I soaked up my view above the clouds. As far as I could see, a fluffy, chalky-white duvet smothered the earth's surface. The only thing poking the cloud cover, seventy kilometers to the west, was the nose of Mount Meru. She, too, was a stand-alone, dormant beauty. I smiled and rubbed my hands together, wanting the friction to warm them. *Somehow, I made it this far.*

A few minutes later, the onset of pressured chatter overpowered the morning teatime. I noticed the staff and other climbers beginning to huddle in front of the cooks' tent. Next to the cooks' door was a plastic bucket holding a stack of tin bowls with remnants of disregarded oatmeal. *I'd better get a move on.*

Last night, five climbers and four guides planned an early take-off time, the key to reaching the summit. None of us knew each other before the start of the trek, but we all meshed well and felt like a team—a fortyish couple from Arizona and a father and his son from back east. Aware I needed to be up and ready to go, I dug through my rucksack at full tilt and tracked down my gear for the day. For a fleeting moment, I remembered when I purchased this backpack. It was at the last REI member's sale. I spotted it under stacks of other used items, tagged as gently used. Forest green, perfect in size, and manageable. I was delighted to imagine its previous adventures and the person who carried it. Most of all, I love getting a bargain.

I donned multiple layers and swathed nude-colored Elastoplast over the dark navy-looking nail bed of my throbbing, angry big toe. *The nail will grow back.*

Now dressed, I unzipped the top pouch of my rucksack and removed a sandwich-sized Ziploc bag. Inside was a white piece of paper folded in fours. I stowed it deep in the chest pocket of my purple parka and secured the snaps. With the laces of my hikers tied, albeit looser, on the right, I headed to the group of climbers.

The guide stood before the group, dressed as if he were in an advertisement for The North Face—logos everywhere, thin and fit, not his first rodeo.

He began his instructions with, "Our mantra for the day, '*Pole, pole,*' which means 'Slowly, slowly' in Swahili." Taking long, exaggerated steps, he put his right leg forward, then his left, and paused. He looked at the group of eager trekkers, shot us a big smile, and shouted, "Pole, pole. This is how you do the step, step, pause dance to reach the summit."

To get to the peak with such intentional movements. *Interesting.*

What was more critical: the climb, or standing on the summit? *Would any of this make my life feel fun again?*

In my childhood, I faced a humongous peak. I was a kid, always looking for the pinnacle of safety. Unable to distance myself from Barb physically, I found solace in my imagination, ignoring her blows and silently mocking her insults—all smokescreens. I was teetering at the top when Ric and I concocted a plan to leave it all behind. That day I packed my brown paper bags and walked hand in hand out the door with him. To my new home, my new life, my new peak.

But the summit with Ric was different. My ascent was effortless and painless. It was a crown with a panoramic vista of the vast and breathtaking world beneath us. There was ample room for both of us, on our mountaintop, and I yearned to tether myself to his presence. It was where I longed to take in the sun, awakenings, and slumbering—a perfect spot to watch the moon peeking out from behind the backlit moving clouds. It was a venue to witness our changing seasons, marvel at the migrating birds, and watch the marmots balance on their back haunches. He was the one who encouraged me to climb, who meticulously checked all the ropes, secured my harness, and laughed his way to the summit. I wanted to stay, never leave, to die there. I wanted to linger there until my final breath, allowing the vultures to claim me piece by piece.

Then, one year ago, it all changed on a sunny, bluebird-sky day. Ric breathed his final sigh on his handmade couch, under his handmade quilt, and the summit we stood on trembled, cracked open, and exposed the earth's core. His death made me tumble and somersault uncontrollably, colliding with jagged rock after rock as I plummeted to the bottom. I felt like I had sprained both ankles, run out of water, and landed at the bottom of a crevasse. I struggled to get up, but I couldn't. Day after day, I planted my feet firmly, gripping the rocks of hope, until my knuckles bled. I coiled the shredded rope of the future around my wrists to get better traction. And with each incremental progress forward, I regressed to my starting point.

The past.

In the months that followed, my sorrow kept me anchored in place as if my very essence mired in the mud of my grief. Everywhere I looked, I saw groups of climbers making their way up the mountainside, their world carrying on like usual. I tried to call out, though it felt like a shout in my mind, but no sound emerged. I called out again, but they continued to ascend, oblivious. I felt the weight of my wounds and the steady march of time as I gazed at the mountain that once was a home shared with my soulmate. Maybe Kilimanjaro was my new peak. I didn't doubt I would make it; stubbornness is one of my best qualities. I wondered if it would fix me, reset my clock, and return me to happiness.

And so we began, one step at a time.

Initially, the group trudged together. About thirty minutes later, we were all scattered, seeds in the wind. A few black dots ahead of me and a few below me, all slogging up the mountainside to their internal chanting.

"Pole, pole," I repeated out loud with each calculated step. I nudged myself to drink water. *Most failed summit climbs are because of altitude sickness, often due to a lack of hydration.*

So I continued my dance, repeating the exact words: "Step, step, breathe, pause, pole, pole, and then again." The frigid air felt fire-like as it entered my lungs. It tickled the back of my throat and made me cough. The winding, loose dirt path hugging a rock cliff to my left metamorphosed into a slick, snow-covered path. I wondered whose legs were dragging up this slope.

To take my mind off my breathlessness and the increasing pang in my big toe as it jammed into the front of my boot with each step, I allowed my mind to float back into the theater of my past. Ric.

Our years of marriage and devoted friendship made me believe I somehow snuck into the back door of happiness and safety. We had an ideal life. I had a profession I loved, an adoring husband who worked just a few doors down from me, two goofy Great Danes, and a used Volkswagen. *What more does one need?* Life with him camouflaged my mother's dereliction of duty.

Our marriage worked on so many levels. It made me think of the leafcutter ants I once eyed while hiking in the dense forests of Costa Rica. I was mesmerized by their march in a single file, on the heels of one another, up a tree, down a rotting log, over the moss-covered boulders, and close to the river's rushing waters. Sometimes, a new leader took over, while others politely stepped aside. They continued, marching without pausing, fighting, or stuttering; they trusted the process. There was no drama, no pushing and shoving. No one taking the role of the constant leader. They followed each other's vibrations and chemical receptors to communicate: We were the ants, Ric and Sheila. Ric used to say, "It's like having a best friend, and you also get to sleep with them." Our march never went astray.

Early in our relationship, in our twenties, our college studies consumed our week, followed by a weekend hangover. We were typical twenty-year-olds. Monday through Friday, Ric wrestled with the periodic table, and I wrestled with the mandatory white nursing pantyhose. I hated those things. (Too tight, too white, and never without a runner.)

We also had part-time jobs, squirreling money throughout the week for our Saturday night bash. At five o'clock each Saturday, I slapped my physiology books shut as Ric did the electric slide across the floor in his socks next to my chair, his cheek resting on mine, asking, "Ready? How much do you have, Sheil?"

Fumbling in my bag slung over the arm of the chair, I said, "I have eight—Wait, let me check my coat pocket." I slipped out of my chair and checked the pocket of my last-worn coat on the entry coat rack. "Oh smack, a five," I said.

"Race ya to the car," Ric said as we ran toward the car and slammed the screen door behind us.

Our Jetta seemed to know the way; we knew the aisle and the prices. We returned home with "our stash," and in what seemed like minutes. Ric's best friend, Butt, appeared at the door in his usual flannel shirt along with his petite bubbly wife, Beaner. We gathered at the oak table in the kitchen. Its surface paraded the previous Saturday nights, stained circles of red, blotches of built-up dripped wax, and three or four burn marks by the glass ashtrays.

Someone, usually Ric, snapped open the cassette player, and the tunes of Creedence started the party. Randomly shaped glasses from the thrift store emerged, followed by the peanuts. Songs we knew by heart, songs we belted out, the ones I still sing—lyrics embedded in my memory. The four of us spent the night talking about nothing and everything. As they say, we were young, free, and in love.

In our thirties, after finishing our education in Philadelphia—Ric's at Temple and mine at Penn—we headed West. We were proud new federal employees on the Pine Ridge Indian Reservation. Before leaving, we heard all sorts of negative things about this reservation—dangers, stereotypes about the Native Americans. And the list went on—opinions from those who stayed close to their homes. But together, we set aside the chatter and packed anyway.

We swiftly became proper adults there, exchanging our Saturday night stinky ashtrays for healthier hobbies. Ric created furniture in his wood shop, and I explored the world of warp and weft. Through all of this, we remained each other's priority.

The Indian Health Service provided us with a cookie-cutter rental on the reservation: a two-bedroom ranch with cheap tan carpet throughout. It was basic and clean, with an expansive view of the South Dakota prairie. Upon arrival, we pounded holes in the drywall to broadcast our new fancy framed degrees—paper confidence, at best.

Growing up, I knew I would end up doing something in the medical field. At an early age, I scoured any science magazine I could get my hands on, enthralled with blood and guts. The high school frog dissection fascinated me, although I disliked the acrid formaldehyde smell that lingered on my hands the rest of the day.

Raised on a farm, I couldn't wait until the veterinarian visited one of our dairy cows. I grabbed a hay bale and silently watched the vet as he donned his gloves, which reached to his shoulder. When he cracked open a canister he brought, it spat out white fog. He flapped his hand to remove the swirling whiteness that obscured his view, and then he selected one of the many foot-long glass straws and quickly shut the lid. Then he inserted his gloved arm into a cow's backside while his other hand inserted the straw with the contents. I now know he was artificially inseminating the cows to bump up the breed qualities. At that time, I wondered what magic his gloved arm was performing. But hands down, the best was when I got to help Dad pull a stuck calf from a laboring heifer. I knew then obstetrics was in my future.

After finishing my RN training, I worked for a few years as a floor nurse and in the ER, but I was not a fan of taking orders or wearing white pantyhose. *And the swooshing sound of my thighs rubbing together.* I tried nursing administration for a couple of years as a head nurse of an ICU, but found myself bored with all the meetings. At that time, a friend introduced me to a nurse practitioner who worked in her private practice and allowed me to mirror her for a few days. In no time, I was determined to follow in her tracks. So I returned to the university and completed an advanced degree as a nurse practitioner and a certified nurse midwife. These allowed me to find the passion I missed in my earlier roles.

As a new family nurse practitioner, I remember trying to hone in on a diagnosis akin to solving a Rubik's Cube handcuffed. Patients on the reservation were tricky. New patients showed up holding plastic bags of old and new prescription bottles; some were full, never opened, and others were outdated. A large percentage had multiple maladies or rare diseases I never treated in my clinical in Philly. So I fumbled, said the wrong things, made mistakes (not deadly), and researched every medicine a dozen times before writing the prescription. But with time and mouthfuls of humble pie, I fell in love with this quirky reservation and the sweet patients who trusted me to help them with their care. I was grateful for my profession, and Ric loved his, and we felt we had something to offer. If only I had known then that years of working on the reservation would be the perfect preparation for my most significant professional challenge to come.

We lived our American dream on the reservation. We spent long hours in the hospital and banked our comp time and new salaries for trips to Asia, Africa, South America, and New Zealand. Regardless of our destination, our only constant was a dog-eared, highlighted *Lonely Planet* guide. Hiking boots or bicycle tires did not matter; as long as we were together, our unity radiated so brightly that everything else faded into the background.

For the first time in my life, I ran into unconditional love. The dangling carrot of my childhood, that overwhelming need to work so hard to be accepted, was now obsolete. No more keeping score. Ric ignored all of my bruises. He buried my self-doubt in positivity and sent my negative self-talk to Davy Jones's locker. He knew my faults and accepted my mule-like determination, my ability to anger quickly, and my competitive side. Most of all, he sensed my tender spots and never poked them. Never.

Ric was an exceptional handyman. He held a flashlight between his teeth and removed my junction box. He cut off the frayed ends of the old black-and-white wires and entwined their fresh cuts—white to white, black to black. Then, left with the copper ground wire, he straightened out the kinks and held on tight, year after year, never letting go, unwavering.

At times during our marriage, I dwelled silently in self-doubt. The self-doubt I carried with me—principles I learned growing up, old wounds from verbal and physical pummeling—I worried Ric would wake some morning and discover I was rubbish and needed to go out with the weekly trash. But I was a master at stuffing this lifelong uneasiness back into my pocket, purging it out of my mind. I avoided putting the bucket into the old well because the water I drank tasted candied and plentiful. My new world gleamed with kindness and love. Wite-Out slathered all over the past. My tormentor erased. I was broken but felt bionic with him. We had the world by the ass.

An annoying hammering between my ears brought my concentration back to the vertical climb and the view of the first glacier. Coughing from the biting air forced me to stop. I regarded the towering ice shelf with the glittering facets of many-hued blues—such a poor prognosis for their future but, at this moment, imposing and breathtaking. Less than thirty meters ahead, I spotted the flags fluttering at Uhuru Peak—the crown. Adrenaline ignited my urge to dash to it, but I continued to "pole, pole" to guarantee my victory.

At the summit, the force of the wind pounded the shredded multicolored flags advertising success. Another pertussis-like cough left my lungs from the lack of humidity in the air. I snapped a photo to prove I had made it. Then, I pivoted and walked to the north—far enough but not out of sight of the other climbers. My bent knees struck the crusted snow.

Hunching forward, I leaned on my gloved hands. Sounds gurgled from my mouth for heartache, fear, bitterness, myself, Ric, life, and exhaustion. I unzipped the breast pocket of my parka and pulled out the Ziploc baggie.

Using my teeth, I opened the bag, dizzy from the altitude. The wind tried to seize my words, but my grip said no. Unfolding the paper, I began to read.

Dear Ric,

If there is a heaven and you are there, I might get closer to you if I climbed a towering peak. Here I am. You told me to think of you if I saw a bird after you died. It would be you checking in—no birds in sight.

Over the past year, your absence sidetracked me. I have even taken some major off-road journeys. I have faced some eerie demons and looked down into too many pitch-black, gloomy holes. C.S. Lewis wrote, "No one ever told me that grief felt so much like fear." I get it now.

Before leaving on this trip, I made mincemeat of that old pink bathrobe I wore nonstop after your death. For months, the belt of the robe strangulated me whenever I attempted to put on proper clothes, holding me hostage in our dark house. No more dimly lit living rooms, wrapped in my pathetic bathrobe, aimlessly walking around the house listening to that Goddamn skipping record. Ric is dead. Yes, you are, but I am not. Kilimanjaro proves to me that, beyond a reasonable doubt, I am alive.

So, going forward, my closed curtains blocking the essential vitamin D are now wide open, and there is a whole bucket of fresh cleaning rags in the garage— pink. You told me before you died, "Sheila, you are the strongest person I know." How lucky I was to have twenty-five years of your encouragement. We worked hard to fill our bucket list—my job is to continue the momentum. I admittedly stuttered, but now, listen closely. "Plunk." Did you hear that? I just added some- thing to our bucket: Kilimanjaro. And I will continue.

My eternal love,
Sheila

Still kneeling in the snow, I pulled off my right insulated glove. I poked my fingers into the icy, sharp environment, moving them from side to side to dig a hole. And then, I pressed my words as deep as my hand would go.

Getting to my feet, I felt lighter as I kicked snow over my promises. The skin on my face stung. I gave my nose an upward salute, wiping the drips on the cuff of my long underwear. My body spent, and my mind was in that good postadrenaline moment. Both were triumphant. I never doubted my physical body; I was athletic and determined as a bulldog. I turned around and saw the rest of my climbing party posing for a group photo, arms in the air, cheering for their success. My dull headache lingered, but I gushed with a new sense of confidence. I waved to the group and began my descent.

Now, enough of this nonsense. It's time for a change.

CHAPTER 5: STILL A WIDOW

Mid-December 2009

I couldn't believe I was back from Africa, often referred to as the Mother Continent because of its status as the oldest inhabited landmass on the planet. My expectations that climbing a mountain would somehow reset my perspective failed miserably. After a round-trip of 12,762 nautical miles in coach class from Elmira, New York, to Mwanza, Tanzania; a few packs of lousy peanuts; a couple of Diet Cokes; and a middle seat with chatty passengers next to me, it all seemed in vain.

I was determined to recoup my former self; I underestimated this inevitable crash and the strength of my mind to stomp on my newfound vigor. And as they say, "What goes up must come down," and I did; I plummeted back into the abyss of loss. Abandoning my thoughts of killing myself, blowing my nose into tissue after tissue in the therapist's office, and conquering a mountain peak held my score to find peace at a dismal zero out of three.

All far from stellar.

Standing at the bathroom vanity washing my face, I gave in to the Dove's lather that forced my eyes shut. The radio spat out a burst of static and then broadcasted, "The world remains deeply shocked over the King of Pop's death, the senseless loss of a talented musician reported earlier this year . . . Outpouring of . . ."

I searched with soapy fingers for the toggle switch. *Please turn it off*, I thought, before NPR pitched any more depressing stories into my bathroom.

Click.

The dread of kicking off another day was sufficient in my world.

Does chronic insomnia begin like this?

I yearned for sleep. The only attribute that resembled it was me crawling into bed, supine, with a pillow supporting my head. Then, a hasty prayer to the sleep gods instantly followed a psychedelic hamster wheel of memories, destroying any hope of a peaceful sleep. Round and round, until sunup, the affirmation; I lost the battle.

Drying my face, I stumbled across the pine floor toward the closet. My foot accidentally kicked the laundry basket overflowing with dirty clothes, including faded jeans and a ratty blue sweatshirt. *I wore these yesterday, maybe even the day before.* A swift, reassuring sniff, and I threw them over my head. While putting on Ric's socks, I started thinking about how long it would take for my toenail to regrow.

My lousy attempts to break free of my sadness—shutting out the world, contemplating suicide, scaling a summit—felt both desperate and hollow. I was running and searching for some relief. I woke today, like yesterday, and certainly tomorrow—still a widow. Every step felt uneasy, and everything awkward beneath my feet.

Esther yawned from her rug in the bedroom's corner. Gladys rested her head on the haunches of her companion, eyes hollow. Gladys, like me, has found it hard to focus since Ric died. We shared the same affliction. We divvied up the useless chores for each day. Her four legs go in one direction, whimpering, sniffing, and hunting for her master, convinced Ric's hiding somewhere, like in her puppyhood hide-and-seek games.

My two legs rummaged through another section of the house, only to find myself standing in Ric's closet. Arms hanging at my sides, eyes closed. I welcomed the soft cotton touch from his shirts as they brushed against my face, breathing in his lingering presence, dizzying inhalations. I was a bloodhound for his scent—that fading, evocative smell. I yearned for a signature pink harem Jeannie costume. I envisaged slipping it over my head, squinting, arms folded over my chest, and with one intentional nod, shazam! Ric reappeared to rewind our lives to whole again.

My slouching rucksack stared at me from the corner of my room, still advertising the MWZ to ELM twisted airline tags. It hasn't moved from where I dropped it the night I returned from Africa. Unpacked, dirty clothes were still inside. The musty smell was a letdown and reminded me of defeat. Touching it reminded me of my magical mystery tour on a high summit, meant to mend my melancholy, which did not work or even put a dent in my mood. I wondered whether I was being unreasonable for being pissed off at a backpack. *Everything else annoys me in this world, why not the backpack?*

Death snuffed out my sunny attitude, now buried in bitterness, engulfed in pessimism, and muffled in despair—all my gusto, gutted. Seeking someone or something to hold accountable, I glanced back at the nylon bag and my slothfulness in dealing with it. *That green adventure seeker will spend the rest of its time on a nail in the garage. A dust collector. That will show it.* I grabbed the shoulder straps and dragged it down the steps to its final resting place.

After ridding myself of the backpack in the garage, I entered the house from the back door and stood in the kitchen. *Now what?* I opened the refrigerator and spotted shriveled carrots in the bin, an expired container of cottage cheese, and a swig of soy milk. I drank from the milk carton and chucked the empty in the garbage. Anger replaced my doldrums. *I need groceries—time to venture out on another solo excursion as a widow.* I despised the word *widow*. It brought to mind an older woman in a somber dress, wearing clunky orthopedic shoes, sweeping debris piled at her doorstep while the neighborhood cat observed her from the window. *Relicta*, an antiquated term for a widow, stems from the Latin root *relictus*, meaning "left behind." Bullseye.

Right after Ric died, I submerged myself in all the "firsts": eating alone in a restaurant, changing my tires, going to a celebration, or taking a road trip. The first came right after I hit my thumb with the hammer and realized no one was there to question me: "You okay?" Followed by the first of asking myself, not Ric, "Do these pants make my butt look big?"

Up until now, I mainly avoided these scenarios. But the necessity of eating forced me routinely to the dreaded grocery store. Continuously feared. Persistently uneasy. Before, I relished my trips to the grocery store. A hub for finding fresh recipes for Ric's indestructible hunger, who devoured each dish with an "mmmhh." Whereas now, shopping for the relicta was soul-destroying. Turning off the house lights, I walked to the car and buckled up. There was no need to leave on a light; I was pretty sure the house would look the same upon return—vacant. I was off to put food on the table.

I parked far away from the entrance and the other cars, hoping to reduce the number of door dings in my VW. I headed toward the grocery store entrance and pulled a cart free from its lineup, quickly passing the store greeter with a trailing, forced smile. I pushed my way through the veggie section. The lettuce looked sweaty, and the apples were too smooth under their coat of wax. I told myself I needed to start eating better.

My cart squeaked its way from aisle to aisle, still big and empty. Pausing embarrassingly too long, I scrutinized couples as they exchanged tender touches and endearing expressions. They were laughing with each other. My need to buy groceries wilted. On my first pass tonight, a green-eyed monster followed me around the store. Observing couples sharing that can't-wait-to-get-naked-with-you-tonight glance felt like a sucker punch. My self-wallowing reminded me of how I reacted after a high school breakup, those days after being dumped. I wrapped myself in a blanket and played sad, sappy love songs on my cassette player. Does revisiting the circumstances that trigger an intense emotional reaction help us heal? *No.*

With a 180-degree about-face, I swung the metal cart back into its corral. It struck the side rails with a loud clang. *This sucks!* Buying nothing, what a wasted trip.

Skillfully, I balanced the chip on my shoulder and stomped toward the parking lot. I knew then it would take more than Listerine to get the bitter taste from my mouth.

I hit the gas and shouted to the empty parking lot, "I hate every minute of today."

My edginess dwindled as I drove from the store. Distance, my fail-safe cure. I concentrated on taking deep breaths. *In and out, repeat.* During my final appointment with my counselor, she suggested, "Focus on happy memories to counteract negative emotions." I told myself to try it as I motored along the winding back roads home.

I concentrated on my grandmother. She was a happy memory and the grand epitome of all grands. My father's mother. Short, fluffy, and buttery soft skin. Big bosom pearl hugs, custard pies, iced coffee (way before Starbucks), late-night rummy games, followed by her tucking me into bed for the night under the weight of four quilts that took me to sheep-counting bliss. A dairy farmer's wife, filled with creativity, a passion for everything, and a pre-YouTube DIYer. A zero waster—a trait I hold close to this day. I called it economical; my friends called me cheap. With her eagerness to turn old recipes into new ones, find a better technique to gather a skirt, or discover the best mix of manure to plant her dahlias, she displayed her unstoppable energy and insatiable curiosity for life. I think this rubbed off on my dad. I took some of the leftovers.

Grandma and I were like two squirrels in the late summer and fall. We rummaged in the garden and woods to fill our baskets with nature's goods. I remember the ease with which she entered the nests of blackberry briars. One moment, she was there, and the next, she was gone. When I did not see her, I wondered what I would do if she did not return—an unnerving game of peekaboo. And then, the weeds wiggled, and I spotted her fingers bouncing from one bush to another. "Bring an empty bucket," she hollered. While I worried about getting lost, swatted mosquitoes, battled the thorns, and fretted about the possibility of losing her, she held an overflowing bucket of berries.

We also picked apples, so it was much more accessible. No thorns, no losing Grandma. Bent at the waist, her fleshy hands rifled below the ground cover of tired brown and yellow leaves, chucking apple after apple into her basket. The ancient apple trees' wartlike trunks supported unreachable brittle branches that creaked in the wind, teasing us. Her summer straw hat guarded her pale skin. Her crisp, floral handmade button-up and creased, baggy navy ankle-length pants were always spotless. Her black puckered-toe granny shoes made her five feet tall, barely.

"Pick everything. They are all good," she said. Not wanting to disappoint her, I followed orders.

Then, with my index finger embedded in the weak, fermented flesh, "Grandma, what about this one?"

"Throw it in because we can find the good and make a tasty pie."

Once back inside her tiny, functional kitchen, I pulled up the metal step stool next to the laminate countertop to help. Her short, knobby knuckles turned circles around each fruit, filling the bowl with citrusy ribbons. Nickel-sized rust spots did not slow her down. She plunged the tip of her oversharpened paring knife around its demarcation and separated the two. She plopped the rusty flesh into an aluminum waste bowl. I grabbed the prettiest, unblemished apple from the bucket. As my knife split it in half, I saw a nut-brown, grainy highway leading straight to the core, with squirming rice-like creatures inside.

"Ew, Grandma, that's a worm," I said.

"It's nothing," she chortled, with her ample bosom jiggling. "The rest of it is good."

Sometimes, the damage is on full display, while other times, you only discover it after cutting the apple in half. Hidden. Lodged next to the core. But as she preached,

"They all have a little good left in them." Humans and apples bear some resemblance.

Growing up, I believed this seventy-year-old woman was my silent cheerleader. She provided me with an unfaltering sanctuary.

She would call me weekly and say, "Ask your mom if you can walk down to my house after school and spend the night."

No doubt, I was her special project. She never opened my can of worms. Barb did not ask about my time with Grandma, and Grandma reciprocated. I was pretty sure they despised each other. My two worlds did not collide. The "loser" was my undisclosed tattoo; I needed to keep it close and out of my grandmother's sight. I did not want her to see it. I trusted her but mistrusted myself, scared stiff that this wise woman would eventually come to the same conclusion as Barb.

But Grandma and I were battling the same monster, my self-doubt. I did not know it until now. I thought about self-doubt—my wounds from childhood. How did the physical and verbal insults in childhood mold my adult belief system? Now, compounded by my loss, it was making me feel unworthy, unlovable, and a big fat loser all over again. I believed this never-ending noisy loop was forever lodged in my pores, a booger on my finger, impossible to shed.

Looking back, I thought Grandma did not see my deep sadness. Now, I believe she did. Her actions showed me she knew I was wounded. Her gentle approach avoided a power struggle with my aggressor at home. She silently picked up my pieces. She wrapped me in her arms and pressed my head on her lavender-scented chest. She knew I was not all those things; she was trying to help me forget it. Show, not tell, right?

I noticed I had nearly reached home without fully recalling the trip. Meditative driving. At the stop sign, I admired the picturesque farm in front of me: a white two-story with black shutters and a sign by the mailbox advertising their homemade cheese. The last time I stopped, I bought a hunk of cheddar and ate the whole thing before I got home. As the rhythmic beat of my left turn signal clicked, I refocused the route to backtrack along the two-lane road to my earlier starting point. I turned the wheel and pressed on ahead.

Like Grandma's theory, the counselor's insight resonated with me. Focusing on the good to redirect the negativity, the counselor's insight suggested that if I could just accept my damage, focus on the good that remains, and move on, I would survive. We all had that worm somewhere close to our core, chewing away at our innards. It may be about recognizing and confronting it without fear before it consumes me. The theory seems obvious, yet challenging to put into practice. It was unimaginable right now.

The crunch of the gravel under my tires told me I was home. *Yep, dark.* I took advantage of my inability to count sheep and fired up the computer. The desktop of my screen resembled the past eleven months of my life: disorganized, nonsensical links and shortcuts scattered haphazardly. I saved shortcuts to my bank, phone provider, electrical company, and various site links with possible ideas for my future. Daily, I shuffled through this jumbled mess, no order, nothing that was first or second, just chaos. Links stirred my romantic appetite of how I toyed with moving permanently to Alaska, considered building a home in place of the Rambler and living off the grid, and contemplated turning my Upstate NY farm into a sanctuary for goats—all potential pathways for my future.

A lone shortcut beckoned me in the lower right-hand corner of my screen. A white square bearing the iconic red side profile of a man running, the iconic symbol of this non-governmental organization (NGO), Médecins Sans Frontières (MSF). MSF, commonly known as Doctors Without Borders, was a medical humanitarian organization I aspired to join. It was not a new dream, long-held and now tinged with a hint of attainability. Nothing to hold me back. Working internationally, immersing myself in my passion, exploring a new culture, and taking on a challenge—why not seize the opportunity? I hesitated to apply months ago after I contacted them about the application process because they told me it was easier to get into Harvard than this organization. So I put it on the back burner because I did not have enough gumption to fill in the application or get let down. With no other options in sight, I flung a dart to see what would happen.

The first question on the application was, "Explain why you want to work for an emergency humanitarian organization?" The cliffhanger for acceptance. Typing with vigor, I explained my years of working in rural medicine on various Native Indian reservations in the US. I introduced my long-term goals, my Ivy League education (humbly), my savvy clinical skills, and my stubborn drive to succeed. Rereading, I wondered who this person was. *Could I get back to her, or did she leave permanently with Ric? Did I have what it takes to do this?*

I placed my hands behind my head, lifted my chin, yawned, and hit send.

What do I have to lose?

Right then, it felt like nothing.

CHAPTER 6:
THE FUCK-IT BUTTON

End of December 2009

"Osteosarcoma," the vet said, sitting on the floor next to her in the exam room, caressing Esther's shiny black coat.

"Unfortunately common in the giant breed," she added.

"I can't let her suffer." Choking out my response.

The benefit of euthanasia. No long, drawn-out battle to fight the incurable; a conscious choice before the suffering begins. I left the vet's office, a leash in one hand and a collar adorned with a red dangling heart medallion engraved with her name and a phone number for Ric and Sheila—evidence of the latest disappearing member from the family as I once knew it.

The restlessness of Gladys, the silver Great Dane, already troubled me. Immediately after Ric's death, she was inconsolable, unable to sleep through the night without sniffing and searching the house for her master. Like humans, losing her buddy Esther renewed her old trauma of losing Ric.

Shortly after Esther's demise, I was changing the tires on my SUV in the garage when I heard the stones crunch under the tires of an unknown truck approaching the house. I got to my feet and walked toward the middle-aged man, who was sheepishly walking toward me.

"Do you have a gray dog?" he asked.

"Yes, she is probably around the back of the house. She stays close," I said, smiling confidently.

I whistled, and before I called her name, he interrupted, "I think I just killed her."

He helped me pull her limp body out of the ditch and place her in the back of my rig. I thanked him for stopping—it was probably miserable for him—and drove her into the back field close to the barn and parked. Exiting my vehicle, I entered the barn through the side door, climbed the backhoe steps, and turned the key. It started with a slight growl, resentful of the cold air. Sitting in its cab, I wondered what the hell I was doing, knowing what I was doing.

Slowly, I backed out of the barn and drove toward my car. My body lurched with each jerky movement of this mighty beast. The pungent, oily smell that fed the power of the machine made me nauseous. A blue sky and white fluffy clouds appeared to mock me. As I deployed the outriggers to stabilize the machine, I heard Dad's words from earlier instructions when he taught me the safety of driving the backhoe: "Never forget to put these down before you dig."

I placed the massive yellow machine bucket in front of me, hoping it had enough power to penetrate the frozen ground. I moved the joystick and took a small bite; it met the ground with some resistance, teeth bouncing across the dirt with each swipe. The bucket tips scratched relentlessly against the unyielding earth as I continued to try to dig a hole. Then, as if the planet grew weary of opposing me, it parted and allowed me entry.

Each time I placed the bucket, I took more and more of the dirt, digging the hole deeper and deeper, churning it, and piling it around the perimeter of my hole. Until something made me stop, I climbed out of the cab, retrieved the old comforter from the back of my SUV, and lined the hole with it. I struggled to lift Gladys and then gently lowered her into her winter grave. I crawled into the hole, spooned her, caressed her, told her how much Ric and I loved her, and tucked the blanket tight around her gray brindle coat.

I felt nothing and everything.

As I slowly piled the dirt over my last family member, I screamed and motherfucked the universe at whoever deemed it necessary to subject me to this additional loss. Everything that held me to this farm was gone; it was time to go. The end of my dog's life plunged me deeper into sorrow. I should have known that as each season bids farewell, a new dawn gently emerges. But at that time, I failed to realize it was dawn anew because it felt forced, like pushing a bitter brew down my throat and pinching my nose, forcing me to swallow again and again. I know now their untimely and uncomfortable deaths allowed me the freedom to accept a mission with MSF. A new dawn, in a shitty way. I will always believe Gladys took her own life.

I put the backhoe on Craigslist that night.

Months ago, long before the death of my dogs and my submission to MSF, I opted to take on a part-time role with an obstetrician in the local town. Family and friends cheered me on, thinking it would be "good for me." In hindsight, it felt more like playing Blind Man's Bluff. I felt constantly dizzy, unsure of my path, with my arms extended, grasping for a solution. Hoping to alleviate my woes, I planned to dedicate two days a week to something else entirely—a much-needed distraction, but I often could barely remember what I did on those two days. The fog was still too thick.

It was Wednesday. I was off the clock but hadn't gotten far, but I got dressed and left my house by 10:00 a.m. *Small improvement.* Something about cruising to a local coffee spot in a VW instilled a glimmer of optimism within me. Even if I only accomplished one thing on my day off, that was a plus. I dressed in Ric's oversized T-shirt, tucked into the depths of my baggy jeans, and relished the soft cotton threads on my skin, smoothed by his constant wear. The shirt bore the adage he lived by: "Not all who wander are lost." Maybe this indicated that I was progressing, but I still felt like a mock-up of the previous Sheila.

The slight vibration of the engine jiggled my thighs, and a red-circled *P* winked from the dashboard as I stopped. I opened my window as a pale arm elongated from the drive-through window. Black polished nails with three beaded bracelets robotically handed me a steaming wake-me-up. I have rehearsed this many times. Yesterday's spatter of shiny dried drips around my cup holder accepted more. I chuckled because acidity and bitterness were wacky ways to slide into a new day. But then its magical allure saturated my space. I pulled into a parking space to enjoy the first hot sip.

My iOS passenger chirped, and I noticed a 212, a New York area code, from an unknown caller. Still struggling with my relationship with my phone, I hesitated to hit the answer button. But suddenly, it dawned on me that over fourteen days had passed since I sent my application to the NGO, so I tempted fate and answered it. I doubted it would be the NGO—they told me it usually took months before they would decide. The female voice introduced herself confidently as the HR director of that organization. I altered my breathing.

"Are you willing to go to Sudan?" she asked.

Is that north or south of the equatorial bulge? What the hell, it doesn't matter. At least on my chosen continent.

"We believe you would be a perfect fit," she continued.

Before I could respond, she added, "Remember, as a first missioner, you must stay nine months. And often, expats even extend their missions."

"I understand." I blurted out as nausea and enthusiasm stampeded my innards. "When?"

"In two weeks."

There was a slight pause. *Am I doing this?* I rushed to respond, not wanting her to detect my hesitancy. "Ah, okay, I'll go."

"Great, I will email you the logistics. Again, congrats, you'll do great . . ."

There was a minor break in her following words; initially, I thought we were cut off until her parting words came through clearly: "But remember, Sheila, be prepared to be uncomfortable."

Then, she hung up.

Uncomfortable sounded better than miserable. *Plus, how bad could it be?*

As I put the car into reverse, I remembered something from the NGO's phone interview the week after submitting my application. "This is not a good place to hide if you are afflicted with any bubbling unattended emotional issues," the interviewer stated.

"For sure," I agreed, exaggerating my nod of understanding.

I wasn't lying because, after a dozen sessions with the counselor, my health insurance declined additional visits and deemed me cured. They would know, right?

Was there anything else holding me back?

I had two seemingly healthy Great Danes at the start of this month.

Now, there was nothing.

A new electricity collided with my long-standing apathy, and I suddenly wanted to get home. I glanced at my phone while slowly pulling away from the parking lot. A metallic *kerplunk* launched me back into reality as my front tire slapped the curb. *Shit!* Reversing to straighten the wheel, I noticed a stranger smiling at me in the rearview mirror.

Driving home, the memory of months spent live-streaming others' opinions clouded my new sense of achievement. It is free for all, without my solicitation. Each drop, albeit well-intended, slowly suffocated me. It was too much all at once. Remuddling my already muddled wits. Most of their voices echoed in my mind.

"You need to move on, Sheila."

"Plant a tree."

"Most people are better by now."

"Just stop thinking about it."

"The sun will shine someday."

"Did you ever think about online dating again?"

"Don't do anything drastic. Stay put."

"Go back to school."

"Take a vacation."

"Read this book. It helped me when Grandpa died." I responded internally, *For christsake, he was ninety-nine years old.*

There was not an ounce of graciousness in my dead-as-a-doornail heart then. I handcuffed myself to my self-absorbed belief that I was the only person in the world who had suffered the loss of a young spouse. Plus, if I took off this veneer of mournfulness, would Ric slip from my mind?

Would I forget that weekend in South Dakota when we discovered a rock with a half-moon cut out next to our camping site? You placed my neck in the divot and washed my hair.

Would I forget when I left home for a month to an out-of-state clinical site to catch my allotment of births, and you stashed thirty notes in my rucksack, one for each day?

Would I forget the muscles on your back and your body's heaviness on mine?

Everybody's advice overloaded my circuitry. Back then, I could not tease apart each suggestion, especially when I frequently found myself standing in front of the open refrigerator door, questioning my actions. Disturbing and confusing, but not the worst of it. The worst, or my alone-on-the-desert-island feeling after his death, came when my retold stories met others' expressionless eyes. My desperate times when I needed to talk about it again. Then I watched their eyeballs switch on autopilot, lost in their thoughts, probably asking themselves, "Was there enough flour in the cupboard to make cookies tonight, or do I need to stop at the store for milk?" Their reflex was to steady their world, to pull back from my lopsided one. I get it now. But this gutted me, launched me into a pissed-off silence, and heightened my heart-wrenching loneliness. I was ten again.

And in the end, my decision to go to Africa was one of resistance, the path of least.

I was confident in my expertise in diagnosing and treating patients. With years of experience, it felt like an unbreakable foundation, a path I knew well and trusted completely. It was the only attribute I could bank on moving forward.

Unshakable and tested. I learned I gravitated toward what I felt confident in and ran with my hair on fire from those things I did not know how to solve. Despite the many suggestions for moving forward, none resonated with what I truly wanted to do. Not even close. I genuinely did not care about others' opinions regarding my decision. I was on my own. Plus, deep down, I have always been a rebel.

Slowing my car, I executed a swift U-turn on the road to align my driver's side window with my mailbox. Catching sight of my neighbor Becky getting her mail, we exchanged waves and smiles. We shared similar demons. Months after Ric, her young husband received a deadly cancer diagnosis. Ric came in first; Bobby followed in diagnosis and death. Now we were two forty-something widows trying to force a smile. Neither Becky nor I had children, another commonality we shared. Sometimes, when we got together, we reminisced about our lives before death's embrace. Other times, we laughed, cried, sat silently, stared at the wall, swore at the world, shared pizzas, and drank lots of coffee. Once, we even tried to get drunk, but that only led us back down the rabbit hole, so we opted to stick with nonalcoholic beverages. Our bond stemmed from our mutual comprehension of each other's unpredictable and often erratic behavior because we had either recently experienced it ourselves or were heading back in that direction once more.

A blast of cold Upstate NY winter air entered my car as I rolled down the window and reached inside for the pile of letters. *The quantity of paperwork after a death is unreal.* Chucking them on the empty passenger seat, I drove down the driveway and parked in my garage.

Once inside, I put on the kettle. The piercing whistle signaled it was time to unwind. Peppermint tea in one hand, I made my way to the computer. As I settled in the chair and tried to scooch as close as possible to the desk, its feet scuffed the wooden floor and produced a screeching, G-sharp sound.

First, where in the hell am I going? I entered Sudan on Google. I began to read.

In 2009, Sudan remained one of the sub-Saharan countries south of the Sahara Desert. Egypt, Eritrea, Ethiopia, Kenya, Uganda, the Democratic Republic of Congo, the Central African Republic, Chad, and Libya formed a coastline around Sudan. Colonized by Britain and Egypt in the late nineteenth century, Sudan broke away from these early chains and gained independence in the mid-fifties. After that, primarily Arab Muslims settled in the north, and African Christians occupied the south. Lying between these two groups is a swatch of oil-rich land, a fragment of the earth destined to kindle a never-ending conflict. Who owned it, and who benefited from it? The other longstanding tension came from the South, which felt underrepresented by the northern government in Khartoum.

Decades of civil wars resulted from the accumulation of deep-rooted ethnic tensions, religious identity, and resource allocation. These convictions ignited the First Sudanese Civil War, which lasted from 1955 to 1972. In 1972, the Addis Ababa Agreement temporarily paused this civil war, giving the South some control and forcing everyone to put down their arms *after seventeen years of suffering.*

The agreement stopped the war, but the political instability hung in the air, causing sustained, unpredictable outbreaks of fighting and violence. Then, in 1972, the North outwardly reneged on the Addis Agreement and attempted to impose Islamic Law on the South. That arm-twisting sparked the Second Sudanese Civil War, which lasted from 1983 to 2005. During those years, the South formed the

Sudan People's Liberation Movement (SPLA) to protect the citizens of the South against their perceived one-sided government—*twenty-two more years of suffering.*

It wasn't until 2005 that an international group mediated the Comprehensive Peace Agreement. Over two million people lost their lives in the fighting between the North and the South between 1983 and 2005. The International Coalition forced the SPLA and the Sudanese government to sit at the same table and agreed to allow the South to hold an independence referendum.

I added up the number of years of suffering in war since 1955, which is almost forty, with no actual periods of peace in between. *That's a long time.*

Four decades of trauma handed down through generations. Four decades of once-traumatized adults attempting to raise their children. The cycle of intergenerational trauma. When I worked on the Native Indian reservation, I saw this. I took care of kids who carried nicks in their stress responses and coping mechanisms by no fault of their own. They often lived as if they were still under attack from a hidden, passed-down genetic scar.

Would the Sudanese be angry, bitter, or resistant to outsiders, especially considering the ongoing traumatic events? Unbeknownst to me, I would witness how they gracefully allowed life to unfold, accepted their inability to control wars or the drying up of a borehole, dealt with the lack of food from an invasion of locusts, and swallowed the bleak reality that many Sudanese kids under the age of five did not make it to six.

She mentioned I would be working with the Nuer tribe. I continued to read.

The Nuer tribe was the second-largest ethnic group in the South. They are pastoralists by tradition, and many are

Christians, thanks to the European missionary efforts. In every reference I read, the summary included "among the poorest and least-developed countries in the world."

I bet this is where the uncomfortable comes in.

I had no idea just how uncomfortable I would be. It's peculiar how we arrive at certain places in our lives. Sometimes, we enter through the front door, and other times, we get catapulted through the back. I believe this might be the latter.

I recalled my last weeks of graduate school. A guest speaker showed up; I don't remember when or during what class. But I can see him. He was a bit of a leftover hippy guy, bearded, wearing clean but well-worn khakis, and he stood at the podium and talked about humanitarian work. Soft-spoken, humble, and articulate, he mesmerized me with his experience working for an NGO in Africa. I scribbled this exciting job with a permanent Sharpie on my life's to-do list. And now I am here. *Good job, Sheila.*

My head inundated with information, I pushed back from the desk and remembered I had not told Lisa my news. I unearthed my mobile from beneath a pile of papers and dialed her number.

Picking up on the second ring, I blurted out, "Guess what? I'm in!"

"In what?" she asked.

"They want me to go to Sudan in two weeks," I said, tilting my head and swigging the last drops of my cold water.

"But you could die there. It is dangerous." I heard a deep sigh signaling her doubt.

"I have nothing to fear, Lisa. The worst has already happened."

"I know," she replied, followed by a forced congratulations. I felt her fear, but I would never admit it.

After hanging up, I felt torn between the thrill of embarking on this new adventure and the vulnerability I was about to face. I reflected on Lisa's words about the danger of possibly dying. My first momentous departure was from my toxic childhood home with Ric at my side. I can recount that scenario with crystal clarity. Even before it took place, I dreamt of my freedom if it all went as planned.

The whole thing began in the family room of the house I was living in after my parents' divorce. Ric and I, two twenty-somethings, stood hand in hand, facing the kitchen, wondering if the next few hours would change the trajectory of our lives. We devised a plan earlier: We would walk away together if this conversation went astray. I believed then in love at first sight and still do.

We locked our eyes on the woman at the sink moving about. The large ceiling fan whirled cool air. Typically inaudible, but now, the silence exaggerated its rhythmic *whomp, whomp*. The white noise dispatched puffs of cool air on my goose-bumped arms. The greasy hamburger smell lingered from yesterday and overpowered the grass I had just trimmed—one of my many duties.

The middle-aged woman at the sink wore an old work T-shirt speckled with coffee stains. She rattled and clinked the dishes she was washing. She was pretty, even with the flecks of forgotten mascara scattered below her oval eyes. The waist-high bar in front of us was a barrier between the conflict zones and a hiding place for our knocking knees.

Hand in sweaty hand, I glanced at my new partner of four months. He shot me an everything-will-be-okay signal. I wanted to believe it, but this was his first introduction to my world. *God, I hope her actions don't scare him away from me.* Our brief time together had not yet shown me how far that worry was from the truth.

"What's your intention with my daughter?" she asked as she dried her hands.

"To love her and care for her," Ric responded. He smiled, lifted his shoulders in a half-shrug, and squeezed my hand. His typical approach was gently, calmly, and humbly entering a tough situation.

Leaning over the counter with a frown of disgust, she pointed her incriminating index finger at him. "This relationship is finished. Sheila, you are not leaving this house."

I licked my dry lips, resisting the temptation to peel the loose skin from my lower lip. Barb always yelled at me and said, "Stop picking," and I didn't want to hear those words again.

"If you walk out this door, you will lose everything I buy for you."

I looked at the Cabbage Patch doll propped next to the fireplace. "A keepsake, one of a kind," she told me as I tore off the festive wrapping paper years ago. I didn't get it then, and I still don't. I thought the damn thing was spooky—period.

Then she stumbled over her words, and I stumbled over the meaning, which I rarely heard: "You know how much I love you."

Words I longed for in the past, she now tested their ability to glue me in place. An attempt to tack me down and affix my needy edges to her world. A place that never embraced me. Cruel sarcasm invaded my thoughts as I played back her words.

I pictured her on my make-believe stage, wearing a floor-length, shiny, blood-red crinoline dress with a tight corset.

Breasts are overflowing. She threw her arms in the air and, in a melodic voice, said, "How do I love thee? Let me count the ways?" Dramatically, she recited Sonnet 43. Then, the curtain falls without clapping: silence, nothing from the crowd. A flicker, and the lights switched off.

Even if I pined to hear those words from her, the vulgar insults, the repetitive groundings, the welts on my body, the taste of Ivory soap on my teeth, and the inability to comb my hair after another one of her tirades cast doubt on their authenticity. I wasn't a bad kid. I did well in school, my teachers liked me, and I never got in trouble with boys, drugs, or alcohol. But she, the woman who shared her nutrients with me for nine months, the same woman who heroically pushed me through her birth canal, never failed to deem me as insufficient.

I had a typical universal kid trait: the need to be loved. I craved reassurance that I mattered and that I would achieve success. But something was missing, a void, maybe in me. I don't know. As a kid, I was desperate to get her attention. I remember faking illness before a school day. Barb would forcefully place the glass thermometer under my tongue, stating, "If you have a fever, you can stay home." When she looked away, I touched the silver tip of the glass thermometer to the warm floor register to get the mercury to climb. Convinced if I stayed home alone with her, she might realize I was a cool kid. My trick kept me out of school, but that was about it. A child should not have to work forty hours a week trying to please her parents or beg for their attention or affection. It was a horrible job for a kid, and the endeavor ran me ragged year after year. So, years ago, without a thirty-day notice, I quit this impossible job.

"Get your shit, Sheila. Let's go," Ric said. Louder than I ever heard him speak. He avoided eye contact with her. I think he understood the idiom of attracting more bees with honey was not applicable here.

I hurried to my bedroom and grabbed my "Low Prices, Every Day" brown paper sacks, which held my belongings—stuffed to the brim with jeans, T-shirts, sneakers, and typical clothes for a twenty-year-old girl in the '80s. One under each arm, I rushed to the door Ric held open. As we walked down the driveway, a loop of repetitive dialogue ricocheted off the walls inside the house. We drifted together, away from the noise.

Her desperate cries, "I promise you, you will regret this," faded with each stride.

The last thing I heard was, "You will never have all the nice things I do for you."

"Nice things," I said out loud and expelled a puff of air from my lips.

Is it "nice" to tell your daughter she looks "fat and ugly"?

Is it "nice" to tell your daughter she will never amount to anything?

Is it "nice" to tell your daughter she will never be a good mother?

Is it "nice" to tell your daughter she's a piece of shit or a loser?

I continued to walk away from the house, down the driveway, shoulder to shoulder with a man I barely knew. We were giddy that no one was behind us. But looking back, I was disappointed no one was trailing me out of the house or calling me back. No matter how ugly the situation, we still want our mothers to run after us.

The distance to Ric's truck inched nearer while the perils of harm and her fading last jabs melted into the caress of Ric's hand now around my waist. *God, I love Pennsylvania summers*. Maple trees, palm-shaped leaves with fat trunks covered with furrowed grayish bark—ancient beauties. Their true beauty lies in sharing, one tree transferring nutrients to neighboring trees when one is lacking. A steady breeze flicked my ponytail up and down my back, like a horse's reins, a constant encouragement to keep walking away. I focused on my memorized survival to-do list.

To Do:
1. ~~Leave~~
2. Collect my money at the bank
3. Find a place to live
4. Prove her wrong

Ric parked our getaway at the end of the lane, under the shade of the trees. He bought this 1949 forest-green Chevy truck from his grandfather for one dollar years ago. This not-so-reliable beauty with patches of missing paint, now in mostly tinged coppery tones, served as our primary source of wheels. Approaching it, he tucked my bags in the back of the truck and gave the driver's door a twist of the silver handle. The rusty hinges groaned open.

"After you," he said with a smile. He was clapping his hands and motioning to the open door.

I placed one foot on the wobbly running board. Not a new-car smell. Any journey in this old Chevy could be the last.

"Let's blow this popsicle stand," he said, pressing his thumb on the push-button ignition on the left side of the dashboard. The engine tried to catch it but fell into a loud, constipated, grinding whir. Nothing.

"Oh no!" I said. Ric gave me a big-mouth grin.

"Don't worry. There is more than one way to skin a cat." His words made me laugh. It wasn't the expression; it was the way he said it.

"You wondered why I parked on a hill?" He jumped out and secured his hands on the driver's door frame. He rocked the truck until gravity cooperated, and it began to roll slowly. His skinny legs propelled his body back into the truck, and he slammed the door. A poof of dust from the floor suspended in the air and mingled with the afternoon sun. As our speed increased, he popped the clutch, and with a few jerks, coughs, spits, and sputters, the engine purred.

Gaining speed and distance, I imagined Ric as my Westley. Like a fully armored prince in the movie *The Princess Bride*, glaring out through the peephole of his face shield. Sword drawn, leaving his horse outside, he rushed into the castle and forcefully pushed open every door, searching for me, his Buttercup. When he discovered her, he extended his arms, and she leaped into the embrace of his bulging biceps, finding a sense of security she had never known.

Together, they fled the clutches of the evil queen. They mounted his horse, which was now frothing with anticipation, its four hooves stomping in eagerness to escape. With the wind in her hair, the princess convinced herself that her life had finally reached a state of perfection. Nothing could touch them, but she had to keep the drawbridge closed because they planned to drink liters of wine, gorge on fattening food, and live happily ever after.

That was what I expected.

That first historic departure played out well. But I wondered how my second departure to Sudan would turn out. This felt bigger. Was it an escape or a good decision? If it is an escape, does it become easier with practice? I survived the first, so no doubt I would survive the second. But this time,

I have to do it alone. *Will it be dangerous?* My education and training with talented colleagues gave me confidence in my clinical capacity. So I could cross that off my scaredy-cat list. And really, what did I have to lose? This NGO maintained high standards for the security of the expats, the international medical staff hired by the organization, even in the sketchy war zones in which they work. My fate was in their hands; my first time gambling.

Do I have what it takes to do this? What am I made of?

Too many thoughts mutating, I headed to the kitchen to pour myself a glass of water. *I wish I had a beer.* My fears still circled the wagon, but now in a different direction. I was gnawing on a leftover twinge of excitement, the childhood night-before-Christmas sensation. I chuckled. We have all had it, the butterflies, the insomnia (the good kind), the straining of our ears trying to hear the damn reindeer on the roof, and the wonderment of what will wait under the tree in the morning.

This brand-new feeling energized me. I struck my right fist into my open left palm, akin to a solitary beat rather than the customary three strikes of a rock-paper-scissors game. My gesture conveyed a decisive moment. The instance when I was no longer considering the pros and cons of a decision. My friends knew it as my "fuck-it" button. I slapped my open palm with my fist, and a percussive sound indicated I decided. There was no going back. I had permitted myself to free-fall, not look right or left, to drop into the unknown. My actions were a bit impulsive. I reacted as I always had, guided by the motto, "You will not destroy me." But now, it was all about grief, and I didn't need to say anything—the distance said it all.

I pushed open the sliding glass door, scrutinizing the night sky. The glow of the moon and the sizzling stars evoked memories of long-lost splendor. A symphony of croaking frogs, their chorus echoing through the gentle nighttime breeze. These were the minuscule things I failed to notice over the past months. I was skulking my way through life, deviating from treasures that surfaced nightly as if by magic. My decision to leave would heal my wounds and bring back the buzz to my life.

Back inside, I undressed and tossed my T-shirt and jeans over the back of the couch. I untangled my inside-out PJs and balanced on one leg, nearly stumbling when my big toe snagged the leg opening. I pulled the top over my head. Massaging my temples and the nape of my neck, I became acutely aware of my exhaustion.

I can't go to bed yet; I have only two weeks. Now, where did I put my rucksack?

PART 2:
RUNNING ON FIRE

CHAPTER 7: THIRD TUKUL
ON THE LEFT

January 1, 2010

oly cow, someone switched out my ankles last night. I looked at the shiny skin that had expanded and leaped over the rim of my socks. Sneakers that felt comfortable in REI a week ago now strangled my feet. *I bet yesterday's international flight and salty french fries were the culprits.*

Last evening, my airport accommodations screamed Africa. The pungent antiseptic odor smacked my senses as I walked into the room. Above the headboard on the mint-green walls, a velvet-framed King of the Jungle, with day-glow marble eyes, stared at me. A suspended mosquito net danced to the force of the poorly functioning aircon. My nightstand was an ornate, chunky double wooden bed beside one hard-to-find outlet. After locking the door, I undressed and shook the dust from my cargo pants. The NGO staff stressed in my predeparture orders, "You are only allowed a bag of fifteen kilograms or less." That was not much for a long mission. I hung my clothes on the two flimsy plastic hangers and hoped the wrinkles from the long flight would somehow disappear with gravity.

Exhausted from the time change, I took a quick, tepid shower, climbed into bed, and switched off my internal clamors. Dawn broke, and a yapping Chihuahua somewhere in the building jolted me from sleep. I dressed, then threw water and a dab of sunscreen on my face.

I made my way down the steps to a vacant checkout desk, relieved I settled my bill the night before, and dropped my key on the open guest registry. The pungent odor of cigarettes suffocated the earthy aroma of the coffee warming at the hotel's entryway. The interior of the glass kettle was coated with lines of cloudy residue, hinting at its prolonged exposure to heat. *It was probably made hours earlier; I'll pass.* I exited through the front door. With the help of two phone-scrolling airport security guards, I tracked down my designated waiting area right next to the plane.

Standing on the airstrip, I ignored the kerosene odor of jet fuel and whirling engines because my twin ten-and-a-halves stood firmly on the northern solitary track, leading me to my new-fangled life. The word *north* reminded me of Ric.

On our international biking adventures, we rarely knew our destination. We never relied on an itinerary. Our singular focus was to explore. Because Ric was a powerful biker, he consistently maintained a lead of a few meters ahead of me. When we stopped for a roadside pee or water break, I often asked, "Which way do you want to go?" Turning his head with a broad smile, he replied, "North." Then, without hesitation, I followed my True North.

Going north has to be a good omen.

God, I miss him. I wonder what he is doing. He was probably soaring around the planet like some undiscovered birdlike species, hooting with laughter, spiraling close to the treetops, and gobbling grains from generous strangers' feeders. That was my romantic, paranormal version of the other side.

As I waited, I watched the African sun gobble up the distant, towering dove-gray mountain silhouettes. Squinting, I made out the sign next to the door leading to the metal-roofed terminal: WELCOME TO LOKICHOGIO—KENYA'S LAST STOP. I later learned the locals just called it Loki.

The entry port for the wide-eyed newbie expats, squeaky clean, chatty, and exchangers of life stories. And the exit ramp for the weathered, cigarette-wielding expats bolting to find an internet connection to confirm their overdue vacation spot. Eager to locate a food they've been dreaming about for months. Their weariness publicized by the blue monozygotic twins under each eye. An army of NGOs coming and going. Thinking back to my interviewer's remark, I wondered if these guys have "unattended bubbling emotional issues"—the words of caution from the staff that interviewed me for this position.

Trying to avoid the workers bustling to prepare the six-seater plane, I dropped my rucksack on the tarmac. I made a few tiny, inconspicuous circles, pretending to look like I knew what I was doing. Providing care in these places was a logistical challenge. I was told during my orientation a flight comes to my mission every fortnight, so every ounce of supplies requested by the team on the ground was scrutinized, weighed, and carefully stowed. Months into the mission, I learned how the cargo weight limits could positively and negatively impact our daily activities. Only a quarter of the Sudanese had access to healthcare, and our organization provided 90 percent. *I am proud to be part of that.* I surveyed the piles of supplies resting orderly next to the plane: plastic sheeting, boxes of Plumpy'Nut, tied-down crates, black duffel bags, gray metal sheeting, and a carton of fresh fruit with a pineapple on top. *Is that a crate of African beer?*

As the packers bolted around, I wondered who was the pilot.

Minutes later, a tap on the shoulder answered my question. "Hey, I'm Jason, the pilot. Sheila, right?" I turned and extended my right hand while my left hand shoved my lip sunscreen into my pocket.

His baby face and full-of-life eyes met my hoisted eyebrows. "Don't worry. This is nothing. I used to fly during the winters in Alaska," he said. He hurried back to his duties.

Concealing my overzealous nonverbal cues was not one of my stellar attributes. *I need to work on that.*

Moments later. "All right, your turn," Jason said. Reaching for my rucksack, I realized someone had already stashed it.

"Hop on." Jason set down a typical bathroom scale in front of me. Then he lifted his ball cap and slicked back his hair. *I guess I am also cargo.*

"Sixty kilograms," he hollered to the man holding a clipboard, who stood watching the plane's cargo door close. *Two-point-two pounds in every kilogram. I need to eat more.*

"Let's go," he said as he sprinted to the plane and announced, "You'll be there in a couple of hours."

Swallowing and not looking back, I gripped the metal rail and climbed the three steps into the plane, sat in the one empty seat, and secured the belt.

An hour in, I gave my arms a rubdown to deter the draft-forming goosebumps. *There's no way to get to my bag now.* I refocused and repositioned my earbuds. Fleetwood Mac interrupted my window gazing. It was a song Ric always sang to me proudly off-tune, but I still loved it. *Why can't I shake these gloomy and despondent feelings? They hide at every turn. Shit.* I told myself to refocus and hit skip.

After what seemed like days, the Cessna announced its arrival with a 360-degree swoop over the dirt airstrip. A butt-pinching, close-to-the-ground flyby to announce its arrival. Coppery dirt, bushy trees, and lots of pointy, grass-covered roofs were everywhere. My first introduction to the mud tukul. *National Geographic* worthy.

Looking down from the aircraft window, I noticed the frantic urge of those on the ground to clear the airstrip; kids poked their goats to safety, and women grabbed the closest kid by their arms to drag them to the sidelines. Jason finished delivering the you-have-been-warned memo. And the next pass, he guided the plane to a gentle touchdown. The dust billowed behind us. The whining engine of the airplane quieted, and the blades slowed to a halt. Previously, at a safe distance, the bystanders rushed close to the plane.

Unclicking my belt, I inhaled deeply and bent my head down as I rose. *Holy crap, I am here.* With a metallic clunk, the door opened to a blast of dust and heat. A surge of dust veiled the outside. Suddenly, as though someone had swiped their fingers across their phone's screen, the dust disappeared, and this guy resembling the Marlboro man on a safari stood at the end of the airplane's steps. *He's cute.*

"Hi, I'm Ed, the PC."

Another organization filled with acronyms, but I knew this meant he was the boss. I tried to smile and clenched the hand-rail to avoid tripping, trying to make a good first impression.

"Welcome. Let me show you around." Ed was a stereo-typical Dutch guy with a broad base stance, a head taller than most, dusty blond hair, and evidence that he lacked a razor.

I felt embarrassingly clean. Slinging my backpack over his right shoulder, Ed said, "The compound is only a five-minute walk."

One long stride after another, he spoke, making every minute count. *God, he walks fast.*

"We expect you to abide by security rules at all times, things are unpredictable here."

"Okay." I swallowed.

Kids of all sizes in threadbare clothes followed along, mocking our moves. A potpourri of dogs kept their distance.

"Your staff is eager to meet you, and don't worry about the language barrier, they will translate for you."

"That sounds good," I said, smiling, but he didn't. *Cute but intense.*

A few minutes later, we arrived at the compound, encircled by a basketlike girdle woven from twigs and branches. I followed him as he lifted the latch on the expat gate, which was also crafted from interwoven branches and secured with twine.

"The hospital is only a one-minute walk, straight ahead," Ed said.

I tried to get a glimpse, but he was fast and long-legged and the boss, so I squelched my curiosity and kept up. I glimpsed a man seated in a lawn chair a few meters from the gate. *He must be the guard.* They told me during orientation that all missions have a guard who functions as the ears and eyes of the mission. MSF did not allow guns to enter our hospital compound, nor did they let the guards have one. It was part of our neutrality.

"Keep the expat door shut at all times," he added after we both entered, and he latched it behind us. At that moment, I couldn't foresee the countless times I would enter and exit that gate as I carried out my role in this mission. The aroma of cooked food reached me as I went through the gate.

I'm hungry. It smells like rice.

A group of expats hunched over the large table looked like they were having a meeting. Following a whirlwind of introductions, Ed said, "Okay, let me show you the radio room. Malcolm is waiting to give you the security briefing."

"See you guys later," I said to the group as I chased Ed back through the gate, closing it tightly as he had instructed earlier. *This guy is intense.*

The radio room was ablaze with blinking lights and squawks from fixed radio sets anchored to the wall, facilitating communication between Malcolm and distant locations.

"Sheila, this is Malcolm. Malcolm, Sheila," Ed said.

We exchanged a smile.

"When you are done, find Rupert to finish your first day briefings."

Before I could reply, he was gone.

Security was a priority for our NGO in Sudan because of the unpredictability of the current political situation. In 1983, a guerrilla group formed the SPLA against the Sudanese government in the North. On paper, the South and the North had made peace, but ancient wounds still festered. The referendum was next year, and the South was sitting on a historic moment: their first opportunity to vote and claim its border, cut ties with the North, and call itself South Sudan. If they succeeded, most of the natural resources would be theirs, which did not sit well with the North. Even though I thought I would be gone before the election, the tension was still palpable.

Our organization was transparent about risks to expats. Before I left the USA, I filled out my "Proof of Life" form in MSF's New York–area office. The new expats sat before the HR advisor, who instructed us, "Write five questions and their answers on the form that no one knows except you." So I scribbled the first: "Where was the most annoying mole on my body growing up?" and answered it with, "In the center of my forehead, but had it removed in my twenties." In the event of field abductions, my organization would request the captor's permission to communicate directly with me. Correct answers confirmed I was still alive.

Malcolm began. "The safe room is next to the expat compound." He pointed. "Its walls are made from concrete-filled fifty-five-gallon drums to protect from unfriendly fire."

"What is the roof made of?" I asked.

"Metal sheeting. We haven't experienced air strikes." He smiled.

"Oh."

He reached for a radio that hung on a hook and placed a lanyard attached to the heavy black object over my head. *Like I just received an Olympic medal.* Then, at breakneck speed, he rattled off Oscar–Kilo lingo, explaining how to operate the thing, change the batteries, which channels to use in the day, and which never to use at night. He turned the dials to the right, left, off, and on, and then asked if I understood. He looked in a hurry, and I did not want to be that pain-in-the-ass first missioner, so I nodded and smiled, convincing him I understood. *I will figure more out as I go.* As I walked away, I mumbled aloud what he told me.

"You go everywhere with your radio.

"You keep it on at all times.

"Never wear earplugs. You must be able to hear your surroundings." Ten meters from his radio shack, and after my first lesson on security, I was already annoyed with the lanyard that dug into the nape of my neck from the radio's weight. *At all times?*

I returned to the expat compound in search of Rupert for

my next briefing. Rupert looked up, excused himself from the table, and motioned me to walk with him toward the tukuls as he explained the dos and don'ts of expat living. I attempted to find a sliver of shadow under the tree, but the lubb-dupp in my shoes reminded me of the impressive heat. *It must be the hottest time of the year. I bet it will get cooler.*

With short stature and a T-shirt that did not hide his previous gym membership, Rupert explained in a loud Welsh accent, "The third on the left is yours." He gestured toward my tukul, maintaining his wide stance. Externally, he looked tough, but I had a hunch that I would like this guy.

I noted the eight tukuls, each equidistant from the other. Our homes formed a crescent moon around a rainbow of freshly washed clothes flung over scores of suspended lines—the soil below being chased by the drips above. Aluminum buckets still held the bubbling evidence. Two towering neem trees, side by side, kept each other company, sharing roots and a bird's-eye view of the newcomers.

"Go ahead, get settled," Rupert said, reassuringly patting me on the shoulder.

"When you are done, come join us for lunch." He returned to the table to finish his meal.

I grabbed my backpack, knocked off the dust, and headed toward my new home. Ducking my head to avoid the straw overhang, I passed through the open door; it felt cooler inside. Two tiny windows, both supported with embedded vertical sticks, prisonlike. The sun's reflections and shadows cast an avant-garde portrait on the opposing earth walls. A recycled wooden pallet, now repurposed as a single bed, supported a thin mattress that displayed a significant dip in the center—an unopened plastic package laid at the foot of the bed, a deterrent for the nighttime feeders. A lopsided shelf was opposite the bed, next to a white plastic chair with the word EXPAT written in marker on the backrest. A tan, two-tone, plastic woven rug decorated the center of the dirt floor. *Oh boy, how cool is this?*

I let my rucksack fall to the floor. Then I unzipped the main body of the sack, dumped my fifteen kilograms of possessions in the center of the rug, and began sorting out my newly discovered life, shooing away the flies that drifted freely in and out of the tukul door.

My plan is going to work. I feel better already.

CHAPTER 8: SETTLING IN

Late January 2010

My habits didn't change easily, even on an unfamiliar continent or a different time zone. I was already a few weeks into it and always the first one awake. I believe my early rising was ingrained in me, perhaps a trait inherited from being raised as a dairy farmer's daughter. I strolled around the empty maternity clinic, stomping down the high spots on the packed dirt floors as I waited for the day to begin. My dad always told me that if I failed graduate school, I could get a job stamping out forest fires. Jokes about my size 10.5 feet, which made me want to hide them, but I think he was telling me that every situation had hope.

There was a stack of lawn chairs in the corner, a rickety table stabilized by the folded-up piece of cardboard under its back leg, and an exam table built from what looked like the same wood pallets used to create my bedframe. Off to the side was a floor-to-ceiling metal cabinet, its body bearing the indentations from numerous relocations. The cabinet's base bore a rust ring, evidence of the rainy season's influence from the waters that seeped into the clinic and left their imprint. Dangling from the cabinet's metal cutout was a locked padlock with the key still inside. *Meds should always be locked; I'll have to talk to the staff about that.* I grabbed the key, forcefully wiggled back and forth until it gave way, and stowed it in my pocket. I learned later that I wasted a lot of space in my rucksack, bringing along my strict Western morals.

Just past the entrance were cartons of Plumpy'Nut, a high-calorie supplement for our severely malnourished pregnant women. Behind it were our congratulatory baby gifts, an oversized burlap bag stockpiled with new mosquito nets.

We brought on local staff from the community to support our medical efforts, referred to as national staff. Their combined skills and life experiences were incredibly diverse; some were unimaginable, others too profound to describe. But consistently, they showed up with curiosity, loads of flexibility, and a contagious sense of humor. Many of them were raised in refugee camps after observing heinous acts of brutality that forced them from their homes. Some confided in me they witnessed the killings of their parents, siblings, or neighbors during attacks on their village. Many watched their village set ablaze after the assaults or another round of war. With nowhere to go and no reason to stay, the parentless kids walked, hid from other dangers along the way, and ended up hundreds of miles from their home in the safety of a refugee camp. Most had limited education, and some graduated from high school, but the majority only had on-the-job medical training from the years of our NGO's presence in this village.

I asked myself daily how this happened. How these fantastic packages of goodness showed up for work every day, squeaky clean, clothes pressed, begging for a fresh experience. They portrayed an exuberance for life without evidence of the heartaches they suffered and worked diligently for our NGO. Keen to contribute, the staff were eager to gain knowledge and develop skills to serve their community. I loved these guys. Our Maternity Department consisted of me, a family nurse practitioner/certified nurse midwife, and a dozen national staff. Period. Back then, I didn't realize grit was more important than schooling.

Early on, we often struggled to understand each other. As the obstetric manager, my job was to increase the community's access to care and foster cross-cultural understanding by bridging the knowledge gap. The gap was enormous, mine probably more significant than theirs. This community, including the staff, believed the baby was the one who decided when it was time to set foot in the world. They did not give credence to the physiology of contractions initiated by their hormones and how they strengthened over time to an irreversible peak. The prevailing belief was that a baby's forceful kicks propelled them into the world.

They rejected the theory that the programmed maternal time clock signals the end of the pregnancy, typically around forty weeks. In doing so, the hypothalamus secreted oxytocin, then shuttled it to the posterior pituitary to flood the bloodstream. This natural process set forth the muscular, bodied uterus to begin its much-admired oeuvre. Initially, contractions were haphazard, often with a dull backache, but then built into a thunderous, agonizing rhythmic activity. One after the other, each one stronger and longer as the child descends deeper into the pelvis, forcing the door of the uterus, the cervix, open for the child's expulsion. A fundamental concept in modern obstetrics is that contractions begin slowly and build up over time. I planned to address this misconception in one of our first training sessions.

Benches that soon would hold hordes of patients sat deserted. I caught wind of a high-pitched *tsee tsee* and noticed two birds flitting on and off the bench—a pair of red-cheeked Cordon-bleus. I knew the species because I found a dog-eared bird book in the expat shelter the day before and read about them. Tiny, finch-sized beauties with a vibrant electric turquoise body and a milk-chocolate-dipped effect on their head and wings. The male flaunted a quarter-shaped, cherry-colored circle painted on each cheek, imitating eighteenth-century theatrical makeup. *Spectacular.*

With nothing to get ready in the clinic, I had no reason to get here before everyone else; it was my deep-rooted belief that early preparation would result in a more orderly day. More control—my scheming companion. Here, our supplies were minimal, our diagnostic tools were limited, and patients carried their own five-by-five cardstock charts. There was only one thing to control here: myself. I fiddled with my pen, scribbling precise circles on the back of a torn piece of paper on the table, coaxing the ink to come alive.

Liz, always the first national staff member to arrive each morning, strolled through the door. Approaching me with an outstretched hand and a big grin, I shared a "*Maale* (How are you)?" Both of us responded, "*Mal le mi goa* (I am fine)." She concluded her greeting by placing her flat palm on my upper chest, delivering a few gentle pats.

She glanced inquisitively at me and asked, "Sheilee, does your husband miss you when you are gone?"

Oh crap, the conversation I have been avoiding.

Then, her arms rested on my shoulder. I sensed her gaze, waiting for my response.

A few weeks in, I learned nonverbal gestures were more powerful in Nuer's social interactions. Physical affection, including hand-holding and embraces, dominated their communication. Initially, my muscles tensed; but slowly, I transformed into an engaging magnet. Americans called it an "invasion of personal space." *What makes us maintain that underground electric fence?* In this small dusty village, the culture demolished "mine" and mutated it into "ours," giving everyone shared and ample space. A collective effort to celebrate joy and dilute pain. It was such a better way. But at that moment, her stare and question felt like a spade in my soul, and her embrace felt like the confines of a prison cell. Gut punched again. *Don't cry.*

I focused on steadying my quivering chin, willing it to cease its trembling. For the first time, I found myself physically constrained. Logistically trapped at 8°36N 33°4E. Yet despite this physical limitation, in my mind's eye, I sprinted down the synthetic rubber track, my spiked shoes keeping me between the two white lines—my reality and my delusional state where Ric was still alive. Both adhered meticulously to the regulations of the race. Yet, glimpsing the finish line brought me back to Liz's question, leaving me speechless. Concentrating on my breathing allowed me to gather myself. A simple question, a smell, or a particular word still held me hostage and possessed the power to hurl me back into the vortex of hell. *It is still there.*

I examined Liz's white handkerchief, cinched at the top of her head. Wisdom peeked out at her temples. Flashy faux-gold hoops adorned with a delicate heart charm suspended in the center hung from her ears. She wore a floor-length piece of yellow synthetic cloth tied at the right shoulder, protecting her dress. *Who am I to whimper?* She was a mother, grandmother, a woman who had grown up with the horror of this war-torn country—a natural survivor. Unlike the younger female staff member who worked in our clinic, her face revealed the ancient tribal custom of scarification.

"The elders picked with a knife," she told me when I touched her face last week, raised skin-tone dots that formed connecting patterns of tribal ribbons on her forehead and cheeks. It was her story, her forced preadolescent passageway into her society. A free ticket for an outsider to gawk at the pinpoints of the heaped-up skin. Evidence of her ownership. On display and revealing. She bore no shame or bitterness when she told me the story and delivered the facts without pride or judgment.

Finally, I mustered enough courage, looked at her, and lied, "He keeps busy when I am gone."

My cowardice and inability to say my husband was dead shocked me. *Dead.* I blamed it on wanting to avoid the awkward moment of silence that followed my admission of the truth. That familiar split second when the questioner wishes they could retract their query while both parties stammer and stutter, eyes fixed on each other, scouring their brains for words of comfort. The conversation's conclusion, with their "I'm sorry" met by my "It's all right," always bothered me; the truth was, it wasn't all right. That whole nervous energy exchange where everyone walks away, wishing it had not happened. Like asking a woman when the baby is due, only to find out she is not even pregnant. Back then, it was my lame excuse.

I found the Sudanese way of asking questions captivating—a penetrating gaze that held you until you answered. It was an honest pause, listening, waiting silently, and then watching your response. Had I revealed the truth, I undoubtedly would have received a gentle hug while Liz dabbed my tears with the corners of her wrap. Instead, I missed out on an authentic exchange.

"That's good," she replied, but I sensed she did not believe me.

I heard the clatter outside as the rest of the national staff gathered for our daily rituals: exchanging greetings, sharing a cup of tea, and engaging in the customary barrage of questions, none of which pertained to clinical matters. The Sudanese questions were never a malicious interrogation; they all shared a childlike curiosity. I wondered if motherhood felt like this, a responsibility to answer the child's innocent questions as the spirit of inquiry oozed from their pores. Most days, I loved this part of the job.

"Come on, Liz, let's get some tea." With arms linked, we walked outside. At the clinic entrance, the rest of the staff sat in a circle. I approached the group with an outstretched hand and began at one end of the circle.

"Hello. Maale?"

"Mal le mi goa."

By now, I knew almost everyone's name. But as I did my last "maale," I shook hands with an older woman. *Who is that?* I reminded myself to ask one of the staff members later on.

Puffs of smoke from the wood fire followed the wind currents. A ring of black soot rose on the dented aluminum teapot as it balanced on the mud bricks above the flames. As the heated water expanded, a hiss escaped the kettle. A dozen chipped glasses floated in a rubber basin of cloudy water. Sue, a nursing assistant, plunged her hands in the water, probing each cup for yesterday's grounds. With a quick side-to-side *swish*, she lifted the entire glass and flung its contents over her shoulder. She handed the "clean" glass to another female staff member to fill. (Nuer men never participated in preparing drinks or food.) Not adhering to my Western standards of hygiene, I put confidence in the fact that the intensity of heat would intercept any freeloader aiming to make me spend a night at the latrine.

Not wavering from our usual daily routine, we sipped the sugary, piping-hot, amber liquid while I reminded myself to try to relish the moment. I wanted to hurry this along most days because we had so much work. Today was one of them. Plus, they often asked the same questions about life in my country, growing up, and attending a university. Thus far, I have been spared; there have been no inquiries in the group setting regarding my husband.

"Okay, go ahead," I say with a forced smile. Most days, it went like this:

Them: "My husband's co-wives keep us company and help raise all the children. Isn't it difficult with just one mother in the family?" (Polygamy was the norm here.)
Me: "No, in the US, we typically marry or commit to just one partner." They give each other a shocked elbow nudge.
Them: "Is everyone rich and educated in the US?"
Me: "No." Everyone's eyebrows knitted into an exaggerated *M*.
Them: "Do all women have many babies in America?"
Me: "Some women don't want to be moms. They instead focus on their careers."
Pity pulls their bottom lip forward.
Them: "How many cows did your husband's family have to pay to your father to marry you?"
Me: "None. Women choose who they want to marry, and no cows are involved."
Them: "None?" they yell. "No cows, no cows," echoes, and a back-slapping laughter fills the room—uncontrollable, hysterical laughter with tears leaking from their eyes. "No cows," they repeat, tilting their heads back and whooping.

Answering this question was always a favorite, prompting laughter until work intervened.

The laughing and questions didn't offend me at all. They carried no characteristics of mockery. I bet my responses were incomprehensible to their customs. We were two different cultures bumping into one another without violence or insults. It was a harmless joy to peer into someone else's way of life and not feel ashamed of what we love, live, and honor. It revealed their innocence and desire to know—a refreshing quality.

The NGO hired me to find solutions to enhance access to care for mothers and babies in the tiny town where I lived and the surrounding villages. However, the job description I signed on the dotted line did not fully capture my role. Early on, I failed to recognize the value of the minor details, dismissing them as insignificant time-wasters, such as the morning greetings and the teatime, followed by an onslaught of questions from the national staff. As always, I focused on the end goal and fulfilling the purpose of getting the job done. I didn't realize initially that my get-the-job-done attitude provided another benefit, which was apparent later on. That one that promised, if I immersed myself in the task at hand, head to the grindstone, I wouldn't have to think about *that*.

That old wound.

I found myself fantasizing about the moment I would board the plane to leave this mission, proud of all I accomplished. As the plane took off and I looked back at the tukuls, with a newfound understanding, I was a clean slate—a new Sheila, unshackled from the burden of my past. That was what I expected. Glancing up from our tea, I saw the empty bench filling with various-sized belly bumps.

"Let's get to work," I said, pushing my damp bangs out of my eyes. *Will I ever get used to this heat?*

The circle of staff dispersed, chatting loudly about their assigned tasks.

Back inside, Liz was by my side. A different staff member shadowed me each week, and it was her week to work with me.

"Liz, please bring me the BP cuff," I asked.

"Yes, Sheilee." She scurried out of the clinic and returned smiling proudly, gripping a chair and proudly positioning it in front of me.

"You know that thing you put around the arm?" I gestured a circle around my bicep. *Christ, it's hot in here.* I forcefully yanked on the neckband of my T-shirt, enticing a cool breeze to waft in.

"Yes," she said. Off again, and seconds later, she returned with a patient's chart, still grinning, as she handed it to me. I sighed. How am I ever going to get this work done? *Every day starts the same way—time lost when we could be training.*

I tamped down the internal monster who stood at the door, wanting to rant and rave, reminding myself that if I opened it, I would look just like my DNA. Then, her innocence ignited a surge of empathy within me.

Counterclockwise, I felt like I was standing in the kitchen of my childhood home. I was the "stupid" kid peering into the eyes of disapproval. I was a child trying to prove myself to an authority, striving to please the woman before me with every ounce of my inner being. But then that kid accepted the impossible and succumbed to the burning handprints of her mother's perpetual disappointment.

But Liz was not like me. For her, it was a game of charades with no self-disappointment, judging, or lingering shame. Freedom from guilt. Maybe she never learned shame. *Are we taught shame?* Liz was willing to go out on a limb without concern for taking a nosedive. She trusted herself and whatever came next and carried no expectations. Her eyes glistened, and dimples formed as she dared me to ask again. I had a sneaking suspicion this was a better way to approach life, but the other side of my seesaw was heavier—the urge to get this clinic in working order.

Moses broke our silence as he hurried into the room, a stethoscope around his neck. A "lost boy" at one time, but now a nurse in training and an armful of good spirits. Fleeing his home during the war after watching his parents die of unnatural causes, he ended up in various refugee camps. His "luck," as he calls it, brought him in contact with teachers of multiple languages.

Last week, I overheard the staff engaging in a friendly competition to see who spoke the most languages. Moses, the perpetual unspoken leader, began with a universal dialect, dactylonomy. In front of his group of peers, his wide stance and his two outstretched fists silenced the room. Enunciating "English," followed by extending his right index finger, brought the staff to their feet. Each added finger turned up the volume of his admirers. A display of pure joy for their colleague. His slender fingers continued, Nuer (middle), Dinka (ring), Bande (pinky), and Bari (thumb), Swahili . . . until his knowledge exceeded his anatomy. But for me, his prowess to root out so much good in something so wrong was more impressive than his tongue dexterity. *How did he manage that?*

Liz quickly settled into the chair she brought and kicked off her flip-flops. I stood holding the chart.

"What's up?" Moses asked. I grinned and elaborated on our predicament. He glanced at Liz. "Come on, Mama," and then, hand in hand, he guided her to the enigma.

Returning together a few minutes later, Moses explained, "She did not know the word." His simple spirit of inquiry annulled my Ivy League perspective. He deconstructed the moment and found the answer, exceeding my expectations that she would just understand. All the while, Liz took one stab after another in cracking the case, so much better at the game of chance than me. *I am such an asshole.*

As the day ended uneventfully, I trotted back to the compound for supper. Scarfing down a heaping pile of rice, I neglected the other mystery dish. With just a few rice grains left, I flicked them into the trash bucket, rinsed the dish, and threw the plate on the overflowing drying rack—time for shut-eye. The faint scent of sandalwood incense I burned last night greeted me when I entered my tukul. After multiple headbobs and retrieving my book from the floor, I called it a night.

Switching off my torch, I thought about Liz's scars, the day her appearance changed forever. Years ago, I read in one of my coveted science magazines about the African spiny mouse that lives in these parts of the world. Mouselike, in all ways, except for its magical ability to regenerate tissue. It can heal like no other mammal in the kingdom. If caught by their enemy, their brittle skin tears easily, which allows them to escape the danger. While the aggressor stands holding a palm full of fur, the bugger scoots away. The miraculous transformation unfolds as they single-handedly repair their skin, sebaceous glands, and fur—devoid of any scar. Their regenerative capacity is an extraordinary scientific anomaly.

But I wondered, with or without a visible scar, did their trauma still teach them a lesson? Who can they trust, what should they run from, and how can they relax and move on? We are all wounded in some way. African spiny mice, scarless. Liz's scars glistened in the sunlight, out in the open for all to see. My scars, an invisible abscess leaking over time. *Who was better off?*

Gabor Maté wrote in *The Myths of Normal,* "Trauma is not what happens to you but what happens inside of you." I know now that was the key.

I detected a faint *whoo, whoo.*

A bird? An owl? Ric? I buried my head under the pillow.

CHAPTER 9: EPONYM

January 31, 2010

With a steaming, creamy, beige drink in one hand, I slid the inside bolt of the expat entrance gate to the side. The door swung open and grazed my coffee cup, splashing a few drips on my clogs, the hottest on my right forearm. "Glad I bought brown," I muttered only loud enough for myself to hear, followed by, "Shit."

I hurried past the guard shack, delivering big puffs of air on my arm and trying to calm the sting. The guard must have thought I was a sight; I'll surely be the main topic of his dinnertime chat. I could hear him discussing with his family, "Every day she walks past me in this big hurry, wearing those funny oversized shoes, and today she had her head down, blowing puffs of air on her arm. I wonder why *they* do that?"

Maybe he did not use "they," but I have often pondered a question similar to that about others, realizing how frequently I've framed it using the pronoun "they," a practice that oversimplifies and generalizes an entire category of humans. It's remarkable how easily people form opinions about other cultures based solely on superficial observations without genuinely understanding the culture.

Halfway to the clinic, I gave up blowing on my newly formed blisters, knowing I could not soothe the sting because it had a lifespan of its own. Understanding that flies flocked to any open wound around here, I drew a mental note to remember to find some type of bandage in the clinic.

Slowing my pace to avoid another incident, I took a swig of coffee and thought about how I had adapted relatively quickly to some aspects of this place. Usually, I was an espresso connoisseur, a lover of a dark-roasted bean that yielded a full-bodied brew with notes of chocolate cherries. Dark as motor oil, forced by high pressure into a tiny cup, crowned with a velvety crema on top that left a hint of mustache with each sip—perfection. That was the start of most of my mornings at home. Here at dawn, a game of hide-and-seek for matches in the kitchen to ignite the gas hotplate, with fingers crossed, the previous expat refilled the water filter dispenser. Then I filled the kettle, set it on fire, tripped over Felix the cat, who was scrounging for scraps, and began my hunt for the instant Nescafe and Nido. Nido was a yellowish powdered milk that emitted a slight aroma reminiscent of Parmesan cheese when you popped the lid. The two were not my drink of choice, but the preparation was now my reliable ritual. It granted me that initial sip of the day, a structured and comforting kick-off. I hadn't fully grasped how a basic routine provided me with a sense of security and stability in the chaos of my current reality until it vanished. I think it was that control thing again.

At the clinic, I grabbed the lawn chair someone had left outside for the night. I plunked it down in my spot to casually observe passersby as they began their day and finished my coffee—that airport people-watching, without an airport. I felt like an undercover agent, observing the Nuer women as they went about their morning routines—posterlike beauty and posture perfection, strong like no other.

The morning light bounced off their lean arms, accentuating their spherical-shaped deltoids and prominent biceps. Deep onyx skin tones passed down from their Sudanese ancestors. Heads of hair formed into basket shapes, towering halos, and triple buns, artistically perched in an eye-catching position, and still able to balance a full jerry can of water simply by using a rolled-up cloth for support. National staff members reported that most of their decorative headwear was handmade by other women late at night, a time for skill-sharing and local gossip. Tall, thin, able-bodied physiques adorned with wrapped dresses moved about. Bold, geometric shapes outlined in black and colored in bright orange, red, and lime green were showcased on the attire. Their ankle-length hems swirled above the ground as their flip-flops padded the dry earth. I observed recognizable outlines of their babies tightly swaddled on their backs. However, the only moving parts of these tiny hitchhikers were their wee heads and bright eyes moving side to side, trying to catch the activities of the village.

I must remember to ask Moses the name of that woman I couldn't place at our last tea gathering.

Obligations assigned to the Sudanese female gender consumed their day. Their routine began as soon as the light of dawn scattered on the parched, fissured earth. Their priority was to collect water. From my vantage point, the borehole supplying their water was visible. The queue of women lengthened as the persistent squeak of the manual hand pump extracting water from the underground well remained resolute. Every Nuer woman possessed a yellow, indestructible container made from high-density polyethylene. A jerry can.

What a hammer is to a carpenter or a scalpel is to a surgeon, this indispensable jug was their lifeline for survival. Women started each day by walking to the closest water source, filling a forty-pound jerry can with water, lugging it on their heads, and returning home. A nonstop task. Water-fetching duty: their customary role, always done in good spirits, with no opposition and no complaint box to hold their concerns.

One day, I observed something more than their beauty: their cunning life strategy. Amid their daily duties of caring for their husband and children, rummaging for firewood, grinding sorghum, and supervising their livestock, they serendipitously infused joie de vivre. Throughout the day, after several tiring trips to collect water, village women frequently made a pit stop at our clinic. Sick or not, pregnant or not, it did not matter. They grabbed a place on the long wooden bench outside the clinic. Tightly stacked next to each other, with a tarp partially blocking the sun's rays, they waited. They were pandering to the moment.

Their waiting was not an inconvenience; it was a luxury. No scrutinizing looks at our medical staff, no customary verbal grievances like, "Hey, my appointment was an hour ago. I don't have time to wait," leading to an, "Oh, forget it. I'm leaving," while slamming the door and exiting the building. They exhibited a sense of enjoyment and wholeheartedly embraced old and new companions now in their circle. This was all they could control, a fleeting moment of peace in the now.

I needed to improve in mastering the art of living in the now. If I tried to focus on the present, it propelled me to the past. And the past forced me into the future, the one without Ric. My world has taught me that stargazing was a waste of time. My culture and childhood prepared me to keep my eye on the prize, never fail, concentrate on the next vacation, my growing IRA, or a potential raise, and always focus on my golden years. The snowball of hell. It was always about reaching for the next star and neglecting carpe diem. I did not know that someday I would learn that today was not just a means to get to tomorrow. It is not a bridge but an opportunity in itself. Only when I conquered the apprehension of the future and could smile at the nostalgia of the past could I bask in the moment of now. I did not have more burdens than these women; I just lacked the know-how to manage them.

This brief pause in their day released the women from their sense of obligation, giving them a moment of tranquility and weightlessness—literally. Maybe their riddled pasts have taught them this gift. Their tomorrow could be the start of another civil war or an attack from a neighboring tribe attempting to steal their cattle. Enemies could set their tukuls on fire, leaving stains on the soil, which had already held too much DNA from the past. So they captured the best of every single now.

Just then, a donkey in the distance captured my attention. It stood in the middle of a pile of rubbish, jaws moving from side to side, wondering why the cardboard it was chewing had no taste. *Poor thing, nothing to eat.* Ten meters from its rib-lined thorax and patchworks of nude skin that showered its body, I spied a chain of yellow, unattended jerry cans propped next to the vine-covered wooden fence at the clinic's entrance. No doubt waiting for their next trip to the community pump, but for now, jerry cans be damned. A yellow line of growing resistance was forming. Our clinic was a haven for women to pause, catch their breath, and savor a little of today. *So clever.*

A cacophony of high-pitched laughter, early morning chitchat, braying donkeys, and a rumbling language I did not comprehend resounded through the air. I always felt

Africa had two speeds: turbo and off. When it was awake, it was an ear-splitting racket; when it was off, it embraced the surroundings in a peaceful hush. We were on turbo right now. *Time to get this day moving.*

From the moment I hit the ground in Sudan, the staff bugged me about when I would begin teaching them, keen to learn. I intended to start that day; I just hadn't surprised them yet with the news. My initial goal was to grasp their understanding of labor and delivery and, with them, explore new strategies to encourage women from far-off villages to use our clinic for safe deliveries.

I was about to become a teacher without any formal training. Knowing I had to wing it, I took comfort in the staff's curiosity and eagerness to learn. It motivated me to showcase my finest attributes and forced me to confront my dwindling supply of patience that was tested daily by the oppressive heat, the workload, the damn flies, the lack of almost everything, and the language barrier. The accumulation of these hurdles made me fret that, at any moment, I could snap into someone I promised I would never be.

Her.

As a kid, I recognized that Barb's coping mechanisms were not the most effective for navigating life. I vowed not to become her. But even with that sacred promise to myself, I always had to do some self-talk on tough days because there was still an enormous gravitational force trying to get me to emulate her behavior—the profound impact of parenting.

Taking the reins as a teacher made me weigh in on my life's teachers. Teachers came in different forms: mentors who lit me on fire, and detractors who believed I had no fire. Both types left an unerasable stamp, prompting me to nurture the genuine lessons and untangle myself from the snarls of the forced falsehoods.

Initially, my mother taught me self-doubt—a master of demolishing self-esteem. I handled her with the only defense I knew how to muster up as a kid: camouflage, imagination, and internal chatter to spur me on. My middle finger to her negativity. Head down, determined to prove I was not the words she called me. She added fuel to my fire unintentionally. I should thank her for that.

My Kimble heritage schooled me in curiosity. My dad and grandmother introduced me to this novelty and the gravity of valuing every human in my path. Their sweet-tempered lessons often lacked words, but kids were astute observers.

My husband anchored me to the real magic of life. It started when I met him and continued throughout our marriage. He was a consistent friend, a gentle soul full of energy, who always sported an infectious smile. His confidence in me rekindled my dwindling flame and fueled my abilities. I worked hard to succeed, but it seemed easy with him holding the pom-poms. *I can be a positive mentor for this fantastic staff.*

Teaching the staff was crucial, but our biggest obstacle was our inability to connect with the surrounding villages. We lacked a lifeline to pull the high-risk pregnancies into our clinic to deliver. Normal deliveries in the villages weren't the concern. It was the complicated cases, the births that lasted for days, the "stuck" babies, the ones that gave up and stopped moving. It was the relentless flow after the birth, the constant trickle that depleted their bodies into another statistic. The dreadful delay in seeking care.

Many factors impacted the delay in accessing healthcare. The distance imposed a logistical nightmare. Many women did not know about the services we offered, while others were aware but trusted their familiar practices. Most villages lacked a trained healthcare provider. Therefore, no one could identify early warning signs of labor or high-risk pregnancies that might need our assistance. The cultural obligations also played a big part in the delay. Their society expected women to care for their men from morning to night. Nuer men did not cook, clean, carry water, or care for the children. It was taboo for a man to lift a finger, leaving them paralyzed without their wives.

I remembered a woman whom we admitted to the ward after a delivery of twins for a few days of deserved rest. Her husband arrived hours after the birth and insisted I release her from the hospital. Using Moses as my translator, I explained why she needed to stay overnight. Her husband asked, "Who will get me a drink of water at night?" Initially, I scoffed with a little laugh, but then swallowed it because I realized he was serious. He took her home without our permission, pulling her by the elbow. Exiting the ward, he said, "She belongs to me." Our birthrights are subject to limitations or empowered by possibilities bestowed upon us from our country of origin.

As the staff filed in to start the day, laughter, back-slapping, and loud voices filled the clinic room.

"Guess what you guys?" I said to the group as their laughter ceased.

Dozens of heads snapped to look at me, their eyebrows questioning what would come next as they quickly finished with the Maale moment. I never anticipated how much I would yearn for this greeting after I left Sudan. Over time, I cherished this ritual despite initially feeling like it was a big time-waster. The tradition was inclusive and extended to everyone in our space. It was a shared touch, an observation into the essence of another, conveying a simple gesture of human bonding.

"Training this morning," I said, followed by a big whoop from the staff.

They promptly collected themselves in the small clinic room, ready for the start of my questions.

I began, "What happens if the woman in the village decides to stay in her tukul for the birth of her baby?"

Their waving hands shot into the air as they yelled out responses.

"She dies," I heard from the front of the room. I thought it was Sarah's answer because the staff behind her were patting the top of her head.

"Baby gets stuck," another shouted from the front of the room. Before I recognized who gave that reply, Moses raised his hand.

The chatter in the room subsided, and he added, "Dirty sorghum stalks to cut cord, a problem."

"Yes, good!" I said as I wrote each answer on the whiteboard.

A room full of eager minds, over half the battle already won.

"Next, how can we get more women to come to the clinic?" I asked.

Waiting for them to respond, I noticed Sarah beside the same mystery woman. She was thinner and older than Sarah. As Sarah translated in her ear, the woman nodded her head. Then Sarah raised her hand.

"Yes?" I asked.

"Ahieu just told me we need to meet with the TBAs." A TBA is a traditional birth attendant, a century-old custom for the Nuer women.

"Who is Ahieu?" Knowing we did not have an Ahieu on our staff, my scrunched-up eyebrows again highlighted my lack of transparency.

"Her." Sarah pointed to the woman beside her, index finger on Ahieu's right temple.

I let Sarah continue. "She is the head TBA, the leader."

Ah, the woman I couldn't place at the previous meeting.

Most women in this community opted to deliver their children in their villages with a TBA. After the delivery, the TBAs cut the umbilical cord with a sorghum stalk, knife, or razor and tied a tight cloth around the parturient's waist with a knot strategically placed over the freshly emptied uterus. They put the baby on the breast, and the woman ate sorghum and fermented milk and returned to her household duties hours after birth. Most of the time, this all turned out fine. Babies flew out, and life continued.

Sarah proceeded to fill in the blanks. "She said she could bring the TBAs to meet you."

"And you can teach them too," Moses added, shaking his shoulders with laughter. His outstretched arms beckoned the staff to join in his enthusiasm. The group burst into a buzz of excitement—a spirit of shared unity—as everyone cheered on each other's potential. I wanted to bottle that trait, a collective community spirit.

"Okay, when?" I asked, walking closer to the two women.

"Ahieu will walk to the villages, send messages, and spread the word of the meeting."

Their heads touching, Ahieu looked at the ground while Sarah translated.

Sarah looked up and said, "Four Wednesdays from now, five o'clock, the TBAs will come."

Smiling, hopeful but doubtful, I asked, "Please ask Ahieu if the TBAs can write the number of deliveries they participated in over the past month and bring it to the meeting."

Sarah and Ahieu exchanged more words; Ahieu smiled, turned to look at me, and touched her heart.

No phones, roads, or electricity exist, and most villages were a day's walk from here.

This will never happen.

Someone yelled, "Come to deliver, Sheilee," which interrupted my awkward smile of trying to look optimistic about what felt inconceivable. It was already hot outside, and it made our space unbearable. I never got used to the trickle of sweat that started around my hairline and ended in my shoes, which immediately sapped my energy and stripped me of my rare eight hours of uninterrupted blissful slumber. When they told me it was hot in Sudan, I thought, *How hot could it be?* It was a boiling inferno most of the time.

Being in this steamy setting reminded me of another similarity Ric and I shared: heat intolerance.

For most of our vacations, we choose mountains over beaches. Once, we took a night train from Uyuni, Bolivia, close to the Andes Mountains, toward Chile. With only two aisle seats across from each other open when we boarded, we took them. Next to me was a sleeping local woman, and next to Ric was a stack of burlap bags. As the train chugged to our destination, the temperature dropped to freezing inside the train. Before boarding the train, we were told to expect this and had come prepared. As I wrapped my scarf tighter around my neck, I noticed Ric's flushed face, and he started to complain.

"I am so damn hot," he said.

I hoped he wasn't getting sick. As the temperature dropped on the train, he kept mentioning how uncomfortable he was with the heat. The next thing I knew, he was on his hands and knees, fiddling with something under his seat.

Rising from the floor and dusting off his hands, he said, "The heat source for this train is under my seat."

Reaching around the bags that occupied the seat next to him, he tried to crack the window but quickly shut it because of the groans of the Bolivians, awakened by a blast of frigid air. He sighed and sat back down. Eventually, I dozed off and awoke hours later; as far as I could see on the train, everyone was sleeping. Weathered-faced Bolivians wrapped in layers of striped woolen blankets, wearing chullo hats with earflaps, and adjacent to me in the other aisle seat was the love of my life, sitting in his underwear, shirt off, pants around his ankles, mouth open, sawing logs.

I missed his authenticity. The world would be a better place with a lot more Rics. I doubted a lot at that moment, but that was something I would never doubt.

When I reached the delivery room, Kate, a timid national staff member, stood at the end of the table, wide-eyed between a laboring woman's legs, one hand resting on the patient's flexed knee. She wore gloves, but her fingers were not long enough to fill the tips. I opened a package of sterile gloves and wrestled my sweaty hands into each glove. As half of the crowning head took a needed rest on the perineum, I noted the silent mother-to-be staring at the ceiling.

"Tell her to give us one last big push, Kate."

Kate translated my message. The woman lifted her head, wide-eyed, and then quickly snapped her eyes closed and connected to her power source.

"Watch closely. The next delivery is yours," I said, and Kate smiled back at me.

With that, the slippery, sputtering infant slid into my hands. His puckered face suggested he was not happy on dry land. I wiped his face with gauze. He hooted for attention, and I placed him on his sweaty mother's chest. Then Kate and the new mother exchanged words.

Kate asked, "The mother wants to know what she should call him?" I learned later that asking the person who delivered the baby for a name was their tradition.

"Call him Ric," I said.

After removing my gloves and washing my hands, I thought of my teaching role in this mission. I felt more confident than ever, especially knowing Ric's namesake had just taken his first breath.

CHAPTER 10:
KICKING YOUR WAY

February 1, 2010

I chuckled, pondering how "Ric" fared through the night and if he possessed the same voracious appetite as the Ric I once knew. I'd wager the mother and baby were still in the ward unless they seized the opportunity to leave early this morning to evade the heat. If they opted to stay, as many of our women do after birth, they'd probably wait until midday when the sun's intensity lessens before embarking on their walk home. A whiff of coffee caught my attention as I passed the guards' tukul.

One unarmed guard sat at the entrance of our gate twenty-four hours a day, the organization's eyes and ears. Facing each other, the two older men swapped shifts and handshakes—one eager for sleep and the other rejuvenated for the day ahead. I waved casually as I briskly passed by at my customary pace.

As I neared the clinic, I spied Martha, an older, rounder, chatty staff member, sitting outside. One of her flip-flops rested on the ground before her while she massaged some-thing shiny onto her foot, which she had casually propped over her opposite knee. The Nuer women use whatever they have on hand, either petroleum ointment or cooking oil, to soften their feet both in the morning and at night. *Looks like cooking oil.* With a grin, Martha rubbed her hands together, slipped back into her flip-flops, and rose to her feet. We exchanged our customary morning greetings.

"What happened to your arm?" she asked.

I stretched out my right arm and displayed what she had mentioned. She reached for my forearm to scrutinize it.

"I spilled coffee. Burned it," I said, looking down at my pale forearm. I glanced at the quarter-size blister that formed yesterday, now taut with a red boundary.

Martha made a clicking sound, a noise you make with your tongue in the back of your mouth like a giddyap when riding a horse. Then, a "ptooey" as she directed a small puddle of spittle on top of the bulla. *Did she just spit on my arm?* I offered her a tight-lipped smile and glanced down-ward, noticing the fine drops of spit reflecting the sun's rays. I told myself to look calm.

Spitting was a traditional part of daily life here, more so for the women than the men. It was customary for women to spit when taking a break in their dialogue; it highlighted the seriousness of their story. To me, it was their exclamation point. My prearrival research also revealed that Nuer spit on each other's wounds to speed up healing. They also spit on the heads of children they want to bless or have not seen in a long time. Reading this and experiencing it was different.

"Come quick. The baby is kicking," Liz called from the delivery room. Rescued again.

I jogged around the corner and flicked aside the dang-ling curtain that served as our door, noticing the familiar metallic scent. Mayian's gloved hands supported the head of the newcomer, slippery puddles at his feet, looking for the drain on the concrete floor. My short time here has taught me that *kicking* and *labor* were synonymous with each other, both guaranteeing that at least one body part of the infant had exited the mother. Two innocent words that now revved my engine. With a smile and a reassuring nod, I moved in next to Mayian.

"Tell her she's almost done. Give us one last push." Then, in the position of an upside-down luge racer, the glossy child landed in his outstretched arms—a gurgle followed by a full-blast shrill cry announcing her entry. And here we were again, back to that kicking thing.

The Nuer believed the child kicked its way out of the uterus. This belief always evoked a delightful and comical scenario in my imagination. A chubby, full-term fetus deciding on some random day as it floated around in the warm, amniotic fluid-filled sac, "All right, today is the day I will kick a hole in this bag of water and get out of here." Subsequently, the Jean-Claude Van Damme infant launched into a kicking frenzy and absconded from the uterus. Imagine! This cultural belief squashed traditional researchers' theories and rewarded the child with a real sense of honor during this undertaking. If only I had the same instinct as a baby, knowing exactly when it was time to make a move, to kick my way out of my funk with that type of innate wisdom.

With the last delivery out of the way, it was only mid-morning, and we still had ample time to begin our training. This misconception of "kicking" drove me crazy and would serve as an effective educational strategy for discussing the early signs of labor and the following stages. I called for the group to come to the delivery room, which was now free of any activity.

As I sorted through the crumpled papers I had stuffed into my bag earlier that morning, the staff settled into various lawn chairs. The last thing I added to my rucksack before leaving home was a printed stack of papers with "Basic Obstetric Principles." It was my way of using the last printer ink before my nine-month departure. I wasn't sure if I would ever use them, but it felt good to be zero-waste, just like Grandma.

"Are you guys ready to begin?"

Wide-eyed, the group sat poised with anticipation.

If the staff fully understood the early signs of labor, their counseling message to the patients might aid in better outcomes. Understanding the gradual onset of labor was crucial to overcoming our primary challenge: distance. Teaching the patients to recognize the early signs of labor might make more women skedaddle earlier to our clinic, reducing mortalities.

"The three stages of labor, important stuff to know because our patients live so far from us." I rifled through my handouts and began passing them to the staff.

MSF pointed out the isolation of this mission before I arrived. But I had already packed my bag and poo-pooed that information, like the heat and the flies, and had never thought about it again until now. I understand now that I had resided in a village not recognized on most maps, a dimple in the sand on Google Earth. From a bird's eye, the only signs of life included spattering tukuls, herds of unfenced cows, and meandering, well-trodden footpaths. I wondered if it was human nature to ignore things until we were forced to put on our glasses.

"This will teach us how to counsel our pregnant mothers," I said.

It took me many months of living in this place before I realized, despite the obstacles of this place—the isolation, heat, and suffering—this tiny village still shared many similarities with other parts of the world. Friends and family gathered to tell ancient stories, children played in the dirt and skinned their knees, dogs howled at the moon, and women still did most of the household duties. Across the globe, humans share numerous commonalities, but the striking disparity here was their limited access to healthcare, compounded by the unforgiving climate.

Globally, healthcare providers attending to expectant mothers aim to convey sound advice to mitigate unnecessary risks and support women as they grapple with this seemingly endless undertaking. A mantra easily slides off our tongues about early signs of labor, warning signs, and kick counts. A consistent message like this almost (*almost*) guarantees fewer sleepless nights. I remembered a case from my last practice in the USA. I received a call in the early morning hours from a pregnant woman because she had "lost her mucus plug," convinced the loss of this slimy thing constituted labor. I desperately wanted to ask her if she had looked under the bed, but I hesitated, recognizing the responsibility likely fell on me for not educating her on this topic. Here, the handheld radio replaced the early morning phone calls with crackles, snaps, and buzzes, announcing a patient had arrived with a "kicking" baby, which prompted me to dash across the hard-packed dirt path to the maternity ward. I yearned for a setting in the world that had a middle-of-the-road approach.

I read from the handout, "Each stage is determined by distinct characteristics, exemplified by the centimeters of cervical dilation, the child's position in the pelvis, and the placenta's expulsion."

"James, could you continue to read for us?" I pointed out where to start on the poorly xeroxed copy he held. James, a clever-witted national staff member, stood facing his colleagues with a wide stance and began reading aloud. "There are two phases in the first stage, latent and active. The progression of dilation of the cervix defines which phase the mother is enduring. The passageway opens at the end of this initial stage, and the mother is ready to push."

"Keep going," I said.

He cleared his throat and continued. "The second stage of labor begins when the cervix is fully dilated, ten centimeters, while the woman pushes out the child. The stage is terminated with the delivery of the baby."

He glanced my way, and I gave him a subtle nod, signaling him to proceed with the reading. All eyes in the room were watching his every move.

"The final stage of labor, or the third stage, is emptying the uterus. This is when the red, disc-shaped infant's life-supporting organ is expelled. The entirety of these stages is 'labor.'"

"Can we review this concept over the next week?" I asked. The group stood and applauded, thanking James for his participation.

Throughout the week, I drew life-size pictures on the whiteboard of one uterus after another, filled with colorful infants surrounded by muscle fibers. For the stages of labor, I generated time-series graphs and plot points. I gave impromptu animated lectures and threw in the relationship of the maternal hormones, the initiation of labor, and the circuitry of all the physiological relationships that played pivotal roles in birth. I was a broken record.

We returned to our circle a week later on the final review day.

I asked, "Do you get how it works now?" as my head delivered an encouraging wag to each individual.

Then, I noticed the unanimous nodding of the entire group.

"Do you guys understand that it is not the baby that decides when labor will occur?"

"Yes!" they yelled politely in unison, the group still nodding.

"Because contractions start slow and build over time, we need to tell our patients to come to the clinic as soon as they notice changes," I said, my head still moving up and down.

"Yes, yes." The group still mirrored my gesture.

Now, with a room full of grinning, assenting staff, I believed they fully understood.

"Let's get to work. James and Kate, please come with me."

The three of us approached the day's first patient, sitting alone in the exam room, clutching a torn cloth. She flicked the towel rhythmically in front of her face to deter the flies from landing. *Damn flies.* I swatted the ones she sent my way.

"Please ask her how far she lives from the clinic?"

After a bit of exchange, Kate replied, "Three hours in the dry season." The rainy season and trudging through the night would add hours to the journey.

Then I asked, "When was her last period?"

James jumped in, "She knows when the baby will come. The moon and the seasons will tell her." End of discussion. I never pushed this; they always knew when the baby would come consistently and more accurately than an early ultrasound. There was no way to prove or disprove this theory; my diagnostic tools consisted of a retractable measuring tape, partially torn at the three-centimeter mark, a fetoscope, and my two hands. I let that one go.

Last question, the moment of truth. That kicking thing.

"Does she know when to come to the clinic to give birth?" I asked.

In unison, James and Kate announced, "When the baby begins to kick," which caused us all to burst into laughter. I never knew if they were joking or serious.

Sarah's entry interrupted our comical exchange. Wide-eyed, she said, "Sheilee, there is a patient in the delivery room. She is not in labor, the baby is just moving." (A.k.a., kicking its way out.) I smiled. Back to square one.

Entering the room, I asked, "When did your labor start?"

Before the patient could answer, she gripped the delivery room table with both hands, extended her head to the sky, and closed her eyes. I touched her rock-hard abdomen and noted a river of sweat dripping off her prominent neck veins. *Looks like labor to me.* A minute passed, and the patient composed herself, glared at me, and through translation, said, "Tell the *khwaya* (foreigner, i.e., me) I am not in labor." Followed by her sending her "exclamation mark" five centimeters from my foot. Then, she quickly hopped off the table, straightened her skirt, and grabbed her son's hand.

"I will return when I am in labor," she told the translator. Her son, who was recently diagnosed with kala-azar, a deadly disease caused by the sand fly, needed his daily injection—one of the thirty painful treatments. The mother and child silhouettes exited the clinic, leaving nothing more to be said.

I quietly followed her to the injection tukul, exam gloves in hand, and waited behind her in the doorway as the staff prepared the child's medication. Suddenly, without a peep, she lifted her arms and clutched the doorframe. She dropped to her knees and, without warning, started to bear down. I smiled and donned my gloves, and with her tremendous strength and one push, the screaming child dropped into my hands. *Not labor, right?* As I held the newborn, our eyes met, and I lifted my chin, pointing to the delivery room. She smiled. The three of us hobbled back to the delivery room, still attached.

Despite the staff's endearing attributes, I could not teach, cajole, or persuade most of the national staff in the obstetric ward and the patients who came to the clinic for delivery that my message was well-founded. My explanation of labor and contractions was just words. Gibberish. I needed to rethink my strategy.

My growling stomach told me it was time for lunch. I headed for the compound.

Haven't I learned that I have so little control over my life?

My need to control the narrative only frustrated me. Haven't I learned the dangers of it? Sure, the message to the staff was important, but force-feeding would not work. All of my stubborn bones believed the facts were the facts—kilometers from reasonable, my inability to see anything but black or white.

Have I not gained insight in this brief period? Here, women orally transmitted narratives and information. I must trust this incredible force, let them talk, and relive their positive experiences from birthing in our clinic. This teaching could motivate them to encourage their cousins, nieces, and aunts to consider our clinic. My understanding needed to be adjusted to better suit this context.

My counselor's advice came back to me. According to her, individuals who fail in their efforts to shape the narrative find themselves chased by unfulfilled expectations. When I heard her say this, I anchored it to others, but now I realize it had been directed at me all along. My days would be less stressful if I concentrated only on what I could influence and let the rest melt into curiosity and acceptance of the uncertainty.

Talking to myself, I marinated in those thoughts.

I cannot control their cultural beliefs.

I cannot control the lack of access to care.

But I can control my early morning sprints to the maternity ward, catching baby after baby as they kick their way into the first light of the African mornings.

In hindsight, I should have extended my focus beyond my everyday responsibilities. I should have explored the dynamics of relinquishing control with my more significant issues—the baggage I carried in the mission: grief and self-doubt. This realization made me wonder if I could have attained inner peace sooner. I wish I had known to give myself more grace and time, trusting that I would "kick my way out" through the suffering when the time was right.

Nearly reaching the compound's entry gate, I noticed I was alone. I covertly zeroed in on a dirt patch next to my left Dansko clog. I readied myself, gathered saliva in my mouth, puckered my lips, and aimed. A slow string of bubbles dribbled across my lips, off my chin, and cascaded down my chest, with the last drops landing on my pant leg. While I had secretly envied the accuracy of the Nuer women's marksmanship, I've realized that I should stick with what I am good at.

CHAPTER 11: THE FATES

March 5, 2010

Resting in my tukul, I heard the generator's hum, followed by a rap on my tukul.

"Ready?" Rupert asked.

Our night's routine was the same as usual. Rupert and I wrapped up the day by taking showers (separately) and filling our bellies with rice. In the first three months, Rupert and I developed a brother-sister relationship. We shared age, a love of DIY hobbies, early mornings, and a sarcastic sense of humor. Similarities attract, cliques form everywhere, and this mission was no different. We proudly spoke of our partners, acknowledging their importance in our lives. I spoke of Ric in the present; Rupert never asked, and I never clarified. It was more enjoyable in the present. It felt like "good grieving," a soothing balm. A rehearsal for reality, trying to outlive the words Ric's living survivors spoke to me at Ric's memorial: "One day, you'll be able to talk about him without tears."

He recounted his sailing adventure, and I told him about my bike trips on various continents. We shared the effortless capacity to sit together in silence, embracing the rolling thrill of the red-throated bee-eaters that buzzed around the compound. He gave me a sense of security like Ric, but more like a real brother I never had. And if Ric's promises held, "After I die, when you see a bird, think of me. It will be me watching over you," I was convinced that the owl who hooted at me nightly would be pleased Rupert was around to keep me grounded.

I liked most of the expats but avoided a few because I knew spending more time with them could change my opinion. It was challenging to assemble a group of multinational workers, drop them together via a small plane, and expect them to seamlessly integrate, sharing living spaces, meals, and basic facilities without eventually finding someone who grates on someone else. Our primary aim was to maintain harmony among the team because we were there to deliver vital emergency health services to the local community.

During our year of working together, Rupert and I indulged in a few bottles of Jameson, keeping it clandestine within the sacred bond of our mutual trust. When I arrived at the mission, I brought two bottles; the team of expats quickly consumed the first. So, I selfishly hid the other to drink at a later date. Early on, I felt guilty, but I learned everyone had a secret or two in their tukul over the years of doing missions. Frequently up at night with maternity calls, I found myself privy to the expats who discreetly shared living quarters in the wee hours of the night. It didn't take long to understand why some men were whistling come morning. Rupert learned of my secret of stashing a fifth and replenishing our stock after one of his holidays, buying two, donating one to the team, and hiding the other for our evening routine.

"Coming." I stumbled out of my tukul and tried to catch up with Rupert.

It was essential to secure one of the four community computers quickly. However, the amount of fuel available for the generator restricted our time surfing the internet, leaving no room for lollygagging. Walking briskly while curling my socked toes around the thongs of the flip-flops was challenging, but socks were essential to deter night-biting insects from reaching your ankles. Rupert cleared his throat to get my attention. He raised his eyebrows while hoisting the two mugs he carried in a gesture akin to a toast. We laughed.

We grabbed the free chairs and the last computer and began our search.

"I need to buy a watch, and I need your help to select one," he said.

"A watch?" I snickered, watching the computer boot up slowly.

He planned to order the item online, ship it to his Welsh residence, and collect it during his next brief vacation there. It was such an absurd object in a place where ancient customs prevailed, where the passage of time blurred. Brisk on the surface and agonizingly sluggish at the same time. While the other expats spoke to relatives on WhatsApp in the same space, we shopped, compared, laughed, and savored our modest rations that forged our unique bond. I laugh now, remembering how he held up his muscular forearm next to the dusty screen of the Lenovo.

"What do you think?" he asked, as if trying to visualize each watch adorned on his wrist.

It was trivial, but now a cherished memory. What was it about this watch? It had nothing to do with the watch. We could have searched for a stuffed rabbit or a set of tea towels. It was a moment to marinate in comfortable predictability. Our connection—secret whiskey and the watch—was a getaway from reality and a way to replace the day with something more manageable, funnier, and accessible to digest.

This mission had a cumulative effect. Day after day, month after month, staring into the soul of agony was heavy. Rupert and I had forged a haven where two weary friends met and tried to replenish their spirits before the generator cut out. This moment clouded the catastrophes we yearned to erase and marked the passing days until our return home. Our silly obsession with the watch was our escape.

At this moment, I can't recall if he ever bought one. Years after this mission, I stood in a parking lot on some continent, passing time before I left on another mission. I called Rupert to catch up, and during the conversation, I asked, "Do you remember the watch?" I always loved his deep laugh. The timepiece was our combined anchor to sanity.

But that night in March, our shopping ended prematurely with the dreaded radio crackle, and someone on the other end requested I come to maternity. Bidding him a quick goodbye, I stopped in my tukul to change shoes before I dashed down the dirt path I knew intimately. Approaching the clinic, I saw a growing crowd around something. With no emergency flashing red lights or piercing sirens, this village's expanding circle of people was a telltale sign that something needed immediate attention.

Four men, sweaty with straw-like frames, stood next to the homemade stretcher made of intertwined sticks and rope. Two on each side, taking a respite from the weight of their shared burden. I could make out an outline of a body under the wool blanket. Partially uncovered, her decorative braids peeked out from the headscarf. I glanced at the men, their eyes pleading for a remedy. The time elapsed since their summons for help remained unclear. Faced with limited options, they devised a plan to carry her. Now, the dilemma rested squarely on our shoulders.

"Let's move her inside," I said. I turned around to see Moses holding the door open. I had forgotten he was working tonight. *Thank God.*

Synchronized, the four men flexed at the waist, lifted the stretcher, and walked into the delivery room. The crowd dispersed. A fresh trail followed us into the room, continuing the path of vital fluids that linked her to her distant village. The men hoisted her gently onto the delivery table before politely leaving the room, closing the door behind them.

Once in the supine position with her knees flexed, heels close to her buttocks, we placed the metal kidney basin between her legs on the drop-down portion of the delivery room table. A monotonous *ping, ping* echoed as the metal basin steadily collected the source of our problem. It was the first time I witnessed fear twirl in the pupils of Moses's eyes as we both observed the soft, squishy mass extending from her vagina, one side still clinging to half of the dilated cervix.

Typically, with the assistance of the national staff, I could navigate through most obstetrical situations. But this was different; I was reluctant to ask for help when it intruded on someone's leisure time, especially when we had such limited amounts. Plus, I detested facing my limitations. Over time, I learned the simplicity of seeking colleague support when necessary. I discovered expats were always ready to lend a hand without criticism or backlash, even if it meant interrupting their free time. It doesn't make one an unworthy clinician to ask for help; instead, it makes one clever.

The patient's insistent placenta was not waiting for its turn. The urgent need for a C-section was clear, but with no access to an operating theater or nighttime air travel, my pleas fell on deaf ears—a scenario of trying to fix a leaky engine with chewing gum. My internal sirens launched into a frenzy, and I radioed for help. Minutes later, Hanna, my Dutch colleague, strode in. I referred to her as my "tall sister." Incredible competence mixed with a tender heart were her most impressive traits, and I welcomed both. We had previously tackled challenging cases in the inpatient ward, marked by seamless teamwork and mutual respect. Tonight was our first case together in maternity, and I harbored no uncertainty that it would be just as successful as our previous endeavors.

"Thanks for coming," I said as we watched Moses loosen the roller clamp on the IV tubing, which dangled below the warm, deep-crimson bag overhead. Owing to our skilled lab technicians' expertise and the development of safe protocols, we could collect blood from one donor and promptly transfuse it into another. This new donation, still warm, freshly retrieved from one of her porters, inched its way through the sterile IV tubing to a foreign land—an attempt to fill her empty tank and give her and her baby a chance. We were already at the *C* of the ABCs of resuscitation. But the nonstop *ping, ping*, a metronome of fifty beats per minute in the metal kidney dish, reminded us of the unresolved hurdle.

"What if we rupture the membranes?" Hanna said. "It might allow the baby's head to engage in the pelvis and tamponade the bleeding." Then she paused with her hands on her hips, chewing on her bottom lip.

"Then we could add oxytocin to speed up the contractions," I added, moving toward the cabinet to retrieve the drug.

Softly, the patient started to mumble.

"What is she saying, Moses?" I asked.

"She's praying," he replied.

Her prayers for all to hear; mine, voiceless.

Hanna, Moses, and I recycled the options and unpredictability of our plan. Our eyes collided, and our heads nodded. We had no other choice but to chase this child out. Needling the amniotic sac, we strong-armed the amber fluid into the metal tray, which diluted the congealed red to pale pink, and allowed gravity to help the head of the infant settle deep into the pelvis—similar to a blockage in a drain. Simultaneously, we collectively drew in a deep breath. The three of us sat on overturned buckets at the foot of the bed. Our eyes counted the slow drips of oxytocin while we waited for it to stimulate the uterine fibers and escort the child to safety. The airless room intensified the oppressive heat and my stench. As the time stretched endlessly, the mother expelled a soft moan and adjusted her position on the table.

We all stood and elbowed each other with a smile. Then, just as Mother Nature intended, first a round head covered with slicked-back glistening curls, then the infant's body, and finally, the placenta entered the African night. Sweat and tears dribbled from the tips of our noses onto the child.

That night, we refrained from saying our unconvincingly optimistic words—"At least the mother lived." These words were like those interjected after Ric's death, trying to dull the sting: "Well, at least you didn't have children," or, "You can always find another husband." The understandable anxiety that can take hold before humans have a chance to sift through their words.

I think our exchange about the mother's living also made us feel more worthy, like we actually "saved" someone, and our hours at the bedside were worth it, strengthening the driving force that motivates many healthcare workers to show up each day. Facing the fact that I could never save Ric was a sobering moment. I knew I couldn't alter the course of his disease. My sole focus became ensuring his journey to the next place was as pain-free as possible. One of my biggest worries was that he would die suffering. But through administering medications and comforting measures at the end of his life, I believe I spared him from unnecessary agony, and that gives me the sense, I *kind of* saved him.

Afterward, the patient sat, taking sips of water from the cupped palm of another woman. I wondered if we outsmarted the instigator tonight or if the universe tilted in our favor. But the only thing we heard, standing under the glow of the dim lightbulbs, the door ajar, allowing the night breeze to creep in, was a hypnotizing cry—loudest from the newborn, discrete from us.

Some might call the situation luck, but that overlooks credit for the villagers' perseverance. When this patient's plight was thrust upon them, they confronted fate and the unfolding of circumstances beyond their control. They carried her.

Confronting fate head-on may be the catalyst for unveiling our authentic selves and coming to terms with the profound reality of life's unpredictable journey. A new and improved way to enjoy a great day, and never be disappointed that it did not last forever. A practice of letting go of our needy ego and its desperate grip on control. No expectations, only hope. It brought me back to a day, about three months into Ric's chemotherapy. He had finished another weekly treatment, and we trudged hand in hand to our parked car. Ric ambled, showing his fatigue.

After getting into the car and buckling up, Ric said, "Look at that guy."

He lifted his chin to point where to look. A man, about thirty, was sitting on a bench under the shade of a tree adjacent to the hospital entrance. The lower part of his belly hung freely over his jeans. He held a Coke in one hand and a cigarette in the other.

"It does kind of suck that guy will outlive me." He closed his eyes and pressed his head on the seat rest.

I waited.

Then he opened his eyes, grinned, and said, "But I have no one to blame, not the doctors, or a higher power. This is my fate."

I leaned toward him and kissed his cheek.

"Let's get out of here," he said, smiling. *Always smiling.*

Ric took an active role in his fate, finding acceptance and purpose in how to spend his remaining days.

The villagers who carried the woman, like Ric, accepted that certain events were out of their control but opted for an active stance in the pregnant woman's destiny. They made a collective decision and carried the patient to the hospital, hoping, not expecting, that she and her baby would live.

This made me think about the Greek Fates of Moirai, three weaving goddesses in Greek mythology—the mighty women who held the reins over birth and destiny in a thread of time. Clotho was the spinner of the thread, Lachesis was the measurer of the thread, and Atropos was the one with the scissors. Atropos had the final say. She determined at what point to sever the thread of life. For no other way to explain tonight, I believed Clotho and Lachesis were hard at work, and Atropos misplaced her scissors.

Switching on our head torches, I threw my arm around Hanna's waist, and we retreated to home base. I told Moses to call me if he had any issues throughout the night. His big grin stuck permanently, and he tipped his head in agreement. I now realize why I admired Moses: He shared that irrepressible smile with Ric. Ric would have liked Moses.

As I walked out the door, Moses yelled, "Don't forget we meet the TBAs tomorrow."

I had already forgotten. "That's right. Thanks again, Moses. Great job."

Hanna and I, a couple of very tall women—one entirely Dutch, and I, with a slight spattering of Dutch from my forefathers—trudged back to the compound. Now giddy, exhausted, and still replaying what had just happened, we welcomed the fresh night air and admired the lights that flickered through the pinholes in the black cloth of the sky. It jolted my mind how I found camaraderie in one of the most challenging places I have been. I imagined more "tall sisters" out there; I just had to let them in. The world was more accessible to tackle with others.

A bitter mustard-like aroma hit me as we passed through the gate. *Turmeric again.* A rhizome from the ginger family—vital for curry. But for the record, it was not a standalone spice, not in small quantities or by the tablespoons. Our hired Sudanese cooks tried to determine what the international expats would eat. They happily showed up for work, cooked with unfamiliar ingredients brought in by our plane. They attempted to serve us a proper meal—no doubt challenging because a Nuer's standard meal was sorghum and fermented cow milk.

They added corn to the spaghetti sauce, mixed canned cream into the overcooked pasta, and served fried and boiled eggs and omelets the same day. They reheated the flatbread and goat meat that no one liked from the night before and boiled large amounts of rice for breakfast. Somehow, an enormous jar of turmeric arrived in our cargo, and the cooks in the kitchen transformed most of the prepared food into a deep golden hue. We translated and retranslated, and they smiled and nodded, seeming to understand. We walked away, convinced supper would be different. Last month, I hid the turmeric. But it tiptoed back. Laughable on some days, cuss-worthy on the rest, and deep in our hearts, we knew they were trying their best to please our fussy foreign palates.

"You aren't going to eat?" Hanna asked as we passed the kitchen and saw the food still on the table from supper.

"I'll pass." I was looking forward to a few hours of sleep.

Hanna headed to the kitchen, and I headed toward my bed. I wondered if I would face more clinical challenges like this for the rest of my mission or if tonight was just an outlier. I shuddered to think of the former. More repetitions of tonight would be inconceivable. On edge, I pushed the thoughts from my head, not knowing then that this was just the beginning of a powerful landslide.

Kicking off my clogs, I locked eyes with the photo of my toothy-grinned mate from my past, sitting on my top shelf. Atropos and her sharp scissors snipped him away. *Why?* Why did she sometimes slash the thread, and at other times, she observed? Out of my control, her reasoning, and clicking scissors.

Don't go there tonight. But then I did. This whole fate thing swirled and tangled my thoughts. Was there a different way to look at it?

I undressed, trotted over to the shower, and cleaned off in the last drop of tepid water held in the reservoir.

Refreshed and back in the tukul, I dropped my folded laundry from the mattress to my bedside chair and stretched out on my cot, ushering thoughts of Ric out the back door.

I need to sleep.

A rustling on my shelves interrupted my attempt at deep breathing. I flicked on my torch, and like a sole actor on a stage, a round ball of brown prickly spines looked back at me. A hedgehog—a nighttime feeder, eater of snakes, and completely harmless. My beam of light followed his jerky, stuttering steps, now resembling a wind-up toy, as he hurried under my bed. I thought briefly about letting him be but knew he would stay until formally asked to depart.

As my feet hit the dirt floor, it took refuge in an unreachable corner in the tukul. I spied my umbrella propped by the door, now retired from the rainy season. It was just the length I needed to reach this now pain in my ass.

When threatened, hedgehogs rolled into a ball, a protective layer. I found kinship with this creature. I also wore a thorny exterior in moments of challenge or threat while cradling my tender and softer qualities within. I just did not eat snakes.

The more I poked and prodded, the tighter his protective sphere became. When I finally got the prickly ball in full view, I used my umbrella like a hockey stick. It took a few bounces off the tukul wall until I perfected my swing, and with enough momentum, I scored. He rolled across the dirt, passed the door frame, and, with a *thunk*, made contact with the tree trunk in front of my tukul, now splayed from his tuck and roll.

Shit, I killed him.

Then, as if the kinetic energy rekindled, he skittered into the dark in the opposite direction.

The last critter who wanted to be my roommate appeared a week earlier. I popped into my tukul for my hat when I spotted a fourteen-inch tail of "something" curled next to my metal trunk. Before I dared to discover what creature owned that tail, I automatically grabbed my umbrella. As I clenched my benign weapon, I peered behind the trunk. Looking up at me, like, "Yes, may I help you?" was this lizard, smaller than an adult alligator but more significant than a baby alligator. In my country, I knew what to fear, what was poisonous, and what was harmless. But having lived here for less than three months, I didn't know what would kill you, eat you, or just inflict terrible pain. So, until

I figured this out, I grouped everything into one mantra: "Kick their butt before they have a chance to kick yours."

This considerable-sized reptile was agile on its feet. I initiated the whirlwind chase around the tukul. The problem I faced was that he seemed to think the umbrella was an olive branch. He invited himself onto the umbrella, like someone shimmying up a tree trunk, legs wrapped around it, tongue intermittently popping out of his mouth, inching his way to my hand. I could picture Ric standing there, jumping up and down, laughing and coaxing me to "hit 'em harder, Sheil" in my battle with this unknown beast.

As the reptile climbed toward me on the umbrella, I squealed and dropped him and my makeshift bludgeon. He toppled to the floor and ran behind some other short-term shelter. We repeated this dance multiple times. I eventually figured I would have to invite him halfway up the umbrella and then run like hell out of my tukul—umbrella, and lizard, in hand. As he made his final grasp around the umbrella and slowly slinked toward my hand, flicking out his forked tongue, I ran screaming out of my tukul and successfully catapulted him across the compound. The dust flew when he hit the ground running, and I never saw him again. Message received.

Now, with a critter-free tukul, it was time to sleep. Just before my heavy lids signed off for the day, I felt a pang of foreboding. I consoled myself by silently chuckling about the critters, not wanting to pose any doubt about my decision to come here or what the future may bring.

The night temperature was tolerable. The nighttime symphony began with the gentle calls from my wise, feathered fowl and rhythmic clicks of the nocturnal insects. Yet, as I turned on my back after securely tucking in my mosquito net under the perimeter of my mattress, I swear I could still smell that spice.

CHAPTER 12: IN THE WAKE OF BLISS

March 6, 2010

The morning after the late-night obstetric case, the lack of sleep made me stare ahead, nontalkative with the rest of the expats at the breakfast gathering table. I silently sipped my morning coffee. As usual, after a brief night's sleep, their lively chatter grated on my nerves. It was times like these when I wished I had chosen another career that allowed me to sleep through the night. Even though I loved what I did, the hours could be annoying. Maybe I was just tired. But it was more than that. And the heat and the flies made everything worse. "Damn it," I blurted out, brushing away the flies that landed on the rim of my cup.

As I approached the third month, a creeping intuition whispered, offering me a preview of what lay ahead in the mission's coming months. It was reminiscent of the quiet stillness that settled in after the vibrant energy of the honeymoon faded away. When your bridal gown was laundered and tucked away in the depths of your closet, and you pored over the instruction manuals for the kitchen gadgets gifted to you at your wedding. Meanwhile, a crochet quilt in mismatched colors lay over the arm of your couch, left out for fear the cousin who made it might visit unexpectedly. It was a phase when the excitement dimmed, and that familiar alarm clock rang at 6:30 a.m. As you rubbed the sleep from your eyes, you tried to see what lay ahead.

Something in my gut was sending me a message.

The shadows of the branches above formed a lace table-cloth and choked out the start of the fiery rays of heat for the morning. I sighed. Then the buzzing started; first, a low-frequency buzz as the flies darted about. The poorer pilots miscalculated their trajectory and bounced off the side of my head. I wondered, *Where are they going? Why are they wasting all their energy bolting about in 36-degree Celsius temperatures?* As I scrutinized the flies, it reminded me of how Sudan pulled me into the presence of being in the now. Akin to a theatrical performance that unfolded with exaggerated senses, where whispers felt like roars, smells lingered into the night, flavors assumed the roles of problematic judges, sight tiptoed with cautious steps, and touch yearned for a tender connection. I knew living in the past tormented me, and the future scared the hell out of me, but this being in the now also left me untethered, wading into an incoming tide, and I had no clue what to do with it.

A high-pitched buzz grabbed my attention. Upended flies spun on their backs on the sticky plastic tablecloth, gyrating in circles to right their ship. Frantic, upside down, twirling in circles, and going nowhere. I saw echoes of my turmoil—me at the Rambler, on the summit of Kilimanjaro, and yet again, in Sudan.

"These damn flies," I mumbled, watching the breakdancers on the table.

Holding my morning brew, I glanced at my chipped I Love NY mug. Trained to have a look-before-drinking mentality, I saw two akin table dancers treading water in my drink. Early on, a movement in my cup raised my hackles, but I had adapted to the fly-in-your-drink situation. I inserted my fingers and flicked the two interlopers to the ground. They landed close to my shoe, rolled like wet dogs, rid themselves of the stuck sand, and shot back into the universe to no doubt piss someone else off.

"Bastards. I should have killed them," I muttered to myself, slapping off something crawling on my neck.

Whether a fly, cat, human, or toad, we are all focused on ridding ourselves of the embedded dirt and rushing back to blue skies, even when we don't know where we are going.

Had the death of Ric challenged my true self? That state of neutrality, a feeling of inner peace, humility, and connection. An authentic place where my negative emotions and thoughts existed, but more on the surface, because then I knew I was so much more than those fleeting, disrupting sensations. In that sanctuary of my marriage, my ego took the passenger's seat, reassured by the safety of my surroundings. There, I could unveil every facet of myself, secure in the unwavering acceptance from Ric. I wasn't the child being slapped and told to "stop crying" or "stand up straight, stop slouching." Instead, Ric embraced me as a woman, brushed aside my tears, and tenderly urged, "Talk to me, Sheil. What is it?" But now, my ego, that needy bastard, was at the wheel again. I was searching for a quick fix, attached to outcomes and expectations for this mission, and smothering my true self with perceptions, evaluations, and preconceived judgments. I may have only brought fifteen kilograms in my rucksack, and I don't remember packing this, but somehow it came along.

As the demands mounted and the heat intensified, the thrill of the mission was wearing off. I yearned for the excitement, joy, and ecstasy I felt when I first arrived in Sudan. As the positive vibes dwindled, I began to feel disconnected and judged, and I felt a sense of utter loneliness. Usually, when I looked for what was missing and my ego tried to fill that void, I tied my sneakers and hit the road. That familiar feeling was back again for the first time since I left the US; Barb's voice was louder, and my vulnerability grew. And even in my new world, the coils of her vine still had a foothold on me. But in this context, fleeing was entirely off the table. The mere realization of it was enough to stir up a cyclone of anxiety within me. But amidst my internal chaos, what truly captivated me were the vibrant souls of the local staff, their insatiable curiosity, contagious energy, and their boundless passion for life that seemed to seep out of every corner from nowhere.

Somehow, I needed to fight back.

I saw the mamas in the kitchen and nudged myself. I needed to remind them about our teatime with the TBAs. I rose and liberated myself from the relentless discomfort of my perpetual wedgie that chased me around this environment.

I walked to the kitchen, needing a coffee refill, and greeted the women scurrying around. I wished I were hungry.

"Today at five is teatime with the TBAs," I said. "Would you put water on to boil around four-thirty?"

I previously hoarded a box of Lipton tea bags, a kilo of sugar, a jar of jam, and some biscuits. I pulled them from the pantry cupboard where I had previously stashed them.

"Can we come?" Sarah, the tallest of the mamas, asked while the other two looked at me, awaiting their invitation.

"Of course, just bring everything over at five." The two mamas clapped their hands and grinned. I made another cup of coffee and headed to the clinic, but I was doubtful the TBAs' meeting would transpire.

Hours later, Liz summoned the last patient from the waiting bench and brought her into the clinic for her prenatal evaluation. She expertly delivered care, handed her the monthly ration, a bar of soap, and sent the woman on her way. I sighed, thankful for an uneventful day.

Standing by the door, I massaged the middle of my sore back and saw three mamas from the kitchen, arms laden with supplies, approaching me. Still skeptical but bent on thanking them for their effort, I smiled and motioned for them to approach me. Once at the clinic's entrance, they placed everything on a tarp and prepared our offerings.

I looked at my watch. *Not yet five. Ten minutes to go.*

Suddenly, as if materializing from thin air, a procession of women came into view. Their dresses fluttered in the wind, their faces adorned with broad smiles, and scarves graced their heads. Leading the group, Ahieu. This diverse group of women, spanning generations, many with decades of experience, approached me. The hair on my arms stood on end.

"Liz, look. There has to be at least forty," I said.

She gazed at me with an expression that seemed to say, "Obviously."

I expected none. Liz hoped for many.

Over the past months, I have fretted about our clinic's inability to connect with the surrounding villages. While I was marinating in worry, the national staff discreetly took the puzzle pieces and made a plan. I never heard them discuss this; they just made it happen.

"All of the national staff are here too," Liz said.

I greeted each TBA individually, and then we sat. Through the translator, I thanked them for coming, explained our services, and welcomed them into our delivery room anytime to bring in their patients and work side by side. Afterward, I gave them a tour of our clinic. When I asked them what I could offer to help their situation, they expressed a need for training. They sought the intangible, something immune to expiration, unbreakable, and perpetually transportable—knowledge. We agreed to meet monthly.

We summed up the meeting with overly sweet tea, some stale biscuits, and a jar of apricot jam. I knew the national staff liked incredibly sweet tea, so I brought a kilo of sugar for the meeting, but the cutest part was watching the TBAs pass the open jar of jam, each giving it a quick sniff, digging their spoon in the gelatinous substance, and plopping a big spoonful in their tea—more energy to walk home. When the sun's intensity faded, the group stood, pointing out their need to depart for home before the night fell.

As they rose to leave, they formed a line. Ahieu was first in line with a stretched-out female ribbon behind her. Moses, a proficient translator at my side, leaned in attentively to capture Ahieu's last words.

"The TBAs brought a record of the number of deliveries they took part in over the last month," he said.

"Great," I replied, remembering I had asked Ahieu to do that.

Without pause, Ahieu handed me two bundles of minuscule sticks resembling toothpicks, both easily cradled in my palm. A white string secured one collection, and a black tie bound the other.

"What is this?" I asked.

Moses asked her and began translating, "The white string represents babies they delivered that lived, and the black string represents babies that died."

Each TBA faced me individually, presented their parcels, offered a gentle double pat on my chest with their flat palms, and silently departed. Despite similar-looking stacks, twig numbers varied from TBA to TBA. Later, I learned most TBAs were illiterate but innovative enough to devise another type of tally sheet. Had I expected a piece of paper with the numbers? *What a fool.* It was their ingenious way to arrive at a solution, their resourceful way to keep a correct count. Two wrapped parcels from each TBA, white for life and black for death. All proof of their innovation, obstacles, and the reality of living in the African bush. Counting the tiny bundles afterward revealed there was a little less than a fifty percent chance of surviving a birth in a faraway tukul.

Less than three weeks after the first TBA rendezvous in March, our clinic was already seeing results. It didn't take my bullhorn to ignite this; the national staff initiated it. Word of mouth, introductions, and trust turned our previously slow-moving clinic into a booming atmosphere. We needed additional space to conduct our clinical activities—a remedy for one issue triggered another.

Postpartum mothers and babies filled the overflowing ward. The increase in deliveries forced us to line the ground around the clinic's exterior with tarps. The eight bedframes stayed inside the ward, reserved for the sickest. When we needed more "beds," we spread tarps on the ground and made do. We inserted random sticks into the overhanging roof, which served as a central anchor point to fasten the mosquito nets and IV bags. This area, designated for overflow patients, soon transitioned from occasional use to another outside ward.

Hoping Rupert and I could plan a more extensive maternity ward, I sat at the expats' eating, meeting, game-playing, and sometimes life-counseling table, waiting for him to show. He oversaw the logistics of the mission. He taught his national staff carpentry, mechanics of the generator, and logistical things that kept the mission running. The outside temperature was already on the rise. How did I find myself in one of the hottest African nations? My aversion to heat began during my two family vacations at the beach, where I took refuge most of my time under the umbrella. Try as I might, the intense sun and sand still burned my pale skin. I recalled the vivid redness beyond my swimsuit boundaries. Barb suggested a cream for relief, but when mixed with the gritty remnants of sand that stuck to my body, it felt like sandpaper rubbing against my already-tender skin.

I heard him before I saw him.

Rupert arrived, out of breath from running. "Sorry I am late."

"Don't worry about it," I replied.

A few hours after Rupert's arrival, his dusty notebook held our plans. We concocted a mix of interconnected rectangles and squares to serve as the new maternity unit.

"Structures here are built with branches and sticks, and then we hire local mudders to finish," Rupert said.

"Mudders, what's that?" I waved my hands to rid the flies from landing on my face.

"They fill the gaps between the sticks with wet clay, forming the walls," he said, massaging his neck.

Mudders were community members and experts in their trade. They plunged their bare hands into buckets of wet earth and filled the voids of the stick-built foundation. They relied on strength for the first ninety percent of the task and allowed the sun to bake the final ten percent to perfection.

"We'll start tomorrow," Rupert said. We gave each other a high five and veered in the opposite direction to conclude our day.

Weeks passed, and we tripped over plastic buckets, short-handled shovels, various lengths of branches, and soggy, slick ground. The partially dried soil proved immovable by late morning. The three female mudders sang as they stuffed the wet clay between the arranged sticks. By midday, their hands resembled red plush gloves from the soil that clung to their digits—a peculiar sight in this heat. Packed wet earth in the walls and sopping dirt floors turned each finished space into a sticky, sweltering chamber. Taken aback as I entered the finished registration area—*Did I get a whiff of petrichor?* Typically, this unique fragrance arose from the earth following a rain shower, blending ozone, moisture, and plant oils harmoniously. It was impossible; it was the end of the dry season, but the scent lingered.

The smell took me back to childhood, ten years old and running in a knee-high grassy field in the rain. "Come here, Flip," my mind yelled to my black-and-white beagle as I descended the hill to the pond: Holsteins and dried cow patties peppered the wet grass. My oversized green rubber boots rubbing the calluses on my heels slowed my pace. I had uncovered peace in my less-than-peaceful life by venturing outside, seeking refuge from the turmoil. I embraced these moments of liberation, distancing myself as far as possible from the grand, two-story white house that sucked me in and called me names.

Even as a child, I possessed the capacity to make choices that enhanced my chances of survival proactively. That potential must still reside within me, but I haven't deciphered how to reclaim it. Without Ric, did it suggest I would always have an inner void, a lack of wholeness, an inability to choose a fresh alternative path? Would I ever find a place not influenced by the pains of the past? I navigated solitude as a child and managed. Stepping into adulthood introduced me to overthinking, senseless worries and anxieties, and time-wasting activities kids don't bother with. Or maybe kids can just sense bullshit sooner and activate their imagination and filter out the noise of pretense.

In my memory, the drizzle outside continued, and I took in the odor of dirt, sun, cow shit, and rain. *Ahh, the power of smell and the mind's ability to attach it to a short adventure in a nanosecond.* I closed my eyes, wishing it would last. I stole as many deep breaths as possible through my nose, divine—a brief vacation in this hot, dusty place. With an accidental nudge, my foot collided with a bucket, sending muddy water cascading down my legs, shattering the tranquil moment of nirvana.

On the last day of construction, I woke up in a grumpy mood. Hard to shake. Too many toos: too hot, too much work, too far from civilization, too many mosquitoes, too many roosters in the morning, too many unsettling night-time coughing fits coming from the neighboring tuberculous village, and too many earsplitting, late-night expat parties.

But the pressure was on, and I had an overwhelming, intense desire to be home.

To flee.

Movement quieted my mind. My mind and body were at odds with each other. The movement was a distraction; it made noise. Loud static. Scratchy white noise, which cut the connection with all of my past. My crutch to numb the wound, to delay facing it, hoping somehow it would heal on its own. Coming here was driven by the same need.

Home meant anywhere but here—an excuse to run from the uncomfortable and search for a safe nest. I dreamt of a fan; I craved a fizzy, ice-cubed drink and lusted after a meal without rice or gray goat meat. I imagined sex with Ric, his tall, runner's physique, in an enormous bed filled with pillows and milky, odorless sheets. But more than sex, I truly longed for the way he effortlessly elicited those deep belly laughs from me. The laugh that required a conscious effort to clench certain muscles to prevent a mishap.

We once went to a fancy restaurant with a few other couples— all the women in dresses and men in suits. Early in the meal, one of Ric's friends, Louie, a short bodybuilder, pushed back from the table to excuse himself for the restroom. Slender and long-limbed, Ric popped out of his chair and said, "Let's be like the girls and go in pairs." The group chuckled as the two of them set off together. About fifteen minutes later, Ric and Louie returned to our table. Laughter erupted, enough to cause the waiters and waitresses to stop and look. Ric and Louie had exchanged clothes in the men's restroom. The bottoms of Ric's black pants, Louie's from a few minutes prior, hung just below his knees, and the sleeves of Louie's jacket hit at the bend of Ric's elbows. Louie stood next to Ric, with Ric's cuffed pants rolled three times to adjust for their excessive length. Ric's borrowed white button-down shirt opened to Louie's belly button, strained against his well-defined pectoral muscles. Glancing at each other, they smiled, resumed their seats, and finished their meal as if nothing had happened—those kinds of laughs.

I didn't know before the mission, and I would have never admitted it, but part of me was running away from Ric. I longed to slam our book of time shut on the chapter of our separation and return the bound life story to its place on the shelf, giving me time to contemplate whether and when I might revisit it.

At that moment, I just needed to move to relieve some stress. However, my remote location and the significant logistical challenges made leaving nearly impossible, and that carried some serious weight.

Discombobulated, I untangled myself from the mosquito net; my dry, cracked feet hit the dirt, toes searching independently for the flip-flops I had left the night before. I grabbed my coverup and aimed my body toward the enormous, sun-absorbing black reservoir of water perched on stilts. A tarp hung like a skirt below the container, acting as a privacy curtain. It was rudimentary, yet the shower was a daily highlight. I scrubbed my legs with the last thin sliver of patchouli soap. I could not call off the memory of my nuit blanche, so I cut the bathing short and trudged back to get dressed.

Self-talk did not improve my mood on my walk to the clinic. Mayian, a nurse in training, met me at the door. His perfectly aligned white teeth poked through his enormous smile. He sported a flashy lime-green-and-orange shirt with crisply ironed trousers. The national staff arrived daily in wrinkle-free attire, achieved by heating a flat iron over the fire and then carefully pressing away every wrinkle.

"Sheilee, we have a surprise for you," he announced.

Hesitantly, I agreed to follow. "Okay."

Closer to the clouds than my height, he hesitantly touched my elbow, intent on guiding me to the surprise. Memories of my insomnia and annoyance with the heat evaporated. His brown eyes, crinkled at the corners and fringed with thick, curly lashes, blinked rapidly.

As we entered the new maternity ward, the entire national staff, a handful of TBAs, cleaners, and staff from the other clinics stood there. Dressed to celebrate, they stood facing me in a bouquet of African wax-printed shirts and dresses, beaming like proud parents flaunting their newborns.

"Look at all of our space, Sheilee," someone hollered.

"It is beautiful," another chimed in.

I absorbed the surroundings and tucked my overgrown hair behind my right ear.

Then an ear-piercing "lilililililili," a ricocheting ululation, enveloped every corner of the new ward. Their high-pitched warrior cry expressed the best or worst of times. This time, the best. With a click of a mobile phone, a lively playlist transformed the space into an impromptu dance floor. We laughed together; they laughed at a white woman with ample feet in an ankle-length flowery skirt and a dingy T-shirt as she tried to get her beloved Woodstock moves on. I couldn't blame them.

Once, I secretly watched YouTube, trying to learn how to dance, but I never improved my technique or rhythm. With my societal pressures miles away, I busted out of my superwoman attire. I danced my private kitchen dance—the one I do alone. I embraced the movements, finally showing the world a tiny piece of authenticity. No one was judging me, only myself. My insomnia and moodiness were now a distant memory, stamped out with the grace of this incredible group of humans pulling me into the now.

Needing to use the latrine, I excused myself from the group momentarily. I hurried back to the compound and headed for the WC. As I passed my tukul, I heard a chirping sound that caused me to pause and look inside. Perched on my self-strung clothesline were two feathered fowl telling each other stories and leaving their mark on my pile of once-clean clothes. I wondered if this was Ric's way of showing me that, sometimes, shit just happens.

"Where is my damn umbrella?" I mumbled to myself.

CHAPTER 13: DAY OF REST

May 2, 2010

I had so much to be pleased about. Five months into the mission, our new maternity ward was booming with mothers and babies. The training with the national staff was progressing, and our collaboration with the TBAs bloomed beautifully. The TBAs now had the confidence to refer patients to us and even occasionally join us on deliveries. And it was Sunday, our day off.

Hot dog.

Technically, our Sundays were days off—our day to delve into something other than our work—but the past few Sundays had ticked by like every other work day. On our day off, we clipped our nails, soaked our feet in plastic tubs with drops of peppermint essential oil from our communal bottle, trimmed each other's hair, played cards, and wrote emails and stored them in the draft folder, hoping for an internet connection later on in the day. We read books left behind by previous expats and tried to catch up on sleep.

I have never been one to sleep in or take naps, and even if I attempted, once Africa was awake, it was impossible. The wee hours of the night were typically devoid of sounds, but "kicking" babies often disrupted those moments, my excuse for grumpiness in the morning.

The kitchen screen door emitted a grating screech as I opened it, and as usual, it smacked against the backs of my heels. "Damn door."

I spied two brown eggs on a shelf in the kitchen: mine, all mine.

Guilt for taking both lasted only for a second—the things we do when no one is watching. I struck the wooden match on the limited striking surface of its box. The matchbox deteriorated at the corners from being handled too many times by the wet hands of the cooks. Once set alight, I threw the match on the hissing burner. Lifting the sticky three-liter jug of oil, I watched as the gold-tinged liquid twirled into the aluminum frying pan that still held remnants of someone else's snack.

The table next to the stove held two partially covered greasy bowls from last night's supper, marred by fingerprints that resisted cleaning. The kind of vessels used at family reunions, holding some fruity walnut salad smothered in mayo made by a distant relative. Daily, the mamas prepared and meticulously filled two entrees for each meal, then secured the lids. Typically, one was filled with a whitish mound of rice or *ugali*, made with maize flour and cooked with water to a thick, mashed potato consistency, and the other held goat meat or some other puzzle, dyed yellow with turmeric. Their lids were ajar, with rice and bone-shards trails across the counter, indicating the community cat took his share during the night.

"Gross," I murmured.

The last person who ate was supposed to clean up. I puffed and rolled my eyes at no one, then cracked my two eggs and returned to my happy space—glad I was the first in the kitchen.

Outside, the wind intensified, sending gusts through the screened-in kitchen and causing the curled paper partially affixed to the refrigerator to flutter—a frantic flutter, as if calling for my assistance. I approached it and noticed a xeroxed copy of a calendar speckled with tape fragments, pointing in various directions from previous futile attempts to secure it. The eggs were almost done, but the water was not hot, so I tore a generous piece of duct tape from the roll on the windowsill, using my front teeth as scissors. As I pressed the paper and tried to flatten it with my hand, I saw that today was not only Sunday; it was May 2, Ric's birthday.

I stopped what I was doing, bent forward, and rested my hands on my knees, taking a deep breath. On Ric's birthday, I used to cook up a storm. He did the same for me on mine. The efforts of this undertaking served as the gifts we swapped. We were such sappy romantics. *Will there ever be a day when I can fondly remember him, smile, and continue my day without being engulfed in waves of sorrow?* When did I expect to be healed? Was there an expiration date on grief? After one year? Or two? Or three years? A decade? Those repeated cliché assurances from friends and family after Ric's death, who guaranteed, "Someday you will look back and be able to laugh." I wanted that someday to be today.

I tried to remember Ric with only a grin on my face. In my previous appointments with my counselor in Upstate NY, she told me, "No matter when, no matter where, when grief knocks, let it in." I heard her, but I still wanted her to estimate when I could expect this to end. I asked her, "In general, when do people feel better?" I recalled her kind, empathic smile, and the silence that followed. I know now that certain dates will always drag me back into the depths, and that's normal. As time passed, the gut punches lost their impact, letting me jokingly share stories of someone I'd thought I couldn't live without. More importantly, I learned every human creates a unique timetable for this process.

The crispy, browned edges of the eggs told me I had overcooked them, so I cut the gas on the stove and slid them onto a plate. I made my way to the outside table, avoiding the screen door this time. Devouring my salty, sulfurous breakfast, I watched the showy orangish sun pull herself upward from the horizon, finding a place to start the day.

Another early morning riser, Rupert, walked through the entry gate, his radio crackling.

We nodded good morning and exchanged our routine hugs. From the outset, Rupert took the lead in initiating our gesture. It began as an awkward half-arm deal, both of us experimenting. But by then, it had grown into a full-on squeeze. *I wonder if he looks forward to it as much as I do.*

I missed touch; it felt like something Ric took with him. Still sleeping in a half-curved-C shape, I missed Ric's nestling from behind, the heat of his body, his bony kneecaps pressed into my popliteal hollows, and his arms locked around me. I never drifted off until I felt his deep breaths pushing and pulling the wild strands of my hair softly across my cheek and tickling the nape of my neck. Then, I followed him, easing my body into a slumber.

One puzzle piece was missing, so I welcomed what Rupert and I shared. This daily, platonic, heartfelt embrace grounded me momentarily in this unpredictable place. Human contact was rare, and I understood that sometimes words took a backseat to touch. Ric was the best hugger, and Rupert came in a close second. Although they were different, their warmth and comfort were equally remarkable.

"Don't forget our flight today. One drop and two picks," Rupert reminded me.

That was code for two patients leaving and one returning. The regular plane came every ten to twelve days, depending on the weather. On rare occasions, when another aircraft was flying over with an unfilled weight allowance, that plane would stop and escort a patient back from a medical center or take one out for further medical care. But those occurrences were rare, especially on weekends. *Today, we got lucky. That should be quick, and I can get back to relaxing.*

Crackles and radio lingo spewed from his handset, hinting that the plane was coming.

"I gotta run and get ready. Later," Rupert said as he increased his pace and exited the compound.

Coffee in hand, handset radio slung around my neck, I headed for one of my secret hiding places behind my tukul to grab a few minutes of morning shadows and anonymity before the plane came—a place I gathered myself for the day. I had two hiding places now, actually three: One was behind my tukul, another was outside the clinic, and the third was at the foot of a towering tree at the perimeter of the hospital compound. This magnificent tree boasted curly exposed roots that twisted in all directions, creating a cozy, circular seating area for me. I now know that nothing hid me; everyone knew of my whereabouts. But in my mind, I was alone. Sometimes, that was enough.

The red clay gradually accumulated layer upon layer on the soles of my clogs. With each step, the tacky mud added a few centimeters to my height until it felt like I was wobbling on stilettos. I spied the rock that served as my shoe scraper, dried sheets clinging to its outcroppings from previous delaminations—a sure sign the rainy season had unfolded.

Intensity characterized the mission. Insurmountable

medical cases stacked next to each other, and an endless sea of patients in the waiting area merged with the horizon. Admittedly, there was a lot of good and a lot of bad. These brief seconds alone were a chance to recharge and gain clarity.

On certain days in the mission, I held on to my morning sessions longer, and then on other days, despite how much time I lingered there, it felt like I had bypassed those moments altogether. I embraced the days I left confident, mastering Zen-like qualities. But often, as was the norm in this place, the day erupted into a mélange of uncontrollable noise and the witnessing of horrific suffering endured by others, which stripped my calm composure back to the bone, baring my soul and revealing my truths. I now know the importance of spending time alone, fostering a deep understanding of what makes me tick. Like everything, the more you do it, the better you get.

Is the newness of this place wearing off? I wondered. Perhaps the tussle with the calendar this morning unsettled me, or maybe it was the weight of my expectations—of this mission, myself, and others. When I arrived in Sudan, I did not expect white, polished hospital floors. Still, I expected trained staff, better diagnostics, fewer patients, better patient outcomes, and that day-to-day living would not be so challenging. A crystal-clear memory of past failed expectations washed over me. Haunting me.

"Pinky swear?" whispered the little kid's voice.

Jason, the neighbor kid, had an uncanny intuition for Ric's whereabouts whenever he worked in the yard or garage with the door open. Ric's patient, easygoing personality and chatty stories instinctively drew Jason to him.

Ric sat in our kitchen with his legs crossed at the ankles. He placed his empty mug on the table beside a bear half-filled with honey. He looked younger than his cohorts in the fourth decade with his lean, runner body type and a spattering of knitted wrinkles in the corner of his eyes. The neighborhood boy faced him, scowling, chewing on his lower lip. Below his jean shorts, his knees were grass-stained and visible. A delicate pink line crossed the bridge of his nose. "Nasal salute," the medical slang for kids with chronic allergies. They held each other's gaze. This afternoon, something was in the way of both of their normal.

I watched silently from our living room and stared at the snaillike, intentional movements of their hands approaching one another. Ric's pale, calloused hand, with a blueberry stain under his thumbnail, reached for the tiny, unscathed hand of the child. Each was paying attention to the other. When their two hands met, their first three fingers automatically flexed on their palms while the thumb held them hostage. Then, with only their pinkies extended, their nail beds blanched as they hooked their two digits. Like a treehouse ritual, pin-pricked fingers pressed together, pledging something.

Peering at one another, they held the pose.

Louder than Jason's first request, "Pinky swear you will get better, Ric." He gnawed on his already-overchewed fingernails.

Ric responded softly, unwaveringly, "You don't need to worry. I'll be okay."

"Are you sure, Ric?"

"I'm sure." He lifted his shoulders in a half-shrug and smiled.

I watched Ric's Adam's apple bob up and down, struggling to dance around his unknown future. Jason grimaced and stepped back to get a better look. He tilted his head from side to side like a young art collector, unsure whether the piece was worth buying. Less than a decade in this world, but old enough to read the tea leaves. Unlocking their fingers, Jason lifted his arms. Ric bent forward as the slender, knowing arms of the boy encircled his neck. I overheard a sniff.

Still, at this moment, I expected this to be true because Ric never lied.

And then it wasn't.

Maybe it was time to squash the black cloud of unmet anticipations of what should have been. I wondered if my clinging to those letdowns kept me from adapting to other circumstances or prevented me from appreciating surprises. What a vicious cycle of dissatisfaction and negativity. It likely curtailed my childhood healing and, no doubt, hindered my grief reaction.

First, crackles, and then Rupert's voice from the radio announced my brief rest was over. "Plane's coming. Get your mamas ready to go."

Two maternity "mamas" were on the flight manifest. So I hustled across the empty hospital compound, past the empty waiting bench at the entry into our ward. All childbearing females in this community were affectionately called "mamas"—the cooks in the kitchen, the cleaners, the older national staff members, and the patients in the wards.

The fusion of reverence for the mama figure and acceptance of polygamy echoed the cultural norms within the Nuer tribe. Not a day passed without the national staff openly discussing the benefits of being nurtured by multiple comothers or asking me, "Wasn't it hard growing up with only one mama to give you advice?" *If they only knew.*

Without firsthand motherhood experience, I contemplated whether the weight of child-rearing was less daunting when shared by a group. Additional mamas diluted the challenging days of raising kids, extra role models who've already navigated the hard knocks, and offered valuable insight into better approaches. I wondered how my life might have been different in this situation. Perhaps the task seemed unconquerable for one sole mama. Lacking a supportive network, a single mother might find herself trapped in a continuous loop of emotional responses to her pain and regrets, hindering her ability to fully assess the long-term consequences of her actions on her children. I have no recollection of being "nurtured," yet I vividly recall how a mere spark could erupt her into a tumultuous blaze. That finding emphasized the value of delaying judgment until after a firsthand experience.

Barb told me I would never be a good mother. Those words stung at that time, but I wondered if she understood how the patterns of abuse marked generation after generation. It was probably the best motherly advice she ever gave me. As a teen, I vowed I would never have kids, and after a few years of marriage, Ric also did not want a family. I made an appointment with an obstetrician to add permanence to my decision.

When the doctor asked me, right before wheeling me into the operating room, "Are you sure you want to do this, Sheila?"

I replied, "I am so sure."

Bearing children in the Nuer culture was the norm. The staff often asked me how many children I had. I always explained, "God did not give me any." It served as an easy way to change the conversation politely. The weight of Barb's words undermined my confidence during my childbearing years. It prevented me from seeing that I could parent in a way that differed substantially from my upbringing. I tried to convince myself that I was the one who decided to be childless, but looking back, I think Barb's cruel words had more power than I wanted to admit. Now, I am confident that if I had chosen motherhood, I would have rocked it.

When I entered the ward, our first mama, leaving on the plane, sat on the edge of the metal-framed bed, legs swinging, calloused bare feet, baby on her breast, nuzzling for more. Five months ago, she arrived with a dual diagnosis of pregnancy and kala-azar, a parasitic disease. Both were underweight but smiling and happy to be going home. The mother contracted kala-azar, or visceral leishmaniasis, months ago through bites from female phlebotomine sandflies carrying leishmania parasites. Sandflies sustained themselves on the blood of mammals to produce eggs. The disease caused an all-out attack on the body, generating high fevers, enlarged spleen and liver, weight loss, severe anemia, and a mortality rate greater than 90 percent without treatment.

The Nuer's typical poor, crowded housing provided the sandfly with a buffet for feeding. Global warming and wars also directly and harshly impacted the tribe's daily lives, with the repercussions extending to the health and survival of these communities, and the reality of climate change. Changes in rainfall and temperature have influenced the size and distribution of the sandfly population. Just as humans relocated in response to drought, famine, floods, and conflict, sandflies also adapted by moving to new areas in response to these ecological changes. As families migrate for safety, they could unintentionally land in areas with elevated kala-azar transmission rates, pushing them further away from vital medical care.

Malnourished populations in these regions experienced dietary deficiencies in protein, iron, vitamin A, and zinc, putting them at a greater risk of contracting the disease. Pregnant women, children under five, and the elderly were particularly vulnerable to this malicious parasite. Sometimes, it felt like a big black cloud.

The first mama came to us with kala-azar, proving she was more robust than the disease. Shortly after her arrival, she delivered a tiny, determined baby. Afterward, her body accepted the harsh chemicals of treatment, and her baby accepted another woman's milk—an extraordinary miracle. Today's flight would touch down in a village nearest her home, reducing the distance she'd have to travel on foot if she left directly from our clinic. Two wholes, returning home.

The second mama and her newborn were going out on the plane for a surgical evaluation in Juba. Yet another victim of the healthcare gap. She lived in a village more than an eight-hour walk from our clinic and went into labor—her third. Three days passed with her pushing, other women pulling, and bleeding that appeared unstoppable. It was apparent she would die. The locals tried every trick they knew, but could not help the woman. So, someone took a risk. They employed a sizable iron hook commonly used for fishing and removed the child.

The baby lived but endured a severe facial laceration. I gasped when I learned of this and pulled up my judgment panties. *What a barbaric thing to do*, I thought. *How could they do that?* And then, with a bird's-eye view of the patient's village, I reconsidered their resources: No electricity or running water, no transportation, no phones, no equipment or trained medical staff, just a grim certainty of the mother's impending demise. What would I do? Try something, or just let her be another statistic? I cannot imagine the fear and hopelessness of those trying to help this woman. And I had no right to judge. Another moment when fate was in the hands of the community, and they did their absolute best.

"ETA fifteen minutes," Rupert announced on the radio, telling me I needed to get the mamas and babies to the airstrip.

The child with the facial laceration seemed content as she swallowed the breast milk the mother trickled into the corner of her mouth. I made a "come on" motion toward the door to both women. The healthier women of the ward gathered the departers' belongings—aluminum pans, cloth squares, baskets, blankets, and gourds filled with fermented milk and sorghum. *Did they carry all this stuff because they never knew what the day would bring? Where would they be placing their head for the night?* This guaranteed they could sleep, eat, rest, and care for the infants wherever they landed for the evening—laughter and sounds of items hastily packed in two easy-to-carry bundles filled the space.

I pinpointed the low roar; the plane was making its first pass. With one baby in my arms, I walked alongside the women as they strolled toward the airstrip, savoring the atmosphere of joy. The locals moved leisurely, prompting me to match their rhythm and slow my pace.

As the plane landed and cut its engine, its wheels made deep imprints in the mud. Rupert's responsibility was to ensure the dirt airstrip was safe for landing. He used a wooden stick with a line drawn a few centimeters from one end. Hours before the flight, he'd walk to the strip and poke the marked end of the stick into the mud, like a dipstick when you check the oil in your car. He radioed the pilot to cancel the flight if the mud depth surpassed the line drawn on the stick. The indentations from the tracks of the wheels of the plane told me Rupert had a light touch on the stick test this morning. I wished both mamas the best in English; I think they thanked me in Nuer. We hugged, squeezing the baby between us. You don't have to speak the same language to communicate. We could understand each other's feelings—frustration, contentment, sorrow, fear, shame, panic, anxiety, suffering, and loss—through a universal dialect: the silent one that requires no words or sounds. The two outgoing patients and I just confirmed that.

The engine whined to life as it took a slow U-turn; its wheels kicked up sheets of reddish clay. The overpowering scent of fuel filled pockets of air as the aircraft bounced to the far end of the airstrip. Once, Jason, the pilot, told me our runway was so short that if he didn't initiate the takeoff from the very end of the strip, he could not get the plane off the ground. I wondered what thoughts raced through the minds of our recently boarded mamas experiencing their first plane ride. If these women resembled the Nuer I had met so far, I bet they were capturing every move of the pilot, soaking in the view from above, imprinting mental snapshots of the overhead view of a country they only knew from the bare ground.

Giving a quick wave to the plane, I turned and headed back toward the expat compound for my planned day of relaxation. The coolness of the morning subsided, and the temperature was on a familiar upward trend. Seconds inside our expat fence—I called it the safe zone—the radio crackled: "Sheilee, two in labor."

"Crap." I exhaled heavily and dropped my head to look at my feet. Then I threw back a swig of tepid filtered water from my water bottle, lifted the creaky latch of the expat gate, and proceeded to the ward, greeting the guard along the way.

Entering the delivery room, I saw Sarah, the staff on duty for the day. Before I had time to put on my gloves, Sarah delivered the first patient in labor. I beamed as I watched her carry out the delivery with such confidence. Like the rest of the staff, she was eager to learn and improve her skills. Every day, the staff took notes during our training, posed questions after questions, observed each other with diligence, and then walked onto the stage without fear of failing and rocked it. It reinforced my belief that determination outweighed mere intellect, and perhaps the absence of a fear of failure was equally crucial.

The contractions of the second laboring patients petered out, so Sarah and I started IV oxytocin. Respecting the power of this drug, especially in a setting without an operating theater, I helped Sarah calculate the drops, holding my watch beside the drip chamber. We counted and recounted, adjusting the plastic roller clamp.

"We must be precise, Sarah. Count with accuracy." Speaking those words aloud sent a shiver down my spine, realizing the gravity of each drop.

In an instant, a commotion erupted as the door flew open.

Entering were three women standing shoulder to shoulder, scarves adorning their heads. I recognized two TBAs from our monthly meetings who stood on either side, elbows locked, supporting a laboring woman between them. All three were mildly out of breath.

"Where did they come from?" I pushed my wet bangs out of my eyes.

Each quick-paced contraction of the woman in the middle caused the corners of her mouth to turn down. But amidst this curious tableau, both TBAs smirked, proud of their catch. Secret smiles of satisfaction because they recognized the gravity of the woman's condition, now relieved to have an alternative for a delivery that could easily take an unfavorable turn in the village.

There's a profound beauty in gazing into the eyes of pride, the internal beacon of self-affirmation that brightens your spirit. Someone summoned this TBA duo three hours ago to assist with this tukul delivery. They eyeballed the woman's short stature, and their hands felt the unsettling size of this unborn child. The laboring mother had a two-fold set of complications, so these astute women escorted her to the clinic.

I requested Sarah to enlist the help of one of the TBAs to aid her with the delivery of the woman on oxytocin, who was now actively pushing in the corner of the room. The volume in the room exponentially increased, or maybe it was just in the confines of my mind. I tugged on the other TBA's arm to come with me. I imagined she had delivered thousands more than I had and probably needed me less than I needed her. I smelled the birth; it wasn't bad or good, just familiar.

We escorted their patient to the delivery table, pushed her skirt out of the way, and watched the sizable head of her infant deliver with a stutter. The TBAs were correct in gauging; the baby had a huge head. But it was more than that.

"Oh no," I mumbled. "Turtle sign." The TBA looked at me and furrowed her brows.

The scalp with petite curls slicked down by wetness retracted tightly against the perineum. There ensued a rhythmic dance of pushing and pulling, just like a turtle poking its head out and then quickly retracting it back into its shell. Each contraction and push from the mother attempted to expel the baby, contrasted with the relaxation that resembled someone pulling the child back into the womb. The child's quintessential football-sized shoulders lodged the rest of the body, halting the progress of the birth—a textbook shoulder dystocia. The TBA's hands and mine moved slowly and deliberately as we tended to the situation's urgency. We beckoned our experience and eventually wrestled this mulish child from the womb. And then, at last, a high-pitched wail, the famous one, the sound that lets the birth attendants breathe again. Our smiles locked in a silent relief, followed by another high-pitched rhythmic cry from across the room—Sarah's second delivery for the day.

I glanced around the delivery room. Chaos. Maroon stains and pools of amniotic fluid trapped in the uneven dips of the rough cement floor, mattresses strewn about, piles of muddy flip-flops at the door entry, and newly woven baskets waiting for their loads. The hubbub of visiting female friends, family members, and uninvited curious patients from our ward inundated the delivery room. They filled the space with a symphony of overlapping conversations, earsplitting giggling, babies yowling for their first taste of breast milk, and the thrill of the "lilililililili" warrior cry. All muddled into one, to me, it was Africa. I admired all the players in the room—youthful and wrinkle-free, aged and stooped over, newborns and mothers sharing the sacred exchange, their unspoken pact, promising to love each other. But the unmistakable bond encircling this room was 100 percent women, championing each other with unwavering solidarity. I centered myself on the reverberating laughter and the first voices of the newborns.

I approached today with more expectations: to relax. I clung to the belief *I deserved it, damn it*. Then, the calendar crisis and my inability to let go of the past. I did not soak my feet or paint my toenails; I did not have my head in a cookbook, trying to create a fantastic menu for Ric's birthday meal while thinking about what sexy outfit to wear for his birthday. Instead, I experienced something new.

Then, I had my first coup d'œil of moving forward alone, a glimpse into a better way of creating my future that would allow me to be pleasantly surprised with what the day planted in my lap. I saw a flash of light, a measly internal flicker of hope in the shadows of Ric's memory.

Slowly and not yet proficiently, I recognize the delicate balance between expectations and hope. Expectations, with their rigidity and insistence, often lead us to defeat when they are not met. Hope is a softer approach to life, more malleable to uncertainties. Perhaps reshaping my perspectives could bring greater peace to my life.

I expected the day off, but instead, I fell in love with the day's pandemonium, which took me by surprise and took my breath away.

CHAPTER 14: SAFE ROOM

End of May 2010

Liz and I had just finished a delivery. The new mother sat on the tarp on the floor of our overflowing new ward, looking apprehensive about the crying bundle in her arms that she had delivered less than an hour ago. In most hospitals in the US, a lactation consultant would be at the bedside helping her along, giving breastfeeding tips. Here, without that service, women just helped women. They did not need to know each other before lending a hand. Here, if one woman noticed another woman exerting herself to lift a whole jerry can on her head, unsuccessfully consoling a child, or grappling with a herd of unruly goats, they just stepped up to the plate and lent a hand. Breastfeeding was no different.

Once more, as I observed countless times, I bore witness to this moment. In the ward, another mother noticed our overwhelmed new mother having difficulty breastfeeding her screaming infant. The seasoned mama gently positioned her sleeping infant next to a basket, got up from the floor, and approached the new mother. With her experienced hand, she reached for the unsuckled breast of the new mother and squeezed it. Both women smiled at the tiny drop of clear liquid perched on the end of her nipple. In one fell swoop, the skilled mother repositioned the baby and stuffed the nipple she held into the wide-open mouth of the howling baby, muffling the newborn's cry into a rhythmic sucking sound. I chuckled under my breath.

I found it intriguing to experience a culture where breasts were not objectified or seen as inherently sexual. Here, the women do not feel pressured by societal norms regarding their size, shape, cleavage, or lack thereof. Instead, the Nuer saw breasts as functional parts of the body. Parts valued for practical purposes rather than their appearance. The Nuer women scratched them without embarrassment, pulled them out to feed a hungry child, fumbled with each other's, or let them hang out in the fresh air when it was blistering hot. It was refreshing.

With the new mother in capable hands, Liz and I returned to the delivery room to clean up the mess. I bent over to pick up a piece of trash from the floor when I heard a strange pop outside.

Fireworks?

Car backfiring?

WTF?

I looked at Liz. She kept to her task of washing the items we used in the last delivery and did not look up. Then, another louder single pop. I returned my gaze to her, keeping her in my peripheral vision. This time she paused and cocked her head to the side, trying to make sense of the noise. I always took my cues from the national staff during moments of insecurity and kept my eyes peeled on her. If they looked worried, I was really worried.

In an instant, the sounds crescendoed, drawing nearer into repetitive bursts of pops and cracks, culminating in complete rounds of rat-a-tat. Male voices fluctuated in volume as if they were swiftly moving outside, as fast as the now-unmistakable gunfire. I was still trying to attach something innocent to the apparent sound of danger. *You're not in Kansas, Dorothy.*

Without a sound, I watched Liz drop to her hands and knees and crawl under the delivery room table; it was enough to make me follow her. Footsteps outside slapped the earth, interrupted by more sporadic bursts of gunfire. The ebb and flow of its intensity mirrored my breath, halting as the sounds grew nearer, then exhaling with a fleeting relief as the sounds retreated.

We remained huddled beneath the rusty delivery table. Our bodies aligned so closely that our shoulders and hips touched, sharing a sense of unity. My gaze remained fixed on the entrance door, unlocked and inching its way open with each puff of wind, granting us a widening vista of the chaos beyond. The cement floor was gritty and still damp from the last delivery. I desperately wanted to see Liz's reaction, but we were rooted in this spot. I could only see one eye, and that eye looked worried, and the dimple that typically held her smile was absent. Liz and I had shared all sorts of things over the past months: miscommunication, laughter, and dozens of births, but this was the first time we shared vulnerability.

The outside sounds faded into the background, and I could only hear the drips from our leaky faucet. *I need to get that fixed.*

"What is it?" I whispered.

"Attack," she whispered, motionless.

My nerves wanted me to talk, but I resisted. It could be just a typical cattle raid, two tribes sorting out what was theirs. But the sounds of the automatic weapons supported the ongoing strife between the South and the North, and all that rested in between.

Damn, my knees hurt. As I shifted my body to try to sit, I whacked my head on the underside of the metal table. There were more blasts, pops, and cracking sounds from outside our door, and I soon forgot about the now-growing lump on my head and ceased my movements.

My radio sat across the room on the metal baby scales. *Crap!* I wondered what was going on outside. *I'll have to wait until I hear Ed give us the all clear to move to the safe room.*

"Are you okay?" I asked Liz. My question attempted to instill her confidence in me, but I was clueless about this situation.

"I'm okay, Sheilee." She stared straight ahead.

Our eyes averted each other's uneasiness. I attempted to sneak a glance at Liz's eyes, but they were vacant, lost somewhere else. Perhaps she also had an imaginary safe place to retreat to. I wondered what hers looked like. Mine always had daffodils and green grass. It had been ages since I'd been there. As I stepped out of the door of Barb's house, I left that safe place behind. I didn't need it anymore. As time passed, I realized that while my childlike destinations offered a temporary escape, the long-term consequences of those experiences lingered. I imagined everyone worldwide had a safe place, be it in the arms of another, in the solitude of their imagination, or the puff of dust they kicked up when they ran like hell. I knew all of them well.

We held our silent statue postures. Then, as fast as the gunfire erupted, it dissolved into an eerie stillness that shrouded the surroundings—dead silence with the constant drip of our defective faucet in the delivery room. At that moment, I realized what was missing: the booming daily cacophony—the laughter of kids, the braying of ornery donkeys, the chattering of passersby near the clinic. They all served as the reassuring rhythm of normalcy, a comfort meter, telling me everything was copacetic. I wished for just one hee-haw.

The constant drip gnawed at my patience. Despite my fear, the physical danger felt less daunting than the emotional devastation of a future without Ric. *How twisted is that?*

I realize now how misguided my thinking was back then. How did the made-up predictions of my future, worry of my failure in the mission, and inability to control my grief reaction scare me more than an afternoon under the delivery room table with rebels outside shooting it up?

Was my lack of fear hiding under the table during the gunfire because I was starting to watch and learn from the staff? Early on in this mission, I knew that kicking and screaming did nothing except make you thirstier.

Or was my lack of fear hiding under the table because Ric's death made me doubt risk calculation and statistics? I was now a skeptical Sheila, which stemmed from reading *Harrison's Principles of Internal Medicine* about pancreatic cancer after Ric's diagnosis. Men aged sixty-five to six-nine represent the highest-risk group for pancreatic cancer, with age being the most prominent risk factor. Other contributing factors identified include non-O blood type and a history of smoking. The death of a young, lean, non-O-blood-type vegetarian, a man who biked like a warrior, shattered my belief in the predictability of risk and statistics. So I doubted the risk the NGO told me about of being physically harmed in this mission. Ric's disease made me a doubter.

My calm under the table might have stemmed from a subconscious desire to get it over with. In the hands of another, it might have worked because I had already proven I was too weak to do it myself.

The radio began to hiss. A nonpanicky male voice said, "All clear. Make your way to the safe room."

It sounded like Ed's voice. Our security bunker served as a barrier to the activity outside. Rupert kept it stocked with the essentials, usually a barrage of radios, batteries, meds, chairs, books, water, food, and a bucket to pee in. It even contained a carton of cigarettes and a box of wine. I guess "essentials" could be subjective. It was a place to wait it out or, if it did not, a place to radio for an evacuation of the expats.

I rushed the short distance from the maternity clinic to the compound; the average five-minute stroll took only a few minutes. I crossed paths with no guard, staff, or patients, only deafening silence. The expat gate was unlatched, and I swiftly passed through, descending the two steps into the welcoming coolness of the secure room where the other expats had already gathered. It was big enough to hold eight expats with enough room to stretch out, similar to an over-sized TV room without the TV. Rupert sat wide-legged in a chair, holding an empty one for me. We exchanged simultaneous raises of our eyebrows.

The numerous discussions were interrupted by Ed, the boss, who gave everyone a loud "shuush." He wasn't a very chatty guy, and his scowl revealed how unnerving it must be to bear the responsibility for all of our safety.

"We do not know what the clash was about," Ed began, followed by a swift addition, "We will wait here until it all cools down."

He went back to his radio.

Glancing around the room, everyone had taken on a different role in responding to this threat. The seasoned missioners were already hoarding the comfortable seats, ready to spend the afternoon reading their chosen book. Ed was still fussing with his radio. I told myself to play it safe and keep my mouth shut. I leaned forward, placed my forearms on my thighs, and hung my head—the bathroom thinking position.

Then I heard a cry. Amy, the typically verbose expat who annoyed me most days, was weeping on the other side of the room. Really loud. *WTF?* Huddled in the corner, she hugged her knees, rocking as if in distress. She repeated, "I don't want to die." I caught some shared eye-rolling between the more experienced staff. They had a way of reminding people like Rupert, Amy, and me that we were *only* first missioners.

With the entire team of expats gathered in the safe room, it played like a real-time movie about people who navigated the loss of security and adapted in its wake. Initially, I wondered if we all started in the same place with a threat to our being: in the fetal position, arms around our knees, rocking in place, begging for relief, asking whoever we pray to or have confidence in to make it stop, begging the bogeyman to leave us alone.

After Ric died, my behavior mimicked Amy's. I knew I lost my safety belt; I felt afraid and alone. Fear was fear, regardless of its origin. However, after my significant threat, I had the luxury of privacy, something poor Amy did not have. In my sanctuary, I could unleash my emotions. A refuge to shout into the abyss or confront the raw, unfiltered emotions of my recent loss without inhibition or restraint. But Amy's desperate plea, "I don't want to die," resurrected memories of me pleading for the complete opposite after Ric took his final breath.

In our narratives of trauma, each of us carries the history of the event, a present reality, and a prospect for the future. Previously, Liz, Amy, and I had all experienced unique tales. Liz dealt with war, scarification, and famine. Me, the death of Ric and childhood trauma, and Amy, I don't have her backstory, so I do not know. During the attack, I witnessed Liz reacting to a threat: still, composed, and patient. Normally, I would run, but I emulated her approach under that table. Amy hugged herself and cried. Liz's story has taught her she cannot control life and must live from moment to moment. Unbeknownst to me, I was gleaning life lessons from someone with whom I shared little linguistic common ground. As far as Amy goes, she may someday look back on this experience as I have, and it will also help her navigate life's unpredictable events. *I need to be nicer to her.*

Ed stood and placed his radio on his now-empty chair. He rubbed the back of his neck and avoided eye contact with the rest of the team. The deep lines on his forehead were more pronounced. He knelt beside Amy, placing his hand on her shoulder. It was one of those moments when you try to give someone privacy, but your curiosity and the space do not allow it. His typically loud voice was now a soft mumble. I couldn't make out what he was saying to her. Eventually, she stopped rocking and crying. He walked back to his chair, a boss's job done. After some time, she retreated from the floor, pulled a chair beside him, and sat. Her pleas and tears had dried, yet terror remained etched on her face, and she didn't blink.

I lifted my head and saw Rupert writing in his pocket journal. I grabbed an old *Outside* magazine, blew off the dust, and started flipping through it.

Rupert nudged me. "Remember our conversation this morning?" He absentmindedly clicked his pen in and out.

"Which one?" I asked, closing the magazine.

He tilted back in his chair, almost falling backward. The chair's front legs slapped the concrete, making a loud noise as he regained his balance. The manager looked up from his novel.

"The one about not having a private place here to hide," he said.

"Oh, how I wish," I shot back at him, exchanging a quick smile and returning to my magazine.

I thought back to our morning conversation.

"Do you ever wish you could find a quiet, private place here to be anonymous?" he'd asked.

"Oh God, I miss that," I'd said.

"I wish I could hop in our Jeep and take it for a ride," he'd said.

"Or a picnic by a stream, eating a peanut butter and jelly sandwich followed by a short catnap," I'd added.

I wondered why Rupert brought that up now, but I understood as I mulled it over. Again, our team was experiencing a total lack of privacy. In the safe room, we were on full display to each other. The expat team did everything together; we shared beautiful and gut-wrenching moments, petty fights, shady meals, and GI distress. We were in it together, like it or not. We had no place to get away from each other, no real private place to shut the door and sort out our devils, no actual place to unpop the cork and let unwitnessed bubbles of emotion flow. My few secluded spots offered me only fleeting respite, constantly disrupted by the intrusion of the radio, incoming requests, or the ceaseless clamor of the environment, tugging me back for more.

I never imagined the lack of alone time here would bug me so much. I never even considered this before arriving. Its absence made me appreciate its presence. One would think the shower would offer privacy, but there was always a queue of towel-wrapped expats. The latrine was the same, which was annoying to hear and be heard first thing in the morning. So I planned my poops inside of the business hours when the majority of the expats were at the hospital.

Sometimes, I got a slight reprieve in my tukul or one of my three hiding places, but my choice of profession had its own rules, and babies came when they wanted—*kicking their way out*. I laughed because that felt real and funny. It took this mission to teach me the allure of anonymity. The serenity of sitting on a sunshine-filled terrace in southern France, watching people pass. A place where no one knows you, no one wants you, no one is calling you, and you can stay as long as you like. A place to blend into the potted plants, looking like just another generic woman having coffee and finding peace in the simple act of observation.

Another round of gunfire echoed outside.

I avoided looking at Amy.

Another issue hampering our privacy was our restricted movements because of the ever-changing security challenges in this country. When things were calm, we could move to and from four places: the hospital, the airstrip, the market, and a rare jaunt on an outreach adventure—giving us some breathing room from each other. But after this clash, or whatever it was, I assumed the boss would ban our morning airstrip walks, the market, and, for sure, any outreach activities. The insecurity of the village grounded us like delinquent teenagers.

Access to the airstrip allowed us a back-and-forth walk or run—a smidge of exercise. And for sure, the market would be on the no-go list for a while. When we could go to the market, we went in pairs, with our radios, and left straight after work to be back by the curfew. In the short ten-minute walk to the market, we always passed kids kicking around a partially inflated ball, motionless donkeys dreaming of hay, women lugging water, and men sitting in groups resting in the shade—some propped up, sleeping, using the tree trunk to support their posture. There were only a few steady vendors: the meat guy, the cigarette guy, and the onion guy. They displayed their wares on tables built from scraps of wood. The meat guy was constantly chopping meat with his wooden-handled machete, arranging palm-sized mounds of pink fibers for sale, representing the lack of money in the local's pockets. Occasionally, a soap guy and a T-shirt guy sold sun-bleached shirts that flapped in the wind. Dull as this was, it still served its purpose: a modest taste of freedom. We always bought a few onions and kicked the ball with the kids on our way home, knowing the mamas in the kitchen would be happy with our purchases.

As more cracks echoed outside, a collective sigh swept through the group, a sense of surrender, and most of us returned to our reading.

◉ ◉ ◉

A few hours later, Ed released us from the safe room. By then, locals, kids, dogs, and donkeys were moving about as usual. The happy, safe sounds of Africa before it sleeps had returned.

Ed gave us a quick debriefing at the expats' table. He surmised the gunfire was from a cattle raid, but he wasn't sure. We would limit our movements for a few days, meaning only to the hospital and back.

"Keep your ears and eyes open," he finished, rubbed his stubbly chin, looked at each expat, and retreated to his office.

Seconds later, Amy returned to her loud, bubbly self as she yelled, "Let's make popcorn."

I reminded myself of my commitment to be friendlier to her and gave her an upturned, pinched smile.

"I'll get the popcorn, I need to go to the stock room anyway to get more D batteries for my torch," Amy added.

I swallowed. *Uh-oh*.

A few weeks ago, I received a surprise package from Lisa, my bestie. A small battery-operated fan that used D batteries was at the bottom, surrounded by packets of peanuts and protein bars. Lots of them. Before this arrived, the only way I could sleep at night with the heat was to dunk my sarong in a bucket of water, get completely naked, lie on my mattress, and throw the wet material over my overheated body. Usually, I could fall asleep before it dried. But when the fan arrived, I took desperate measures. I marched straight to the stockroom, filled an empty box with all the D batteries, every last one, and told no one. I never fessed up to the secret agreement Lisa and I maintained, even while residing on different continents.

Amy yelled from the storeroom, "Hey, where the hell are all the batteries?"

Most of the expats simply shrugged, exchanging glances with one another, including me. I held my tongue, knowing I sucked at lying, and knew silence was better. Amy's tendency to speak with a flight of ideas was a blessing, as by the time she returned to the table, popcorn in hand, she had seamlessly transitioned to a new topic. My secret was safe.

The day's events made me think about safety and control, the alliance of the two. I felt safe in my twenty-five-year marriage, in my grandmother's kitchen, eating the custard pie she had just removed from the oven, and handing my dad tools in the barn as he worked under a tractor to repair a leak. The irony was that I felt *kind of* safe with Liz in that bizarre situation, hiding under the delivery room table together. Maybe it was watching her calm, letting go of the uncontrollable, and letting it play out.

I recognized my habitual pattern of behavior. Feeling safe with someone allowed me to loosen my grip on control.

It allowed for the real Sheila to be displayed—laughing too loud, using copious amounts of expletives in my rambling stories, snickering at my silent farts, and shedding any emotion I desired. My true authentic self, harboring no doubt in my actions or words I displayed. In those rare moments, that took all of my energy to ignore the suckers that evolved from the roots of my upbringing and mute Barb's words. With Ric, Grandma, and Dad gone, I had to learn to cultivate trust in myself and find the inner strength to become whole again, even if I had to do it alone.

CHAPTER 15:
BOWELS OF HELL

June 1, 2010

Hearing the expats bustling around and eating breakfast reminded me of my slower-than-normal morning pace. I scratched my scabbed, mosquito-bitten arms and noticed a faint scar left from my coffee burn months earlier. It had healed nicely—maybe the spit was the key. I tried to find my humor, but it wasn't there. Unlike the previous month, which seemed to slip by unnoticed, I lacked the motivation to pick up the pace.

The security situation in the village calmed since the safe-room incident. No more afternoon shootings to force us into that space, nor did I need to huddle under the delivery room table. Plus, I still had a surplus of D batteries, making my nights tolerable. Expats could again visit the market and walk on the airstrip. Our team was back to full speed. My secret humming nighttime fan, the incredible national staff, Rupert's presence, and the owl's nightly hoots kept me grounded. They served as constant reminders of those who supported and loved me. But I was still running out of steam. Almost at the six-month mark of my mission, I was off balance.

Embedded in my memory, I could still hear the comments from my interview with this NGO: "This is not a good place to hide if you are afflicted with any bubbling unattended emotional issues." Back then, I knew that I hadn't fully healed. Still, I clung to memories of enduring support from Ric, who had woven a beautiful tapestry of encouragement for twenty-five years, insisting success was always within my reach. And my fierce determination to defy the narrative Barb attempted to imprint on my soul. My usual tactics—bury reality, run into the world, guns blazing, ready for any challenge—placed unrealistic expectations and demands on my broken spirit.

In hindsight, it was clear that challenges on tough days resurfaced my old wounds—triggers that initiated cyclical self-talk, the self-deprecating voices of the past. But the most staggering revelation was the bloodhound qualities of grief that tracked me halfway around the world. I remember asking myself before leaving, "Do I have what it takes?" It turns out I do, but maybe then, much less.

This place tested my clinical acumen daily. Before my feet hit this continent, I was naively confident in my clinical skills. My privileged education and extensive experience in medical settings with all kinds of support, diagnostics, and subspecialists to consult with gave me a false sense of security. During my flight to Sudan, I skimmed through the *Oxford Manual of Tropical Medicine*, skeptical of encountering the mentioned diseases, but then faced them daily.

International relief work was my dream job, experiencing cultures, traveling to unknown territories, treating tropical diseases, and forming friendships with locals and international staff. This mission was all of that and so much more. But first, I needed to discover my wholeness, my internal power, which I couldn't achieve by constantly battling Barb's words or by dwelling on the memories of Ric's encouragement. I was standing alone once more, now a grown woman, drawing from familiar tools from the past while striving to sculpt a fresh future. But at that moment, it felt like trying to nail Jell-O to a tree.

I gathered my things for a morning shower, hoping to wash the events of last week away. It wasn't about the safe-room incident; it was another clinical nightmare that I couldn't shake. Amy's commanding, boisterous voice overtook the soft chatters of the other expats. Whatever space she occupied, her voice commanded it, filling the room with its presence. I peeked out from my tukul, my sarong wrapped around my naked torso. No towel was hanging over the tarp curtain surrounding the shower, showing it was vacant. I trudged that way.

Inside the shower, the tepid water bounced from the top of my head, briefly diluting my distress. The water flowed over my closed lids as I tilted my head back. Then, as if a demon inside me had awakened, the blackness of last week's clinical situation returned.

Another typical OB scenario—the patient getting to us too late, living too far away—added more depressing statistics to our register book. The patient's history was no surprise: four days of labor and a day of travel by foot. I could not suppress the memory of that situation: the disgust, the foul smells, my heightened anxiety, and the slippery blood on the floor. That case might have been the straw that broke me. I hoped the distance of the shower from the expats' breakfast table muffled my sounds as the incident I wanted to forget replayed in my mind.

◉ ◉ ◉

Drenched in sweat and shivering, she arrived at the clinic seven days earlier. Her baby was soundless. As I donned my rubber boots and transparent white apron, her family went to the lab to find a blood match. I pulled, tugged, sweated, and cussed, but was unsuccessful in the attempts to release the child from the womb with the scalp vacuum. The last resort was a gruesome life-saving technique to evacuate the deceased child and save the mother. Throughout the procedure, I couldn't shake the feeling of being a perpetrator in a heinous act. Quietly, I repeated to myself, *This is to save the mother, this is to save the mother* . . . and it did. Yet afterward, I desperately wished to distance myself from it because it felt inconceivable that I would be involved in such a nightmare, but I was.

Afterward, her two younger sisters knelt on the floor beside her, their hands combing her hair away from her face. Gravity delivered what she lacked as the clear tubing draped over her body, taped into the crease of her right arm, transformed to a vibrant red.

Then I heard it.

That familiar noise of someone realizing what they had hoped for or loved was gone. It was an undeniable warning sign, beginning with soft whimpers that morphed into a blaring siren. Then they wailed.

More often than not, the Nuer were silent in their losses and pain. I selfishly preferred that. And in those rare instances when I detected trouble looming in this mission, I did what I do best: I ran. I dodged the primal, weight-crushing cry from others and let the national staff gather the fragments. But with these grieving women, I was stuck, forced to bear witness and peer into the eyes of suffering. The images of humans facing restricted choices—lacking the means for air travel, the ability to trapeze up a mountainside, or escaping tragedy in other ways—stayed with me.

Looking at the floor, I walked to the far end of the delivery room and stared through the tiny back window. A blast of hot air parted my hair, and I wondered how I could turn the focus back on my struggle at a time like that. Ignoring theirs, I selfishly focused on myself. My renewed soreness took priority, bubbling to the surface when someone else's life was just ripped apart. At that very moment, their newly torn pieces tore up mine again. The hole I dug to bury my past was neither vast nor the layer of earth covering it thick enough to hide the sticky sap on the leaves of Barb, the hollyhocks of Ric, or this new unidentified mystery sprout. An intertwined, screwed-up root ball beneath the surface, with a sprawling mass of foliage above ground. Neglected, long past the time for a trim, but where?

I tried to focus on the staff behind our ward, who were now distributing feed bags full of nutrition to the long, hungry queue of locals. As the villagers departed, they wrapped their lanky arms tightly around their month of provisions, like a long-lost friend embraced after years apart. Every face smiled because they knew everyone in their tukul would sleep well tonight with a belly full of food. Even that could not strip me of my incoming, indulgent emotions.

The chorus of grief from the sisters pierced through my ears, and their high-pitched cries transported me back to my living room over a year ago when I sat cross-legged on a rug beside Ric's handmade couch—his thin, pale body still and pain-free. Two giant Great Danes frantically sniffed for a clue while my uncontrollable spilling of sorrow instigated rhythmic gulps and forced a clamp around my temples.

The devilish bloodhound qualities of grief, back for more.

I learned that grief was a bully. The mean kid on the playground, the one who trips you on a pleasant sunny day. Their leg pops out of nowhere, and you find yourself sitting in the dirt. It has your attention again. A reminder that it is not finished with you. And then you sit there, engrossed in the whys, the bitterness, the past, and the scary future, while you pick out the embedded gravel in your bloody kneecaps through the tear in your favorite jeans.

My heart rate told me this felt like danger. Cold beads of sweat gathered in the fossa above my collarbones, and ripples of nausea crashed into my stomach lining. I heard a voice tell me to "get out of here." A familiar voice.

"I will be back in ten minutes," I told the staff, then shook the water from my freshly washed hands and exited the clinic, making no eye contact with my departure. I made a beeline for my tree, the U-shaped roots that wrapped around me and hid me from this world.

Alone now, I asked myself, *What just happened?*

I hadn't been that close to my past in months. Eerily close. It was so close that I could feel it brushing the hairs on my arms. The day Ric died, something felt peculiar but predictable. Almost like I knew. For the last two days of his life, I stayed on the floor beside him as he lay on the couch. It was late afternoon, another gray winter day in Upstate NY, and Ric was making a low, rhythmic, throaty noise yet remaining entirely still. Before sunset, I had to ensure our chickens and goats were fed and watered, but I feared Ric would die if I left his side to attend to the animals.

Opening the back kitchen door that led to the garage, I grabbed my coveralls from a hook and dragged them inside. As I slid each leg into the garment, I stared at Ric. *He is still breathing.* I returned to the garage, slipped on my rubber boots, and ran as fast as I could to the barn, calling, "Come on, girls," to the chickens as I opened their coop, and they clucked in, following me. I filled their water bucket and tossed the hay from the stack into their sleeping quarters for the goats. Breathless, I bolted back to the house, kicked off my boots, threw them in the corner, and unzipped and removed my overalls. I resumed my position beside him, content that he was still breathing.

And then, as if only seconds had passed, he wasn't.

I remember asking myself, *Is this it?* But what followed was an excruciating agony that morphed into sounds of me choking, gasping, begging his chest to rise and fall again, insisting he open his eyes. The intensity of my raw, unfiltered cry of disbelief sliced through the air, leaving an indelible imprint on my collapsing world.

"Please come back!" I wailed, primal and haunting, desperate for even a few more minutes, my futile attempts at bargaining with the fragility of life.

It was over; he was dead.

Seeing the three girls mourn in the delivery room brought back my loss as if it were happening to me anew. The four of us had different worlds, languages, and circumstances. Yet we echoed identical cries, mirrored anguish, and faced Atropos, wielding a hefty pair of metal scissors, thumb and index finger in the loops, bringing the blades together with a decisive click.

Closing my eyes, I tried to focus on mindfulness meditation, which I had read about but rarely practiced. Pinching my eyes shut, I took air through my nose and blew out through pursed lips. I repeated this until the electricity in my body calmed, and when I felt ready, I opened my eyes. Out of the view of others and needing to return to the clinic and finish the day, I reminded myself I needed to get my act together.

After a few minutes, I thought of the silly distraction game I often played with myself. The one that frequently roused a chuckle. *Maybe that would distract me.* It was a self-made contest where I picked a word, any word, and said it out loud. I then took that word, pulled it apart, put it back together, reversed it, halved it, and used another language's sounds to create a new word—a silly, geeky exercise to invent a new word, a funny sound, or different meanings.

I inhaled deeply through my nose and said out loud, "Okay, a word. Let's try *grief*."

Then, I spelled it backward: *feirg*.

"How about pronouncing with the subtleties of the French language." I sounded it out in French, silencing the *g*, like the proud francophones who waste the letter at the end.

"'Fe' in French sounds like 'feh.'"

"'Ir' in French sounds like 'ear.'"

I impatiently swatted the flies from my tear-streaked face.

"Now, putting those two together, *feir* sounds like fear."

"Damn it, I knew it was hiding in there."

Grief = Fear.

Each amplified the other in an unending spiral. This time, my nerdy game, usually a source of amusement, failed to elicit even a chuckle. I stood, brushed the pieces of bark from my backside, and returned to the clinic to complete the day, fully aware the cut was too deep.

I reached to turn off the tap because I knew I needed to stop hogging the hot water, then I heard Rupert. "Hey, Sheila, are you alive in there?"

Goose bumps rippled across my body as the water evaporated from my skin, and I suddenly felt cold. I reached for my towel, wrapped it around my torso, and tried to talk myself into forgetting this memory.

"Yep, finishing," I replied while patting myself dry.

Get it together. You don't have enough time for this. The mission's workload never gave me time to process messy emotions. Plus, that day was already waiting, so I stuffed my tangled emotions in my pocket with the rest of the shunned notes and methodically moved my body to the next task.

I plodded back to my tukul from the shower, dressed, and artificially composed myself. With significant strides and heavy steps, I headed to the kitchen, glad I paid the extra hundred bucks for transition glasses. After greeting the cooks, I stood to the side as the boisterous female compatriot exited. *I can't take her today. Most days, I can't.*

I opened the refrigerator, now guarding its dwindling coolness. Fuel was limited, so the generator was off all night. The food stench cooled and re-cooled, killing my appetite. I pressed my hip against the door to ensure it was closed and stepped away to grab my coffee cup when I noticed a paper hitchhiker on the sole of my shoe. Bending to release it, I realized it was that damn calendar. A big thumbs-down to staying put.

I peeled it from the sole, blew off my foot track, and grabbed the roll of community duct tape, ripping off a generous piece. *That'll do it.* I fixed the dusty schedule to the refrigerator door, but noticed the date. Like last month's date, it poked the bear.

June 1.

Twenty-some years ago, Ric's aunt's loose curls bounced, and her body swayed in her shiny blue polyester dress as she played the piano next to the altar. My frilly cream gown's cinched waist was too tight as I walked down the aisle to wed my soulmate. We always made our anniversary special because we believed in adventures and shared moments—not paper, cotton, or leather.

Felix rubbed against my ankles, and I realized I was standing in the middle of the kitchen, not knowing what I was looking for. Reminders at every junction exhausted me.

When I was at home after Ric's death, he was everywhere. I couldn't walk five feet without witnessing him: his flashy blue mountain bike, his razor on the bathroom sink next to his toothbrush, and his watch still keeping time. Without his things facing me daily, I could say, quantitatively, I cried less. Time had repaired that constant leak, which I thought was unfixable. But the surprise attacks were still there, jumping out from behind random doors, me never knowing when or where. I had not yet conjured up a way to deal with them because I spent enormous energy trying to usher them out the door.

Eventually, I understood that regardless of my progress in life, memories circled back to me. My journey now was to trust my forward momentum and believe in my ability to rise again whenever I stumbled. But at that moment, I still felt like someone kept tossing me this familiar ball of grief. *Hey, Sheila—catch!* Over the past year and a half, I learned to be a "relicta"; with enough force and the right swing, I knocked this ball of emotions over the fence. A line drive, out of sight, out of my thoughts, wishing a bystander would someday find it, pick it up, and take it home as a souvenir. But no one did; it kept bouncing back.

I heard Rupert clear his throat.

"You want some oatmeal?" he asked, tilting the pot he held to show me a tan, bubbling, glutinous mass.

"I think I will skip it today, thanks," I replied.

Once again, Sudan had diminished my appetite. I had encountered overwhelming clinical situations: obstructed births, arm and foot presentations, retained placentas, eclampsia, breech deliveries, and births complicated by age-old female rituals. Yet, all of this was overshadowed by the vivid memories from last week, now etched in my mind with striking clarity and undeniable permanence. It felt as if the country continually raised the bar, higher and higher.

A loud crackle came through on my handset. I must have bumped the volume on my radio because the request felt intrusive: "Come. Something is hanging out."

And another day began.

"I can't take it," I said as I bolted to the clinic.

Moses did not smile at my arrival. There was that familiar smell of copper, and a patient was on the floor with chapped, peeling lips and her left arm across her face, blocking out the daylight.

She walked through the night after her water broke and the cord came crashing down, the lifeline, the main free-way that delivered oxygen and nutrients to the growing child. Secured to the belly button of the infant and filled with Wharton's jelly, a clear substance that gave the encased veins and the artery a bumper pad. It was well thought out and architecturally designed for a successful nine-month performance between the mother and child. But now and then, as they say, "Shit happens." A pulseless loop of off-white rubbery rope hung between her legs, dusted with sand. Each contraction forced the baby's head down onto this vital structure, pinching off any possibility of perfusion.

I glanced at Moses. "Can you hear a heartbeat?" I asked.

He made a clicking sound by placing his tongue on the roof of his mouth, indicating no. We put the metal cap on the child's head, and I silently crossed my fingers and toes as Moses pumped up the pressure on the vacuum pump, and I pulled.

We did not speak.

We wrapped him in a cloth and handed him to his father. He drew the bundle close to his chest, expressionless and silent, and then he walked out the door of the maternity ward.

Another man, maybe the father's relative, asked us, "May I borrow the shovel?"

The realities of this place. We hold on to hope and patch up what we can, but we keep the shovel in the corner.

Shaking my head, I tried to dislodge and scatter the lingering question, "May I borrow the shovel?" These recycled words were now stuck in my brain, their repetition reminding me not to forget when all I wanted to do was forget.

Every direction took me back to miserable.

I need to get out of here and go home.

Avoiding eye contact with Moses, I hung my head and walked out of the clinic.

What a day. Was it remembering our anniversary or the horrible memory of last week that hit me in the shower this morning? Maybe it was the request for the shovel today? Was it the cumulative effect of the day or just reality that danced on my nerves? Each separately would be enough. All of this had dragged me into the bowels of hell, forcing me to determine if I had enough strength to bounce back. And now I realized the load was too heavy; I couldn't do it anymore.

I had to get out of here to save what was left of my soul.

CHAPTER 16: DAWN DELIBERATIONS

First week of June 2010

A persistent beep . . . beep . . . beep . . . stirred me from another annoying night of trying to find a little cushion on the perimeter of the center dip in my overused mattress. Upon my arrival on the continent, I purchased this watch from a vendor at the Loki market, replacing my iconic Walmart wristwatch that kicked the bucket somewhere over the Atlantic. This new timepiece alarmed at arbitrary times or automatically changed the time and date. On more than one occasion, I noticed the stopwatch function autonomously, clicking through the hours and minutes. Cheap and completely untrustworthy.

I clicked on my head torch and positioned my head so the beam of light was directly on the noise-making object, confirming it was time to wake up. The watch was right on the money—time to rise and shine for my morning walk. Our curfew was lifted at 6:45 a.m. because there had been no further clashes, so with a radio in hand, we were back to enjoying our small piece of cherished freedom to start each day—the airstrip shuffle.

I decided a walk would help me resolve my predicament and solidify my decision to depart. Even last night's sounds of the owl failed to soothe me. He screeched most nights, and once, I caught a glimpse of him and his golden-brown feathers. For some reason, he mostly kept to himself, undercover in the tree's foliage, waiting to break out his songs when moonlight reined in the blazing sun. Usually, the nightly serenade made me smile, but last night, it was different. His constant call from above my tukul while I cursed the heat of this bloody hot country and composed a letter to Ed interfered with devising my exit strategy. I needed to secure a meeting with Ed when he returned from his leave.

Hastily, I grabbed my sneakers next to my bed and gave them a sharp tap to ensure no scorpions were inside before I slipped them on. They frequented the compound, doing the solo sideways shuffle, their tails with the stinger-tipped curls primed for defense. Locals warned us that scorpions had a habit of crawling into our shoes at night, so just like brushing my teeth, banging out my shoes was a part of my daily routine. Additionally, observing and treating those who were bitten confirmed the potency of the venom.

Stepping out of my tukul, I didn't remember hearing the drops on my thatched roof, but the spattering of deep mud puddles around the expat compound backed the theory that it poured in the night. Felix, the cat, batted a winged insect from one side to the next in a puddle close to the kitchen door. As I passed, I hissed and laughed at him; he ignored me, too preoccupied with his partially wounded swimmer. I avoided the deeper puddles as I walked sleepy-eyed from the expat compound to the airstrip. Slippery, glue-like mud and short-lived, tolerable cooler temperatures were the trade-offs for the rainy season.

Two young children with wild orange hair and smudged faces sped past me near the gate's entrance, playfully racing each other. Their colored hair showed that the corn and sorghum crops had struggled in their early stages. Like so many other little ones in this village, they had probably suffered from kwashiorkor at an earlier age—a severe form of malnutrition caused by a protein deficiency. Without protein, the body couldn't synthesize enough melanin, leading to lighter hair or discoloration, often with an orange hue. Their oversized flip-flops slapped the ground, each step sending clumps of mud in all directions. Their hands playfully grabbed each other's shirts, trying to hold each other back—a bundle of two contagious giggles and four knobby knees. I wondered if they were siblings. Meters ahead of me now, they looked like they were running out of steam. Their antics reminded me of my childhood, albeit they would likely go unscathed from a mother looking on, getting ready to show them what would happen if they ignored her instructions.

Barb bellowed at our farmhouse's entry, the screen door resting against her back and her hands on her hips.

"The two of you . . . Here, now!"

Frequently summoned, my brother, who was around thirteen years old, and I, one year younger, carried on with our banter as we approached her.

"Get in the kitchen," she barked.

Fresh vacuum tracks decorated the tan carpet of the kitchen. Barb walked over to the dinner table and sat at the head. Two manila envelopes bearing our school emblem rested in front of her. Reading upside down, I saw Max's name and mine on the other. I remember thinking the ticking of the mantel clock was louder than usual.

"You are both healthy farm kids with rotten grades in gym class?"

She had that look—a penetrating glare. That telltale seething expression of disapproval. That stare, the one I hated, because I knew something was about to go down.

"This is BS," she yelled.

Silence was my best friend during such moments. Max looked at the floor.

She pulled the report cards from the envelopes, opened both, and pointed her slim index finger to each of our problems. Next to the gym class column, Max had a big black F, and I had a big black C.

Typically, I adored gym class, but this past semester, they forced us to change into a black, snap-crotch leotard and then run a few laps around the echoey gymnasium, waiting for the instructions from Ms. Jane, the gym teacher. After the warm-up, she slipped a scratchy 1970s cassette into the player and began with, "Arms over the head, reach for the stars." Her peppy voice told me she must have been a cheerleader in her earlier years.

When I returned home from those gym classes, I whined to Barb about my leotard being too short. She replied, "You're tall for your age and long-waisted. Stop complaining, it's fine."

The entire blame for my poor mark was not totally the fault of the leotard; I also detested the death walk on the balance beam, forcing my body to make a distorted, upside-down U shape of my spine while touching that red, sticky mat that smelled like sharp cheese. I deserved a C, but it was still a passing mark, and I never dreamed the punishment would be severe. I tried to convince her I would do better next semester because we would be dribbling, and I was skilled with that. She ignored me. Max's failure came from showing off while swinging on the gymnastic rings without permission. He probably deserved the F.

"If you're not in shape now, you will be when this is over, damn it," she yelled. "Starting today, I will watch you run to the neighbors' and back."

Our rural farmhouse sat on a hill, with an elevated back porch that served as her vantage point of the dirt road that connected our farm to the one in the distance. As a kid, I did not know the distance from here to there; I just knew the turnaround point looked like a mere speck on the horizon. And just like boot camp, the "captain" screeched from the porch, and the two recruits hit the road. Day after day, the rules never changed. I did not have to ask what would materialize if I stopped; fear coached my quads and reminded them of the perils of stopping.

No one on the porch was waiting to punish me if I slowed down. If I wanted to put the brakes on running away from the mission, it meant quieting my inner fear. The one that made me look around for another space, something softer, more comfortable. My frantic attempts to find solutions, only to realize moments later that I still felt unsettled, sad, lonely, and uncertain about my identity without the man of my dreams. I was so lost in despair that I overlooked the fresh, tender green shoots emerging from the cracks between the flagstones.

I sped past the tuberculosis village, where I heard a cacophony of intense expulsions of air from the wet lungs of the ailing residents. Donkeys lined the footpath, swishing their scraggly tails in a pendulum motion, attempting to keep the persistent flies off their backs—heads down, rooting through the piles of rubbish for a calorie or two. The cardboard eater was not in this group; he hung out closer to the maternity clinic. None of them noticed me or lifted their heads in curiosity. When my sneakers hit the airstrip, I saw scores of hitchhiking flies stuck to my white T-shirt. I grasped the hem of my shirt and flapped it vigorously, trying to shoo them away. These things had become such a regular part of my day.

Coming to Sudan expanded my relicta world. Over the past months, I'd adapted to many things: new clinical challenges, flies, loud expats, and the culture. The intense heat, which was utterly exhausting, was something I would never get used to. Simply impossible. The food was also challenging, but to my credit, I had made headway on a few things. And all of these things, without Ric.

The national staff in the maternity unit kept me grounded daily. They challenged me, made me laugh, and reminded me how to be authentic, because nothing else mattered. Last week at the clinic, I was moaning about the lack of supplies. Moses overheard me and said, "You know what they say, Sheilee, Rome was not made in a day." That made me laugh out loud.

The airstrip ran north and south. Tukuls lined both sides. From the air, the runway looked like bare skin, like someone had adhered a giant hair waxing strip to the earth and ripped away a swath of the town. I noticed tiny morning fires beside tukuls spitting out little puffs of smoke. Homeward bound, a few women carried water on their heads, as a couple of children squatted and defecated in the ditches alongside the airstrip. A random chicken clucked and ran before me, looking over its shoulder as if chased by a phantom. A typical day was unfolding. Packs of dogs scattered on both sides of the airstrip, exchanging scents and choosing their companions for the day. I had known most of them by color. The friendly white one with three legs and the big tan one barking frantically, masking its fear with a show of bravado—the group and the pack leaders. Kids and lanky adults ventured out into the day from the safety of their tukul, their harbor. We all wanted a harbor that emitted an aura of security—sticks, stones, mud, or wood. The structure was irrelevant, but the harmony within was indispensable.

What is waiting for me back at my former harbor in Upstate NY if I leave this mission?

Before I left the States, I found a loving home for my chickens with some neighbors. If I left Africa, the only thing greeting me when I arrived home would be the circle of oil-stained dirt where I used to park the backhoe, now sold, and maybe a few blooming cosmos I planted over Gladys's grave. And within the hollow walls of the empty house that Ric and I lived in, despite my efforts to let in the fresh air, memories stubbornly clung to the rafters—I know because I've already tried and failed to shake them loose. *What would be waiting?*

The epitome of zilch.

Three men walked within arm's reach of me with AK-47s slung over their shoulders. Time had not yet touched their faces, the arms of their T-shirts cut off with jagged edges and threads dangling where patience lost its way. They smiled, elbowed each other, like the typical antics of teenagers, and kept walking. *How can such a dangerous place feel so safe?*

I saw three guys address the blind guitar player walking toward me. I often encountered him during my morning walks. He was usually alone, wearing scratched fake Ray-Bans, and had a huge smile. He greeted me, concentrating on intermittently plucking the four taut strings on his homemade guitar. I let out a "maale" as he passed my side; he slapped his strings on his musical instrument's fretboard, letting out a comical *twang* and *pop*. He lifted his head with his laughter. His humor was captivating, leaving me to ponder whether Ric's spirit now resided in that joyful soul. I turned to watch him walk away, noticing a group of local dogs shadowing me from a safe distance.

At the northern end of the airstrip stood the butchering tree. The men in this culture were the designated persons who had the duty of slaughtering either a goat or a cow. Vultures lined every tree branch next to the killing site, waiting momentarily to steal a morsel of forgotten meat. Empty wheelbarrows formed a line around the butchering site, waiting for the final distribution of the fresh meat. A gaunt, rib-lined dog lay under the shade of the last wheelbarrow, eyes closed, snout aimed toward the fluffy clouds, striving to capture the essence of satiety. When the men finished the butchering, they filled their wheelbarrows and headed to the market to sell their goods. I stayed far away from this scene; it was too much for the early morning hours and even more appalling for a vegetarian.

An image of a harbor lingered persistently in my thoughts. My old one or the possibility of finding a new harbor within me? Before I found a new one, I had to forgo my belief that my identity stemmed solely from those I resided with. Now, without Ric or Barb, that was my quest.

At that moment in time, I doubted my identity all the time because I was so bogged down in feeling this mission was over my head, coupled with the clouds of my grief. But now, and I probably knew then, that deep within me, I was aware I was a damn good clinician. It slipped away from me momentarily, and it took me a long time to learn how competent I was.

Will the real Sheila please stand up?

Was I the Sheila of the Barb Era? The loser, a beatdown kid, who wonders what she did to make her mother despise her. Knowing in her heart, she must have done something to cause her mother's rage. I was still hauling around the self-doubt instilled in her all those years ago. Or was I the Sheila of the Ric Era? In love, strong, confident, and funny? Kicking the world's ass, loving my soulmate, and embracing life. Or perhaps I was the Sheila of the Relicta Era. Confused, scared (actually petrified) about the uncertainty of her future? Running, momentarily touching down, sensing the trembling under her feet, and then retaking flight?

Was I one of these, or had I evolved into a more subtle combination of all three?

The chatter on my radio indicated it was time to head back to the compound. I tried to shoo away the pack of dogs, but they kept circling me and barking wildly. I stopped, bent forward, and pretended to pick up a stone. When I stood up, they scattered, having understood the universal message: A human bending over to pick up a rock meant it was time to skedaddle.

The choice to stay or leave was entirely mine. My walk did not bring me closer to a solution, so I meandered back to my tukul with the same persistent flies circling me, still trying to hitch a ride.

CHAPTER 17:
NO FUCKING MILK

June 16, 2010

The *krree-krrree* and fluty whistles of the vibrant bee-eaters signaled the sun was beginning its work for the day. The classic calls of the Meropidae family flitting about in search of their first meal. A fresh day, with the same old question gnawing at me, tormenting me. Sitting in my tukul, I reread what I wrote in my dusty notebook the night before with the light of my head torch. I tried to give this move time, but the time told me the same thing—there was no repair, no "CNTL," "ALT," "DELETE." I needed to go home. I decided, and that was that. I was out of here.

When the generator started again, I planned to type my handwritten note into an email for Ed, my boss. He would return to the field on the next flight rotation. Amy's vacation followed Ed's, and I was grateful for ten days without her voice. My escape would come after hers; instead of returning to Sudan after my vacation, I would catch the fastest flight out of the country and hightail it back to North America. As I ripped the page out of my spiral-bound notebook, tiny pieces of paper floated around my feet like confetti. I folded the page into a neat package and stuffed it into my pants pocket before heading to the expat table for coffee.

I popped the plastic lid off the can of Nido and noticed the silver-rimmed bottom.

Empty.

"Christ, there is no fucking milk," I yelled and pushed the can forcefully across the table.

A few expats lifted their heads from their breakfasts, looked my way, and returned to their meals without comment—we took turns throwing hissy fits. This was my first.

"When does the plane come?" I asked.

"In nine days," an expat replied.

"If it doesn't rain," someone else offered.

The sound of clinking forks against dishes filled the silent breakfast.

I pushed back from the table, knocked over my lawn chair, and stomped off, even more pleased with the plan in my pocket. *I am so out of here. I do not have the skills to survive this.*

Red-faced and boiling inside, I retreated toward my tukul and retrieved my outside lawn chair that had blown to the far end of the compound in the night, trying to justify my embarrassing behavior. I was in the same old cul-de-sac with failed expectations, excuses, and justification, with a bit of self-pity around the edges. In my time here, I had witnessed others at this point and vowed I would never go there. And yet, here I was, trembling hands, my heart thrashing the underside of my ribs, sweating—a whirling dervish of reactions in street clothes and Dansko clogs.

"Rage over no milk?" I asked myself out loud.

I closed my eyes and flexed forward in my chair, grabbing my mosquito-chewed ankles. *Breathe, breathe.*

During my orientation for this mission, an experienced expat spoke about a situation in one of her past missions. Until then, I had forgotten the story. She had been in the field for months without a break, doing what we all do: working crazy hours and eating terrible food while embracing a love-hate relationship with it. A few days before their planned cargo arrival, the expats gathered to choose food for the upcoming weeks. They shared a list of available foods with each member, and she quickly scanned it, checking the box next to tuna fish—her top choice for the short term. The following week, the plane arrived with everything but her order. As she told the story, she laughed, describing her ridiculous fist-shaking, ear-splitting expletives while opening box after box in search of the tuna. I thought that story was a bit over the top when I heard it. My mishap with the milk finally made things clear. At times, the mission felt like a pressure cooker—hot as hell, with simmering tensions, relentless demands, palpable suffering, and all of us trapped in the same pot. Looking back, I am surprised I didn't witness more tuna tantrums.

Alone in my hiding spot, a sigh escaped my lips. Behind me, I heard the scratching of dry dirt. Moving in my direction, I noticed Rita, the Sudanese cleaner, bent at the waist, sweeping. Her body and vivid green skirt swayed to her melodic notes. She always sang when she swept. Particles of disturbed red dust chased her across the compound as she approached my space. Dust filled my nose.

I want five minutes of peace.

Inches from my feet, she looked up and cocked her head, waiting for my willingness to accept her morning greeting. My self-pity wanted her to go away. This milk debacle had thrown me into a tizzy, and her usual sweet smile could not pull me out of my imaginary suffering. Why could I not look at her, lean into her singing, watch her enjoying her life, sweeping dirt?

Instead, I closed my eyes, tilted my head to the sky, and heard her walk away. I hated myself for doing this and blaming someone or something that was not responsible. That first object entered the room, and you could kick it after a fit of anger—that kick-the-innocent-dog moment.

Why was I angry because there was no milk?

Anger was my bulletproof vest against fear. The instinctive reaction came more readily than exploring the underlying causes. The most primitive part of my reptilian brain remembered what to do when there was a threat: A familiar crashing of my cerebral matter ricocheted from one side of my skull to the other on impact, a contrecoup wildness that cloaked my root cause and triggered my urge to flee. The quickest fix: fast food for the hunger of my discomfort. Anger would distract me from my fears. I no longer had to deal with complicated obstetrical cases outside my expertise, which softened the echoes of a familiar voice that fostered negative perceptions of myself. I could avoid future observations of raw grief that I did not know how to handle. In short: Get angry, book a flight, and the problem will end.

My underlying fears triggered my anger. Milk powder was the only reliable and constant thing in my unpredictable days. It provided me with a mindless nanosecond of plunging my teaspoon into the yellowish, sour-smelling powder, scattering it on top of my bitter instant coffee, and hearing the chink of my spoon-turned circles. Then, I took the drink to my morning spot, where I did not have to mull over anything. It was an enormous white piece of paper with no lines, lists, checkmarks, or duties for that moment—a happy place without the specters that typically lingered in my head. By the bubbling creek, with your shoes off, sitting on the bank, feeling the minnows nipping at your heels. I didn't know then, but I do now: I was becoming a keen observer of my compatriots, the national staff, absorbing their teachings without lectures or a chalkboard and beginning, just slightly, to learn how to enjoy the now. But at that moment, without that damn powdered milk, I had to devise a new plan, and I was planned out.

All of my expectations, tagging along with the fear, led me astray, shaping and bending my reality. These were the tricks I played on myself.

I expected my mother to love me.

I expected to have a long life with Ric, growing old together. And then he got sick. But my clenched fists still did not give up, and I expected he would beat this unbeatable disease.

I expected this mission to lift me out of my misery, fling me into a happy new life, and propel me forward.

I expected to have the clinical understanding, strength, and curiosity to handle the cases here.

And again, I expected we would always have fucking milk for my coffee.

So there I sat in a plastic chair, the sun beating the side of my head, blowing the dust out of my nose, sweat dripping down my butt crack, having my tuna tantrum.

How could I expect that, coming to a war-torn country, I would not see the worst of the worst? Was it realistic to think I could shield myself from ever witnessing such profound grief? Rita probably did not have big expectations for a warm greeting this morning. I imagine this was not the first time she met a yelling, out-of-control expat. Someone mad at the world. She shouldered the interaction, scampered away, broom in hand, and kept singing like today was still a good day. And I can't even replace the coffee with tea.

On the other hand, milk was all I asked for in this job—a tin of powdered milk. I felt slighted. Who could I blame? Who did not tick the box on the grocery list? As I wobbled between blames and whys, I grabbed my hat and stethoscope and headed to the clinic. I felt lighter, knowing each minute ticked by brought me closer to my departure. As I took my long strides toward the clinic, three kids ran alongside me, hands out, smiling, yelling, "*Kwaya*," trying to grab my fingers. It buffered my emotions for a second, and I wondered if it was time to rearrange my thinking, but I could do that once I got home. I had my mind made up, and there was no turning back. North America was in my sights. The smiling kids, unique patients, and lovely national staff could not hold me here.

By dinner, I had calmed myself about the lack of milk; it was just milk and would arrive in nine days, which was no big deal, but I was still going to leave. The screen door clipped the back of my heels as I entered the kitchen. "Goddamn door." I needed Rupert to fix that. I lifted the lid of our prepared dinner.

A gelatinous mound of golden pasta peered back. "Are you kidding me?" I said.

I marched to the stockroom, grabbed a can of expired beets, blew off the dust, and made a pass with the rusty can opener. Lifting the cut edge with my fingers, I dumped the excess liquid in the half-full bucket holding yesterday's eggshells and coffee grounds. The mushy red quarter of the beet split in half, urging me to chase it around in the tin. The air in the kitchen held the odors of old food, heat, and rancid oil. I sat on a crate propped in the corner, stabbed one piece after another, and shoveled the tasteless contents into my mouth, my plan to leave even more steadfast.

What would Ric tell me? I wondered. He would have said, "You are the strongest person I know. Do the right thing." *Was I doing the right thing?* It felt right. That meant increased comfort and reduced vulnerability with my simple escape.

I wish I had known then a better way to ride life's ocean waves, accepting the reality that you sometimes get water in your mouth, salt in your eyes, and a burning sensation in your nose, which causes a vigorous sneeze after a wave smacks you in the face. And then, after a few bouts with life's tide taking you under, you learn a better way to plug your nose, a more secure way to tie your swimming suit to keep your privates covered, and the importance of squinting tighter to avoid the tiny needles of salinity pricking your eyes. And when you finally get it right, on that glorious sunny day, you go back for more, taking on wave after wave because the water is lukewarm, the sun is shining, the sky is blue, and you look hot in your bikini. And that is just enough. You captured the now, that moment of what we all live for, but often miss because we are so wrapped up in the past or prefer to spend hours just sitting on the beach towel, eating Doritos, and looking through our binoculars for tomorrow.

I looked forward to meeting with Ed when he returned from his holiday. *I will ask him to get me the hell out of here, to put me out of my misery because I am incapable of riding this tide.*

But I had to remember to apologize to Rita in the morning.

CHAPTER 18: MA'LESH

June 17, 2010

The generator's steady hum reminded me that I had failed to email Ed about my leaving. A sea of patients trapped me in the clinic. It did not matter if I typed it to him or told him face-to-face; I was resolute about my decision to leave Sudan. Mere heartbeats after I decided to go, the world looked shinier, somehow unveiling unseen previous sights. The weather seemed cooler, the food more palatable, and Amy's voice less irritating. But that did not change my mule-like tendencies; I was set on leaving.

Searching in the morning for Rita proved fruitless. I hoped she worked that afternoon. When I looked in my miniature compact mirror this morning, I cringed. The mirror survived the wreckage months ago when it slipped out of my hands in my tukul, and dusted the carpet with nude-colored beauty before it seeped into the cracks of my rug. Despite the shattered glass, it reflected the truth.

Even while lugging the Rita incident around, the thought of getting out of Sudan made me feel more like skipping than my usual trudge to the clinic that morning.

Exchanging a group "maale" and a one-arm raise, I smiled and scooted past the waiting patients on the bench outside the clinic. The staff had already started their day; some were rewriting yesterday's math drug calculations on the whiteboard, an inanimate object now firmly embedded as a team member. Sarah and Liz were in the consultation room, looking official and taking histories from two patients simultaneously. Moses was swaddling a newborn, who surprised everyone with a quick entry into the day. At every turn, the national staff made me proud.

I can't give up on them, but I am miserable.

That morning, I planned to lecture the national staff about detective work, emphasizing the importance of using one's senses when investigating cases with limited resources.

"Ready for our daily meeting?" I called out to the staff, leaning forward and making a sweeping gesture toward myself so they could come to start our meeting.

The group twisted, bounced, and wiggled into the lawn chairs inside the clinic. They always looked on high alert at the start of a lesson: silent, inquisitive eyes focused straight ahead, ready to absorb any tidbit of knowledge.

"We must be a good detective to figure out what is wrong with the patient," I said.

"A detective?" Mayian asked.

"Yeah, you know, a crime solver," I said.

There was a collective pause as the disruptive donkey's bray outside the clinic declared his beef for the day. Moses and Liz giggled at what looked like a private joke.

"What crime?" Sarah asked, causing most of the national staff to scowl.

Yet another moment was lost in my inability to communicate. Of all the things that frustrated me in this mission, the national staff was not one of them—only myself.

"Okay. Imagine you wake up, and all your cows are gone."

They gasped. "I bet the Murle did it," Mayian yelled from the back of the room. The rest of the group twisted their necks to look at him, nodding in agreement.

The Murle and the Nuer have been ancient tribal rivals. Both pastoralists often clash over the limited resources, water, and grazing areas for their cattle. When they get pissed off at one another, under the cover of the night, they covertly steal the other's cattle. Unmended bridges were not something for me to fix.

"Okay, hold on," I continued.

"You see tracks in the sand, a residue in the pipe on the ground still glowing, and a knife with unknown initials carved in the handle," I added. "A detective would gather all these facts to help them solve the crime of who stole the cows."

Without warning, the clinic door flew open. A staff member from the nutrition center poked his head in and looked around. Furrowing his eyebrows, he shook his head from side to side, shut the door, and left. A group of laughs filled the space. The staff laughed at his comical facial gestures, and I laughed at his interruption.

"Okay, let's apply the detective concept to a patient."

On the positive side of the negative, the lack of diagnostic testing here had awakened my senses, a dying trait in modern medicine—a back-to-the-basics approach. If you asked specific questions, paid attention to your senses, listened, and watched closely, the diagnosis often sat on the exam table before your eyes.

"We have to use our senses—look, listen, feel, smell—and ask lots of questions, using all of that to solve the 'crime' and make the diagnosis."

"Oh, I get it!" yelled Moses. The rest of the national staff, gesturing wildly, shot out of their seats, patting each other's shoulders and loudly repeating their new phrase, "We have to be good detectives." Stomping their feet to the rhythm of a new concept, they shook their heads.

How could I leave this bundle of beautiful energy? I wished I were more like them. They had a connection to themselves—simple authenticity. Indeed, they could freely express their emotions during infancy, bouncing between their comothers in the family compound. They were not required to suppress their feelings to appease their mothers. Instead, they were liberated to be authentic, unshackled by expectations or maternal pressures. No puppetry from the mothers. A society that did not force them into homogeneous humans, the kind that told them to "stop crying and stand up straight." They were given consent to be kids—dancing when the music filled the air, shedding tears when a sibling took their partially inflated soccer ball, and screaming in frustration at the announcement of bedtime. Because of that, they turned into effervescent adults, popping the bubbles of negative self-talk and fear of failure while drinking the pétillant optimism of themselves and each day ahead. Comothering's advantages hadn't occurred to me; from where I stood, I felt a pang of envy.

The group dispersed, but the "I am a detective" echoes lingered. Half of the staff went to the maternity ward, and the other half to the clinic. I announced I would be right back, needing to make that annoying return to the expat compound to pee. Happily, it wasn't often because the environment took most of what you drank. It took two or three liters of water before my bladder sent a pressing message to my brain. As I entered the expat compound, I saw Rita sweeping the dirt close to the entrance. She stopped humming, stood, and looked at me, smiling. Initially, I froze, but then I walked closer to her—it was time to face the music and apologize.

"Maale," I said, reaching for her hand as my body squirmed. She extended her hand and shook mine.

My dad always taught me to "look 'em in the eyes" when I apologized. I peered at Rita's nose and followed the wedge-shaped tissue growth that extended from her conjunctivae to her corneas—*bilateral pterygium from excessive exposure to UV light*. The medical provider came first, the empathetic human second.

"*Caa duer* (I am sorry), Rita," I said.

I refocused, shook my head, and concentrated on my apology. Her brown eyes sparkled behind the triangular piece of protective overgrowth. She slowly nudged closer to me, placed her right knotted-knuckled palm on her heart, and then moved it to mine. She delivered two soft pats.

"*Ma'lesh*." A beautiful Arabic word traveled over her vocal cords. Six letters made the sound, meaning "nothing happened; it's all okay."

I wilted, and we wrapped our arms around each other for what seemed like not long enough. We broke our hug once we received a clue from the other to break it up and walked back to our duties.

I opened the metal swinging door on the WC. The cooler morning stifled the stench that built up with the afternoon heat. I sat to pee and snickered about the staff now calling themselves detectives. Simultaneously, I felt pride in following my father's counsel. Finishing, I noted it was already close to lunchtime, so I opted to play hooky for the rest of the morning clinic. I positioned myself at the far end of the expat table, under the last fading strip of shadow, knowing the staff would call me if needed.

Still holding on to the energy of laughter from the detective moment, I thought more about it. Despite enjoying the challenge of trying to be a good detective, I had often wished for the magical appearance of an ultrasound machine to help make a diagnosis. I would mentally celebrate with a silent fist pump whenever the patient's condition improved. However, I knew that my confidence in making the correct diagnosis and treatment was often fleeting. There was always another looming complex clinical challenge ready to serve another piece of humble pie. This mission challenged me beyond my imagination and then some. It could lift me higher than I have ever imagined and then, without warning, flip my boat and dump my helpless ass in a roaring river without a life jacket and no rope. Over and over, time and time again, it was a never-ending cycle. I know now it is called life and the importance of greeting our fate eye-to-eye, unblinking, with an unfurled heart as we travel down yet another unpredictable path, cradling hope in our palms.

I'd like to know if my new mood allowed me to take pride in how I taught the national staff. When they struggled with a new concept, I quickly found patience—a lot of it. And when my repeated attempts proved futile, my breaking point was a laughing jag. The uncontrollable, giddy, contagious laugh was reminiscent of someone holding you down and tickling under your arms. Nothing amusing, but it felt funny. It always drew in the staff and made them ask, "Sheilee, why do you laugh so much?" It allowed me to reset and erase the whiteboard another time and try to find the best way to explain the lesson. I never abandoned them, as they never doubted my eventual ability to make a comprehensible point. Although I gave them all my encouragement, I neglected to save any for myself. I couldn't blame Barb for that one; that was self-inflicted. Maybe it was time for a touch of self-compassion and a chance to give myself as much grace as I gave to the national staff daily.

The kitchen was now bustling with the clattering of aluminum pans. The mamas were on a tear to prepare lunch. A pang of hunger gripped me, a sensation I had long forgotten. Sitting there, I daydreamed about going home until a clinical case I had forgotten popped into my head, making me wonder how the patient made out. It was another flipped-boat scenario tattooed in my mind.

It began like usual, terribly usual.

Pregnant and living in a village hours away on foot, she went into labor days before, experiencing obstructed birth and excessive bleeding, which brought the fetal heartbeat to an end. Caregivers evaluate the four *P*s of labor: (1) Passenger (baby), (2) Passageway (pelvis), (3) Power (contractions), and (4) Psyche (state of mind) to predict the success of a birth. With that patient, her passenger was in breech presentation, the mother's abdomen was soft, and her pinched eyes hinted at a lingering worry. We had one positive *P* from her previous three deliveries—the passageway. Every maneuver we tried would not budge this child from his mother's womb. I stopped, reassessed, and tried again. The female family members looked on. I was way out of the boat when I reminded myself of the do-no-harm policy. The mother was alive and stable, but if I continued with my futile actions, she could take a turn for the worse. And without a surgeon or an operating theater, there would be no rescue. I backed away from the table.

Giving up felt like a failure, not being able to help her felt like a failure, and not being able to deliver the child felt like a failure. All a big, fat failure. Another expat communicated with a team in Juba, and they agreed to send us an emergency flight in the morning if the heavens did not release a fresh downpour. We gave her blood, antibiotics, intravenous fluids, and all our worries throughout the night.

I kicked stones back to the compound, pissed at myself for not being able to fix this. I played out different scenarios as I collected my soap and towel for a shower. *Will she live or die in the night? Will it rain? Will the plane come early enough to transport her to a surgical center for the cesarean section? Will she become septic in the night? Will she start bleeding again?* A self-induced mental thrashing over my incompetence followed each question.

She lived the night, and the plane whisked her away at dawn. Remembering this, I could still relive the scenes of the night, the sense of helplessness, the wondering of what I could have done, and the disappointment in myself. As Felix indulged in a self-caress on my leg, I reached down and scratched his head. I never heard more about this patient, which was my failed attempt. I was too afraid to ask, but I constantly wondered about her outcome.

I radioed back to the clinic, telling them to call if they needed anything and that I would return after lunch. I felt like I was cheating, but it felt so good. And then I heard an engine. The plane? An aircraft. It was an unusual sound this time of day, plus none of the expats mentioned it in the morning meeting. I ignored it, overcome with apathetic energy. That feeling of having already checked out. *Let's hope it's cargo, with many medications to fill our empty cabinet in the clinic and a box of groceries. Honeycrisp apples,* I imagined.

The steady hum of the engine became louder and then ceased. Then voices, their indiscernible content, left me curious if the group was happy or sad. But then the familiar "lilililililili" cry began. Too lazy to get up, I let my ears do the work. The chanting got closer.

Then I realized the chant was "Where are you, Sheilee?" I thought, *Oh my God, was I in trouble?*

"Where are you, Sheilee?" from the crowd. Nothing made sense until the compound gate flew open, and hordes of women entered, dancing and shouting, "Where are you, Sheilee?"

Unbeknownst to me, my failed attempt was on this plane; the patient who just crossed my mind was returning home. The ear-splitting howls of the women thanking me and celebrating another woman's near-miss filled the air. How they knew the woman was returning on the flight was a mystery to me. The community never judged me. The patient and her family never judged me. In my eyes, I was a failure, and in theirs, a success.

They formed a halo of female jubilation with me at the core. Their knees were high, striking the ground in a rhythmic whirling ring, each taking turns jumping into the center and dancing alongside me. Witnessing the kaleidoscope of spinning vibrant colors of their dresses, hearing their loud-pitch warrior cry, smelling a slightly musky odor of sweat from the group, and feeling the intermingling of flailing arms—both in touch and being touched—blended my senses and conveyed a message to me.

It was then that I pardoned myself from this lingering uneasiness that had been tracking me for weeks.

This moment reignited my desire to remain in the mission, but I recognized its impracticality. I was riding a bucking bronco erupting with emotions, but that still could not rid me of my smile, which lingered for the rest of the day.

The fuel supply was low, so the generator that powered our laptops after hours was off-limits until the next supply plane arrived—no nighttime watch shopping for Rupert and me. We sat outside at the expat table, sipping the last few drops of our stash, while the other expats spent the night in their tukuls. I never knew the exact time Africa turned off its lights for the night. Sudan had two acts for each day: The first act was a gentle symphony for the out-of-sight scorpions and birds performing for the nocturnal hours. Then, as the earth gracefully spun on its axis, dawn emerged with an ecstatic fervor, recharging the atmosphere for the second act.

"Would your partner ever do a mission with you?" I asked Rupert.

"Not her cup of tea," he replied.

"How about Ric?" he asked.

All these months, and I have yet to tell him he is dead. The absence of watch shopping and the effects of whiskey on an empty stomach might explain my confession then. I hadn't put on my socks yet, and I could feel the pricks of the mosquitoes taking my blood as their nutrient source to produce viable eggs. I trembled, both in my body and voice.

"He's dead," was all I could spit out from my parched mouth.

"You beam when you speak of him. I thought he was alive." He stood and hugged me.

And there it was—my secret. My omission was out under the blanket of the African night. Wafting between the trilling notes produced by the friction of the insects' body parts and with no ability for me to grab hold and take it back, my secret pirouetted toward the overstuffed orange moon. It escaped through the tiny glittering stars that punctuated the black backdrop of the sky. I never intentionally set out to hide that from Rupert. It was just that it felt so good to use Ric's name in the present tense, like devouring an entire pint of Häagen-Dazs ice cream and not telling anyone.

Thinking back, I will never again shame myself for this omission.

Still hugging each other, I said, "Sorry, I'm an asshole."

"Ma'lesh," Rupert said, tightening his arms around me.

The following morning, a handwritten note was lying on my tukul floor inside a transparent pocket protector.

To Ric and Sheila, with lots of love—Rupert

"They that love beyond the world cannot be separated by it.
Death cannot kill what never dies.
Nor can spirits ever be divided that love and live in the same
divine principle: the root and record of their friendship.
If absence be not death, neither is theirs.
Death is but crossing the world, as friends do the seas;
they live for one another still.
. . . This is the comfort of friends: that though
they may be said to die,
yet their friendship and society are,
in the best sense, immortal,
because they are ever present."

—WILLIAM PENN, *Fruits of Solitude*

I repeatedly pored over the note, his belated sympathy card for my loss. Rupert proved to be a good detective, integrating his sensory inputs to understand my perspective, interpret my cues, and deliver buckets of sensitivity to my situation. I would give him an A+ in the sleuth department.

My competence was the skill I was banking on to get me out of this funk. I knew I was a good detective in the exam room and relied on my senses when assessing patients: I trusted my fingertips when they felt the taut abdomen of a pregnant woman, indicating strong contractions. I trusted my nose when I smelled the fruity breath, reminiscent of overripe fruit, suggesting the patient had diabetes. I trusted my eyes when I saw clustered white ulcerated lesions on the inside of a patient's mouth, pointing to Koplik's spots, an early sign of measles. I trusted my ears when I heard the deep, primal groan of a laboring woman representing her superpower just before she pushed her baby into the world. I wish I had understood back then that new beginnings often come with fear, and sometimes, it's better to stay and face them rather than run away.

I felt the bile building up in the back of my throat and swallowed hard. At that moment, I did not trust my senses to help me with this dilemma. Rupert, Rita, the community, and the national staff contributed positively to my senses daily, showing me how worthwhile it would be to stay on the mission. And now these commanding senses were in a fistfight with my fear, taking turns slapping my cheeks, trying to get my attention, struggling to show me a way out. But I snubbed them because it felt like they were trying to trick me into doing something I did not want. I needed to give myself some grace. At least as much as I gave to others.

Once I get home, I plan to work on that.

CHAPTER 19:
A WHISPERED ADIEU

Mid-July 2010

In what seemed like a never ending month, Ed finally returned, and Amy left for her vacation on the plane that brought him back to the mission. Trying to be as polite as possible, I gave him a few hours to get back into the groove before pouncing on him for our meeting. At the end of the afternoon, I pulled up the chair next to the table he used as his desk. He looked bored even before I spoke.

"What is it?" he asked gruffly, balancing on the rear legs of his chair with his arms crossed.

Licking my lips, I tasted the remnants of this morning's sunscreen.

I murmured to my soul the vow not to shed tears in front of him, looked him square in the eyes, and said, "I need to go. I can't take it anymore."

He listened attentively. I recognized his expression; it was the one I saw in the safe room when Amy was freaking out. It likely did not signify what I initially believed, his disinterest. It was probably his default mode, his means of survival.

"Are you sure?" he asked.

"I am. I am exhausted and overwhelmed," I added.

I wiped the last drips from my nose on the neckline of my T-shirt. *Damn it.*

Calm and methodical, Ed said, "I understand, but why don't you consider your decision over your holiday?"

He thought a few days away was all I needed. His pressed smile made me think he didn't trust his advice. Not pushing it, I didn't argue and walked away thinking he was dead wrong. I appreciated the time gap between my tuna tantrum and this meeting. Without it, things would have gone differently.

Either way, I would be out of here when Amy returned in ten days.

Time had a funny way of passing in Africa. The future always felt incredibly far off, and then suddenly, it was upon you, leaving you pondering the path that brought you here. I told the maternity staff the afternoon before my departure, "I am flying out for a vacation tomorrow."

I scanned the room, skirting my eyes from one staff member to another, anticipating that someone might see through my deception.

"Hanna will cover for me when I am gone," I added. They clapped and approached me with friendly arm pats, backslaps, and well-wishes. My shame and embarrassment made it hard to keep eye contact because I knew I was sneaking out the back door.

The last thing I heard as I walked out the clinic door in the late afternoon was Moses. His sparkling whites sandwiched between his big grin, he yelled, "Hey, Sheilee, don't forget to come back. We need you."

I turned around and gave him a big, reassuring wave goodbye.

My decision to leave Barb for a life with Ric was a no-regret decision. I boldly let the front door hit me in the ass, knowing I was finally free of her nonsense. She didn't need me, and I thrived in our separation. The sense of empowerment and relief I felt from choosing to protect myself from her was inconceivable. But leaving the mission felt different. The national staff wanted me to stay and "needed" me, and I lacked the strength to tell them goodbye.

The walk back to the compound made me confront the harsh consequences of my decisions. It forced me to scrutinize my actions and their impact on myself and others. This agonizing feeling helped me understand my deepest desires and identify what truly mattered. Right then, I knew I needed national staff more than they needed me, but my plan was finalized.

Rupert and I had spoken about leaving frequently; sometimes, he wanted to, and other times, it was my turn to complain. We just listened when the other needed an ear. But this time, I was serious. He knew I was going to depart, and we agreed to meet up at some other place in the world, under different circumstances, at a different time. Not a permanent farewell, just a pause in what we've shared. Even though he was supportive, I felt guilty—a weak link between the national staff of the maternity and the expat team.

Hanna and I had planned a four o'clock meeting to do our handover. She was going to fill in for my ten-day absence. A stickler for being on time, she sat at the expat table waiting for me. I loved that about her. The heat persisted, and I longed for an escape from it. I flopped on the seat across from her at the table.

"Are you excited about your vacation?" Hanna asked.

"I am."

"Are you coming back?" she asked.

I gave her a half-shrug and pulled my prepared notes out of my pocket to give her the handover for maternity. My notes silenced her further questions. We both knew. We had watched other expats follow the same trajectory, clutching a narrative they did not want to share before their vacation and mysteriously vanishing from the team. Poof, gone, MIA. A new expatriate arrived with fresh tales, a kilogram of cheese, chocolate bars, and a bottle of liquor for the group. Overflowing with enthusiasm, conviction about their strength and talent, and a firm belief that they could change the world.

That night, I dreamt I danced with fresh veggies, a jazzy tune, arm in arm with smiling carrots, their green tops swaying in the breeze, while oranges and apples waited their turn. *How could my body miss fresh produce so much?* I wondered if I could fill the hotel bathtub with lettuce, climb in with a bottle of dressing, and chomp away. Eating something that did not involve a can opener or turmeric was thrilling. Even the thought of a bubble bath during my first night accommodations in Kenya gave me the same euphoria as my college days. Those Saturday nights, I inhaled pungent air through the bubbling, skunky water of the glass chamber, making a gurgling sound that left me searching for spare change in couch cushions and heading to the closest zippy market on the corner for peanut butter cups—my perennial go-to for the munchies.

I knew my itinerary by heart. I had one sleep in Nairobi and then a quick flight to Morocco to explore for the rest of my vacation. Hanna had gone to Morocco on her last vacation. Earlier, she recounted her journey and offered tips for navigating the area. She regretted missing the hammam and the communal bathhouses frequented by locals, rumored to be exceptional. I jotted down her advice for the trip, and she gave me a handful of leftover dirhams.

Suddenly, it was the morning of my flight, and I dug into the depths of my rucksack. I knew I stashed a zip-lock bag with stored going-to-town clothes at the bottom. I dressed in light-colored khakis and a form-fitting tan T-shirt with a faded, distressed vintage floral design on the front. It was a flower-power shirt for a woman in their forties, a semiclassy leftover hippy look. The powerful citrusy bouquet escaped as I tugged the two interlocking plastic strips apart—the evocative power of scent and how it can transport you back to another moment of your life. I hoped this smell etched a nick in my memory, and in the future, when I got home and stood over my washing machine, drizzling that big jug of green liquid detergent over my soiled clothes, I would be transported back to now and this triumphant state.

Smells could take me on a nostalgic journey through time and emotions. I had a previous sentimental voyage with a fragrance of cilantro. It happened when traveling in Ecuador. Ric and I were on a bus the locals repurposed to run on a train track. A burlap bag of greens tied to the aisle seat filled the seat next to me. The only possible way to get to the vacant window seat was to crawl over the sack. Each time the train/bus stopped for a pause, and Ric and I got out for a pee or a snack, I had to scramble over the bag. My weight crushing leaves of what I learned was cilantro. Even today, when I buy that light green bundle wrapped with a bar-coded twisty tie after selecting my bunch, I bury my nose in South America with Ric at my side.

I pulled on my clothes, baggier than when I left home, but I still felt constricted. I swiped my rough lips with a pink-colored ChapStick and gave my lashes a coat of mascara.

Walking out of my tukul, a few expats whistled and laughed. I offered them a bow and a graceful turn, and then heard the whining of the plane.

My stomach did a flip-flop and then sank into my clogs.

This was the moment I dreamt about; I was getting out of Sudan. Finally, my adieu, my definitive sayonara.

Imagining bidding so long to the exhausting heat and the persistent flies felt exhilarating. But simultaneously, a frenzy of conflicting feelings hit me and spilled on the ground. Was this the final goodbye to what I believed earlier would heal my sorrow? *Am I giving up too soon?* This instant felt consumingly swift, tangled, and bewildering. I felt lost at that crossroads, wondering what governed my emotional state. The high-pitched ringing in my ears wouldn't stop, so I shook my head to clear it.

Each mixed-up knot of emotions unraveled and landed at my feet with a big thud, challenging me, mocking me, and fucking with my decision to leave.

Relieved but overly self-conscious.

Calm but electrically charged.

Eager to step on the plane but hesitant.

Yearning for something new but not knowing what.

Thrilled yet overwhelmed with embarrassment.

Would I eventually reflect on this moment as I had on my previous endeavors to escape discomfort? The Rambler, Kilimanjaro, the counselor? I was unsure if Ric would believe this was the correct action. Would I chalk this up to another failure, another self-doubt that would keep me guessing about my choices during a future sleepless night? With the passage of years and what I now consider a touch of wisdom, I know the only person who can make you feel bad is yourself.

I threw my rucksack over my shoulder and walked with a group of expats to the airstrip, surprised to see the maternity staff lined up in a formation to bid me goodbye. *Did they know something?* I should have realized the national staff recognized my deception, but they came to the airstrip to say goodbye because they were braver and stronger than I.

I felt the familiar trickle of sweat make its way between my breasts. *Nothing new.* The fact that Jason was not in the pilot seat disappointed me, but the NGO had started a contract with a new company. Securing my seatbelt, I shaded my eyes from the sun and waved at my team, blowing kisses. The expats were cheering me on but secretly anticipating their holiday. I know because I did the same thing. Ten-day rotations measured our lives in Sudan, sometimes longer during the rainy season if the plane could not land. Each arrival carries the possibility of visitors and patients, wide-eyed new employees, refreshed old employees, medical and food supplies, and—fingers crossed— maybe a package from home. My departure, freedom.

But more than anything, each expat's departure brought you one step closer to your rotation. That moment, you hopped on the plane and tried to forget Sudan for a flash, a time to coerce yourself into turning it off. Freedom with anonymity, just another generic aid worker with dusty shoes and dark circles under your eyes. A time to kick off the chains from this country and recharge your soul. A moment to turn off the guilt for leaving your program in the hands of another expat plagued with a million other duties. This vacation was my first "me time" in a long time. I had ten twenty-four hours, and secretly more.

The vibration increased as the engines readied themselves for takeoff. I expertly crushed the fly that landed on my forearm, a testament to some skills I've refined over the past few months. Glancing at the ebony hair at the nape of the pilot's neck, I observed him touch his forehead, chest, and each shoulder with his right hand. *WTF?* My cheeks hurt from smiling, but his religious gesture triggered a feeling of apprehension. Later, I learned this ritual was customary for all pilots who flew for this company.

I barely whispered, "Adieu, my friends." The words sparked a fiery tightening in my throat, lit by the raging bonfire in my belly.

The last time I muttered that word was to my French teacher at the end of class. He pulled me aside and said, "Does it mean I will never see you again?"

I raised my eyebrows and pursed my lips in a puzzled expression.

"Because it means goodbye forever," he said.

"Remember, 'au revoir' is for simple goodbyes, and 'adieu' is forever goodbye," he added.

For the first hour of the flight, we flew close to the ground, allowing an unblemished view of grouped tukuls, kids running behind animals with sticks, kilometers of winding footpaths, and snakelike tributaries newly formed from the heavy rains. As the plane's power and pitch changed, I felt like something was pushing me back into my seat. I let the back of my head sink into the headrest as the aircraft broke through the layer of clouds. I lifted my face into the trickle of cold air coming through the air vents of the plane. *So refreshing.* Then, white masses choked out my view, and all I heard was the steady drone of the engine.

I felt hollow, like a deflating foil-like, smiley-faced balloon. Pirouetting in circles with the neck of the balloon hissing the word *adieu*, ascending higher and higher, reaching a cumulus cloud, and stealthily disappearing behind its cottony canvas—a fine display of cowardice.

As I drifted off to take a well-deserved cat nap, I wondered, *Does a whispered word wield the same meaning as its out-loud-spoken counterpart?*

PART 3:
RUNNING INTO MYSELF

CHAPTER 20: THE HAMMAM

The last two weeks of July 2010

It was amazing what less than twenty-four hours could do for someone. The overnight stay in Kenya proved to be restful. I soaked in the tub, scrubbed my sore legs with a tiny bar of hotel soap, and filled the bath twice, exhausting the hot water supply. Afterward, I stood before a full-length mirror, questioning whose skinny body stared back at me. Most of my quads had melted in the heat, but now they looked doughy, and my ribs were easily identifiable. If Ric saw me now, he would be alarmed. I pictured him sprinting to the store for pizza supplies, yelling, "Extra cheese!" as he leaped into his truck.

After my soaks, I dressed and meandered in a daze to the grocery store around the corner and bought a bag of apples, too overwhelmed with all the other choices. I ate two on the way back to the hotel, four more lying in bed, and then fell into a deep sleep in the oversized plush bed of my accommodations.

The next thing I knew, it was late morning, and I needed to call a taxi to transport me to the airport to catch my afternoon flight to Morocco. I collected the dried apple cores from the comforter, chucked them in the rubbish, and got myself situated to go. Looking at my clean fingernails, I almost forgot where I was yesterday. No matter how hard I tried to keep the crescent tips of each nail clean during the mission, I lost my battle with the environment. I felt clean without the remnants of the mission nestled beneath my fingernails. Yet, I couldn't shake the unutterable sense of dirtiness I felt for leaving the way I did.

The flight attendant announced our arrival at Rabat-Salé airport. My trusty rucksack stored overhead allowed for a quick exit. I pushed my way to the taxi line. Hanna gave me a list she had used on her vacation for safe taxi drivers in Rabat. I identified the logo on the side of a taxi cab, which she promised was okay to use. Rubbing the sleep from the corners of my eyes, I approached the driver and asked him through his cracked window, "Do you know a nontouristy hammam?" My worn cargo pants now held only my passport and a few Moroccan dirhams. The fetoscope, stethoscope, pens, whiteboard markers, and scraps of paper with written reminders were left behind. I felt light with only my torn, repaired, and re-repaired green partner slung over my left shoulder.

"Yes, come into my taxi," the driver said.

I slid into the backseat, missing the exposed spring on the cushion. I stuffed my rucksack in the footwell behind the driver's seat.

"I'm Ahmed, and I know a place," he said, turning to boast his dentist's dream smile and his thick knitted eyebrows.

"First, would you like to meet my mother?" he asked, taking turns looking over his shoulder at me for confirmation and dodging other cars.

His mother? His offer felt satisfyingly dangerous. As my

first holiday in over six months, I decided to roll with it. Plus, he was on the safe-driver list, whatever that means.

"Sure," I said with a laugh. He joined in, chuckling.

He gassed his one-eyed taxi through the twists and turns of the poorly lit streets. Pedestrians, bicyclists, and donkeys were within our grasp but oblivious to our movements. I focused on our bilingual conversation; his English was excellent, and his French even better. Like a friend I have known for years, he and I babbled about our lives and culture.

When I was learning French, my teacher told me to stop worrying about having all the perfect nuances of the language.

"Use what you have," he used to say. Just like those moments when the refrigerator is empty and you feel like there's nothing to eat. Then, you force yourself to check the pantry and discover a can of artichokes, a small can of tomatoes, and a hidden bottle of capers behind the flour. You gather them as if they were new vocabulary words you had learned in your French class, mixing and stirring the simple phrases and sounds you mastered to create a new recipe. In that moment, you transformed nothing into something. Ahmed and I used what we had; we found a recipe to connect. With laughter, we jumbled our French, English, and Arabic dialects, celebrating our vulnerability.

Our conversation stopped when I heard a slight screech and noticed a tightening of my seatbelt as Ahmed forcefully stomped his foot on the floor and wrenched the emergency brake simultaneously.

"Here we are," he said. Looking out, I saw a modest brown adobe with a garden entryway. His door creaked open, and he exited his car.

Large, flat red stones led the way to a typical keyhole arched entrance. Dozens of flip-flops parked outside the door winked at my arrival. While struggling to remove my travel-worn shoes, I envied cultures that wear footwear without laces. I stepped into the house. What first felt like an unwelcome chin hair was immediately calmed by the chorus of "*Salam alaikum.*" Various ages, eyes of all colors, and a welcoming mélange of beauty, with no hesitation as to why this alien stood in their living room as they tried to watch their nightly entertainment. *Would my relatives be this gracious if the roles were reversed? Doubtful.*

"*Alaikum salam,*" I responded, and followed with a quick, "*Je ne parle pas l'Arabe, mais je parle Français, et vous?*" I heard a few of them laugh. I didn't know what that meant, but I smiled.

I could not identify the mother from the grandmother, sister, aunt, or cousin. It did not matter. Two younger women smiled and started a polite dialogue in French while the other women returned to their dubbed gameshow, cheering on their favorite contestant. *Canny women, I would have done the same, the TV thing.*

I took the seat offered, realizing Ahmed was nowhere in sight. A female teen appeared from what looked like the kitchen, holding a silver embossed tray artistically decorated with wrapped sweets and plump dates. Peppermint escaped the long-spouted ornate teapot she set beside the chubby clear glasses. My eyes returned to the wordless communication between the women mesmerized in front of the television. They held hands and rubbed each other's backs, the magical allure of touch, not limited or off-limits.

After some polite chatter and boosted glycemic levels, an older woman called Ahmed into the salon. It sounded like a mother's instructions, albeit in a language I could not speak. He left and returned holding a neatly folded navy bathrobe, textured exfoliation washcloth, miniature flip-flops, a fresh bath towel, and a bar of black soap. He placed the bundle on my lap, and I waited for the next clue. As the women took in the finale of their program, he motioned me to the door.

Back in the taxi, Ahmed invited me to the front. *Why not?* Thirty minutes later, he parked in front of a small building lit by a lightbulb. Its advertisement hung on one frayed rope in Arabic letters. *If this all works out, this is what I asked for.*

"Just go in. I will be back in a couple of hours," he said.

Like a child being dropped off at school, I grabbed my lunchbox filled with all borrowed hammam-like things, noting the sweet licorice smell of the black soap.

"See you later, Ahmed," I hoped, then slammed the door and walked toward the weathered wooden door. I caught myself in a nervous chuckle, hearing Ric urging me onward with promises of something fun ahead.

The first thing I noticed as I passed through the doorway was a wet, musty odor. In the dimly lit room, a fleshy, dark-skinned woman met me at the door. Her pendulous breasts swung from side to side as she swept the floor. She handed me a bucket and motioned for me to undress. I suppressed my nervous urge to laugh. *It's not touristy.*

I courageously removed all of my clothes. Holding my bucket, I stood, trying to get the woman's attention. I wondered if I made a mistake. The "safe taxi" driver had my rucksack in the trunk of his taxi, and here I stood, buckass naked, my size 10.5 spilling over my borrowed yellow child-sized flip-flops, able to speak only two Arabic words. *Oh, Mon Dieu.*

After finishing her duties, the attendant propped her broom in the corner. She motioned for my hand and led me into the adjoining room. A blast of warm steam and the blurred outlines of women sitting on the Moorish blue-tiled floor filled the space. Female phantoms faded in and out as intense steam distorted my vision. She handed me my gifted washcloth, black soap, and a tin bucket filled with tepid water. No instructions needed. I tried to see what everyone else was doing and figured it would be safe to scrub up.

Covered in gray, earthy-scented bubbles from the black soap, she motioned me over to where she sat on a close-to-the-ground, four-legged stool. She slipped her hand into the mitten-like washcloth, gave my thigh a tug to come closer, and scrubbed my body with force. The more she cleaned, the more of my dead skin splinters curled and gathered around my feet. She tsk-tsked, and I nodded in agreement. Legs, buttocks, arms, back, breasts—she got it all. Then she doused me with a bucket of water and followed it with another bucket to chase my exfoliated skin down the drain. Now polished, she instructed me to lie supine on the heated floor.

The smell of soap nudged my memory to when I was around five, playing on the flagstones in front of my first childhood house. Like kids do, I got in a screaming match with my brother. Seconds later, the house's screen door screeched open, and Barb busted out with a manic look. She approached me with a plastic bowl half filled with water and a bar of Ivory soap. Grabbing the back of my head—hair was her specialty—she twisted her hand to secure her grip and then scraped the soggy soap bar across my teeth. Repeatedly, she made tracks of my teeth in the bar and then dunked the soap back into the water as if to rinse it, like she was trying to scrub me away. The fragrance of the African black soap permeated the room, one with a sweeter, delicate, and more soothing aroma than the caustic, perfumed soap residue I had to scrape off my front teeth as a kid.

The radiant heat of the tiled floor, the soothing humidity softening the air in my nose, and the hum of foreign chatter of the women made me drowsy but still deeply engaged in the moment. Sprawled out, unclothed on the floor of this woman's bath, silent, unable to speak the language, I took mental notes of an unforgettable, graceful interplay between women of all ages. Preadolescents scrubbing the backs of the gray-haired women, teens braiding each other's hair, giggling about something, and middle-aged women gently lathering their toddlers—a witnessing of those taught and those being taught. Uncomplicated tenderness.

I realized I knew very little about my mother's childhood. I remembered sitting in the backseat after each Sunday visit with her mother. Dad was driving silently, and I was happy he no longer smoked with the windows rolled up. My mother's voice tainted the car's interior with harsh criticisms of her mother up the winding creek road. Looking back, the two women did not share any tenderness. My only clear memory of her mother was of her metallic cat eyeglasses; a hand-rolled cigarette balancing on her lower lip; a husky, wheezy laugh; and a Tupperware full of whoopee pies in the cabinet next to the sink. I was afraid of that grandmother for no reason I can recall, and tried to ignore her. Maybe it was the way she looked, always sitting at the kitchen table, leaning forward on her elbows, expelling frequent raspy coughs, a cigarette bouncing on her bottom lip as she spoke, like somebody glued to her lip—bouncing, but never falling as she told stories. *That raspy laugh.* Her dark pupils stared out from behind her black-rimmed cat eyeglasses, bejeweled with tiny rhinestones in each corner. My gut told me to avoid her because I feared she might be an earlier replica of Barb.

Time has taught me that judging is unfair if we do not know the other's backstory, like Amy's reaction in the safe room that day. We often expect others to understand how to do things without teaching them, as if lessons could some-how fly through the air or seep in through osmosis. Like attaching the word *filth* to the coffee-colored fingernails of a child who was never taught proper hygiene. Judgment before facts. I will never forget Barb's card after Ric died; she wrote one word but nothing more. In black ink, diago-nally across the inside of the card, she wrote, "Sorry." One word, double inverted commas. Somebody taught Barb the soap on the teeth trick, but the one-word sympathy card, I never figured out. The note didn't seem like something a mother would write, leading me to believe I know little about her past. I've come to understand that you can only offer tenderness if you've experienced it yourself.

My itty-bitty glimpse into Moroccan and Nuer culture taught me that women were the foundational pillars that propelled their society forward. Their strength and gent-leness, tempered by their unwavering dedication to their offspring, was a beacon of hope for young girls, affirming their inherent worth. They were unapologetically proud, lin-king elbows, intertwining fingers and hands, forging bonds that reflected completeness. They gently taught each other, dropping sweet-tempered clues for the next generation.

Wet-haired and buttery, I dressed in my old clothes. Thank-ing my scrubber, I walked outside and climbed back into the front seat of Ahmed's taxi, now like an old, trusted friend.

"How was it?" he asked.

"Amazing," I said.

We shared a smile, and he hit the gas. My neck effortlessly followed the motion of the acceleration. On the ride home, the radio faded from crystal clear to static, with an occa-sional melody in between and no urgency to fill the space with words. When we arrived at my hotel, I reached into my pocket to thank Ahmed for my unforgettable experience.

"No money, Sheila," he said, touching his heart with his right hand. "God be with you" were his last words to me.

I tapped him on the shoulder to thank him, and he did not flinch. My desire to hug him was countered by my knowledge that Islam discouraged physical contact between unrelated men and women. The sensuous Moroccan night wafted in as I opened the door of his taxi. It awakened an array of goosebumps on my arms like tiny mountains sniffing the air. I stood in the parking lot of the Ibis Hotel and waved goodbye. His taxi belched, and he zoomed out of sight.

"Yep, safe taxi driver." I went to my hotel room, dug out my room key from my bag, entered the room, decorated with a palette of taupe and white, undressed, and drifted into a deathlike slumber.

My only plans for the rest of my vacation were to eat fresh produce, soak in the tub, and explore on foot. I also had a FaceTime date with Lisa, which I looked forward to. We had exchanged only a few emails since I left the US, and I desperately wanted to see her face—her beautiful, bouncy brown curls, baby-blue eyes, and eyelashes that put falsies to shame.

On the afternoon of our planned video chat, the first thing she said before "hi" was, "What's wrong?" She leaned on her elbows, a cheek in each palm, and moved closer to her phone screen.

I had yet to perfect that lack of transparency.

"I am going to leave the mission," I said.

"What?" she asked.

"I can't take it."

Tight-lipped, we stared at each other. She inspected me as if deciding whether I could take the words, preparing to leave her tongue. She drew a big sigh and then delivered the news.

"You need to stop running. Please. Just stop!" she said.

Her unexpected words were a thunderbolt that caught me off guard and inflamed me. My instinct was to hang up, but I took a breath and listened. I folded my arms across my chest, leaned back, and gazed upward at the ceiling. Words meant to be tender, delivered in a stern, motherlike fashion—the ugly truth I did not want to hear but needed to.

"Ric made me promise before he died to stick by you," she said. "He told me, 'She will struggle but will land on her feet because she is strong.'"

I blinked back the tears.

"I trust you. Ric trusted you. Trust yourself."

She held onto Ric's words and delivered them at the perfect time. She was correct; since the death of Ric, I had been running with my hair on fire. Scared of the monster under my bed— me. One thing I had learned after these months, no matter if I shaved my head, took a rocket ship to the moon, got a sex change, or moved to Timbuktu, I would still carry the same sack of emotional shit. I was dragging my psychological carry-on to every continent, in every dark corner of this world. Pain and fear were both gasoline for my fiery impulsivity.

Since Ric died, my actions mimicked the mentality of the cow. That one you see when you are winding through a curvy country lane. I was extending my neck between two strands of barbed wire, thrusting out my lengthy pink tongue, ignoring the thick strands of bubbly drool on each side of my mouth, reaching for that blade of greener grass in the neighbor's field. I was convinced it must be tastier there than where my hooves were—missing out on the fresh, tender growth of violets blooming within my pasture. Sure, it must be better over there because it lacked appeal in terms of sensation and flavor here. Movement was my reaction and action from my past wounds, trauma, and fear—a skill honed from an early age. An impulse dusted off and reused. Driven by the ego of my fractured soul, devoid of authenticity, and disconnected from my true self.

I changed the subject with Lisa, and we seamlessly moved into other mundane news of our lives. I gnawed on an apple as she filled me in on the school news of her kids.

The rest of my vacation passed like a burp—gone before I knew it was coming. This was my second vacation without Ric, and I survived. At first, it felt awkward, like I was trying to squeeze into a familiar role. And then my vacation just unfolded with little thought or planning. I was surviving another first, wishing he were here, but unexpectedly content. Since my phone call with Lisa, I fell into a strange paradox between "I don't want to leave" and "I can't wait to leave" the mission.

The tune of the project floated back into my thoughts. I missed the mamas' songs when they consoled their infants, the nightly performance from oodles of frogs, the braying donkeys, and the sizzling stars. I missed the daily sacred handshakes and smiles from the locals and the half-moon dirt tracks from Rita's handheld broom. But parting ways with the national staff and leaving them empty-handed was my most significant anchor. That's what I thought then, but now I needed them much more than they needed me. And how could I leave without saying goodbye to the owl, the expats, and most of all, my tukul? Plus, Rupert and I were narrowing down which watch to buy.

At that moment, I knew my home was still that tiny village, filled with individuals who embodied gems of wisdom, unyielding curiosity, and unwavering resilience—but most of all, authenticity beyond comparison. Moreover, the national staff remained tasked with lots of work to do . . . on me. My address remained unchanged because I was not done yet.

In the morning, I planned to climb aboard the plane, pointed south, with my bag stuffed full of chocolates and cheese for the expats, a thank-you for doing my work while I was gone. I hid an extra bottle of Jameson at the bottom of my rucksack for Rupert and our watch quest.

I chose to go back, pushing back my ego-driven need to be comfortable, and allowed my vulnerability to help me rediscover my true self in my expanding world.

And crap, I hated to admit it, but something told me Ed's advice was probably right.

CHAPTER 21:
UNFETTERED SMILE

August 2010

I couldn't believe I was back at the mission again. A downpour gave me a few extra vacation days because the plane could not land on our airstrip. But on my first sleep back in my tukul following my near-miss hankering to flee, the owl perched on the branches above my mud hut spent his night catching up, reminding me of his presence with deep hoots, soft coos, and random, high-pitched whistles.

When I entered my tukul, I noticed each comforting detail. This tiny mud hut felt like a familiar crony, a bear hug from the past, transmitting a loving kindness that seeped into my soul. I had the sense the room exhaled and breathed life back into me. When I awoke in the morning, I felt invigorated with that postnap feeling, a renewed energy, and a clearer mind.

What a relief to be back.

Heading to the clinic, I reminded myself of my pledge to savor more moments when I returned. I needed to dial back the speed of my internal turbine to a slow jog, because right after I got back, I told Ed I would extend my mission. Tut, the day watchman, was sitting in the corner of his guard shack. We exchanged a "maale," and I tried not to stare at the scars across his forehead. *Gaar* lines. Six evenly spaced horizontal scars decorated almost every male's forehead—a puberty ritual. Months ago, I heard the national staff men in the maternity ward scrutinizing the straightness of each other's gaar lines. The straightness of each line gauged preadolescent bravery because it demonstrated they did not flinch or shy away from the cutting blade.

In Sudan, delivering medical care was difficult, but understanding the idiosyncrasies of the Nuer culture also challenged and intrigued me. I had a privileged, intimate glimpse into their rituals and lifestyle practices, but I still struggled to grasp many of them. I tried to understand what made them tick, and they were undoubtedly doing the same with me. Both sides tried to tease through the layers of dissimilarity without judging. We looked and acted differently, stealing looks at the other, trying not to get caught. It seemed six months would have given me better insight, but the reality only allowed me a bird's-eye view, regardless of the time. Exploring this complex society, I was often baffled, yet mostly charmed.

As I walked away, Tut called out in broken English, "Tell your dad forty cows."

I turned to see two national staff from the inpatient ward walking close to him, laughing at the words they just heard.

"I don't understand?" I asked them.

They now stood arm in arm, facing Tut.

The taller of the two started translating, "He will pay your dad forty cows to marry you."

I started laughing, but then stammered after looking at the serious scowl on Tut's face.

Trying politely, I asked, "Ah, how many wives does he have?" That was the best I could come up with in that short, uncomfortable moment.

The three had a brief conversation, and the same guy replied, "He has five but promises he will treat you the best."

I grinned and told the acting translator, "Tell him my dad thinks I am worth more than forty."

We all chuckled and walked away.

Decades after my first proposal, I listened to the second in this foreign, sweaty land. I clearly remember the first.

Ric and I sat on our sunken couch cushions exchanging presents on Christmas Eve in 1984. Our old farmhouse was drafty and expensive to heat, so we lugged around a propane heater to each room we occupied. I don't recall what I bought Ric on that holiday, but I remember he handed me my last present, wrapped with reindeer paper. As I slowly peeled back the tape, a pair of cream-colored handwoven alpaca gloves slid onto my lap—a true luxury for two poor college students. I slipped my hand inside the soft wool, but something was stuck in one finger of the glove. To my true nature, I gave the gift a forceful shake, and a shiny gold object flew out and rolled across the wooden floor.

Ric snatched it before it hit the propane heater and handed it to me, asking, "What do you think? Want to do it?"

"Oh, heck yes," I said, wrapping him tight in my arms.

It wasn't surprising to our family or friends; it seemed natural because we were already defying convention.

My recent second proposal amused me; the first made me cry.

Polygamy was the way of life here. In a marriage proposal, the man offered X number of cows to the bride's father. The bride's father had the final say on how many cows his daughter was worth. He could accept or decline the offer.

Once they agreed, the groom could "have" the woman. Most female national staff members were married and had many co-wives. The women openly talked about the other wives without outward jealousy. They viewed polygamy as a pooling of resources; more wives equaled more kids, and more kids equaled future cattle exchange with each future marriage proposal.

The number of cows one owned measured their wealth. Fines were paid, and brides were purchased with cattle. Frequent cattle camp raids occurred, and the Nuer fought to their deaths, defending their stock. The weekly "cattle court" was held in front of the market. Similar to our court system, but outside under a shady tree, the judges were the elder men of the village. The court assessed the offense and determined the financial restitution and how many cows needed to be forfeited. The offender paid up, and life went on. Simple and logical.

In simple terms, a large part of this culture revolved around cows.

Our daily clinic kicked off like usual: morning greetings and teatime, clinical questions tangled with more questions about living in the USA and my recent holiday. We followed this with a quick staff training about postpartum hemorrhage before we broke into groups to deliver patient care.

I harbored no regrets in my decision to return. I was happy about the smoothness of the first day back, especially knowing I was on call for medicine that night. The expats shared this duty, and it was my turn. I finished the first day back praising the national staff for their excellent work and returned to my tukul. Nearing the guard's shack, I hoped I would not have to cross paths with Tut again. His chair sat empty, probably on a break. I picked up my pace to guarantee my evasion of the guard and walked-ran into the expat compound.

Most of the daylight had passed, and the milieu had become more subdued and dimmer. I plopped down on my mattress, suddenly needing a nap. My infamous radio squawked as I opened my well-worn writing journal, pulling me back into medical reality. A male voice stating, "We need you, come," leaked from the handheld's speaker grille.

Nearing the ward, I saw the crisscrossing beams of flashlights from three national staff members huddled together outside. This was not unusual; triage happened under the stars. Each ray of light, seductive for the onslaught of nighttime insects. On the ground was a little girl, about a year old. Naked, except for a traditional strand of multicolored beads tied around her waist. Her body was clammy and rigid, with a small puddle of sweat in her sternal notch. Her jaw and eyes clamped tight, bubbles of drool escaping the corner of her peculiar smile. The touch of our fingers, the rays of our headlights, and the sounds of others around us exacerbated her muscle spasms. Too sick to cry, but holding that unrelenting smile.

Three Sudanese staff regarded me intently, waiting for instructions, while the child's family squatted beside her. I paused to think and waited for their insistence to hurry me up, but it never came. There was no pressure from them; it was just my internal badgering to make a diagnosis. Insects bounced off my headlight, sometimes accidentally flying into the neckline of my scrub top.

Think, think . . . Wet, cold, drooling, barely conscious, lying in this awkward hyperextended position with that damn smile.

What should have been an obvious diagnosis, the lightbulb of risus sardonicus finally materialized. The medical term for a "fixed smile" was not associated with a joyful situation.

I recalled a photo I kept of my siblings and me dressed up for Halloween. Someone, probably Barb, wrote "1968" on the back, so I was six years old. All our mouths were exposed, but we wore a similar Lone Ranger mask. My three siblings grinned from ear to ear. The tip of my nose was bright red, cheeks flushed, teeth clenched, the corners of my mouth falsely hoisted into that position of "please love me," acting out what Barb demanded: "Sheila, stop crying and smile, dammit." So I did.

But this child's symptoms stemmed from the bacterium clostridium tetani. Tetanus is a bacterium found in the soil, dust, animals, and human feces, producing toxins that cause havoc to the central nervous system. A simple break in the skin of an unvaccinated person was a welcome mat. The muscle spasm starts slowly. Over time, the subject's body becomes rigidly spastic. Spasms could affect the laryngeal muscles, leading to desperate situations. Noise, touch, and light can all trigger more spasms, so the key is to treat and get them in a dark, quiet place. As we say in medicine, four "big guns," robust medicines to combat life-threatening illnesses: (1) diazepam for muscular rigidity, (2) morphine for the pain of the spasms, (3) metronidazole to inhibit the toxin production, and (4) tetanus immunoglobulin to neutralize the toxin.

I was grateful I did not suffer from the pain of tetanus like this poor child, but the smile of our childhoods shared similar qualities; we both had no power over it. Clostridium tetani forced hers, and my desire for my mother's love coerced mine.

Now, I can spot a genuine smile from afar. My thoughts were stuck on the beauty of authenticity and Ric's boisterous smile. The unforgettable, toothy grin that awoke before him. When Ric and I biked or hiked, he always led the way, which meant he was the first to greet anyone approaching us. The beauty of my slower pace was that I got the leftovers of his smile hanging on the faces of those who had just encountered him. I have learned that a natural smile comes from voluntarily moving our lips in a well-known upward U shape. An authentic burst of happiness sent from our brain triggers involuntary muscle fibers of the orbicularis oculi, the muscle that causes the outer corners of your eye sockets to squint. The twinkle we can't trick. I saw both gestures on my face in old photos with Ric and, more recently, in a few phone snapshots of myself on this mission. I knew then my twinkle was returning. There was hope.

By the time I figured out what now seemed evident, the national staff had already earmarked the tetanus page in the medical handbook and were punching numbers into the handheld calculator for the child's teeny-tiny doses. In times like this, I wondered if the national staff needed an expat; they were often strides ahead. I bet situations like this were trying for them, having already zeroed in on the diagnosis but holding back, watching politely another fumbling, insecure expat trying to sort out the diagnosis.

We moved her to an isolated space in the back of the inpatient ward, and the staff started her treatment. The last thing I saw was her stretched, strained expression, lacking the emotional congruence expected in a bona fide smile.

On the way back to the compound, my headlight carved out a tunnellike path. Walking past the maternity inpatient ward, I saw the reflection of the single lightbulb in the middle of the ward. The generator hummed in the background. I peeked through the gap between the two mud structures.

The stack of sanitary pads reminded me of last Saturday morning's "pad party," the day the maternity staff came together, rolled, tucked, and twisted cotton wool around a piece of fabric. We tapped our feet to the music that blared from someone's phone. Those Saturdays, I chuckled inwardly as I watched the male national staff methodically and precisely tuck the edges of the fabric around the absorbent layer of our homemade sanitary pads for the women in the community. I think Liz and the other female maternity ward members also enjoyed the scene.

That night, most mothers in the inpatient ward held rattles made from empty water bottles with a handful of precious sorghum inside. Rhythmic crisp clicks bounced in the dark as the dried edible starchy seed ticked the sides of the plastic container while each woman rattled their unique, tender melody, yet somehow harmonizing with the rest of the ward. United, a chorus singing an interpretation of a freshly crafted melody, "I am your mother, and I am here for you."

This exchange always made me envious. But now, I was starting to look at my monsters, Barb and grief, with more curiosity. My counselor advised me to write Barb a letter when I felt ready and then destroy it—a way to rid myself of her nonsense. As long as I clung to her words, I would be stuck in the confines of my potential. I knew then Barb's words commandeered my true self. The first night back, I felt the need to release them, release her. I desperately wanted to cut her vine, severing its far-reaching roots that spread everywhere—to cut where the earth kisses the greenery, freeing it from its underground hold. I entered the empty maternity clinic, repositioned my head torch, and found a piece of paper printed on one side, empty on the reverse. I brushed off the dust, pulled the chair close to the exam table, pulled the pen from my pocket, licked the end to give it some moisture, and wrote.

> *Barb,*
> *I am finished with the tendrils of the vine that ensnare me and echo your criticisms. I understand now that your words to describe me were simply offshoots of your self-disappointments, regrets, lost dreams, and unmet needs.*
> *But I refuse to carry them anymore.*
> *I have permitted the winds of Africa to cleanse me of the runners that constrain me. My broadcasted blessing will take flight and journey from this sunbaked earth over the vast tapestry connecting our landscapes—our only connection. It will move northward, bobbing in the waves of the Atlantic, and eventually reach you, allowing you one more chance to explore your whys, or not.*
> *Thank you for teaching me that I am stronger than an ox.*
> *I wish you no harm.*
> *Sheila*

Convinced that seizing control of Barb's words marked the beginning of my liberation and fresh attitude, I sent them back to her through the trade winds of multiple time zones. No longer my weight to bear.

All year, I stood back and watched hundreds of women curiously on this mission, where the women I encountered had a multitude of daily struggles. But somehow, they endured their lives with graceful finesse. Witnessing freshly delivered new mothers, old crooked women, energetic adolescents, ailing and frail women, and handholding female cousins and sisters, they affectionately showed value to any young person within their sphere. Attending to their needs, cries, and wants with a gentle hand. They showed them love and acceptance, etching this message deeply into the next generation's hearts. These women sparked my epiphany, teaching me Barb's words were her early childhood lessons; I was just her canvas, something she could use to paint her angst and express herself. None of the vile words had anything to do with me. Not a single one of her insults captured who I was. The next day, with tea and the national staff, I would stoke our tea fire with this blessing.

In the morning, I hesitated before entering the clinic to assess the child from the previous night. The mother greeted me and patted the front of my chest with her flat palm, a gesture of thanks when the spoken language differed. Initially, I couldn't see the child's face because she faced her mother, breastfeeding. *Good sign.* Breaking the seal of her child's sucking, the mother inserted her index finger between the mouth and nipple. The child turned and looked up, breast milk dripping from the corners of her mouth. The "fixed smile" was gone. In the night, this fantastic little Sudanese girl went to battle with the disastrous bacteria, and by morning, I declared her the winner; her power was back.

Sipping my early morning tea with the maternity staff, I also basked in a sense of triumph. Laughing and answering the national staff's typical questions, I sported a genuine smile, twinkle and all, as I witnessed my message to Barb erupting into sparks, no longer mine, returning to their roots, soaring back to where it all began.

At last.

CHAPTER 22:
PRINCESS BRIDE

October 2010

A wax-printed cloth hung from the doorway of my tukul. Geometric patterns of reddish purples and lively oranges flitted from side to side on the puffs of wind, resembling a timekeeper's pendulum. Flat-out on my mattress, I extended my limbs and let out a hearty yawn, realizing it was time to head back for the afternoon clinic. Each gust gave me a glimpse of the activities outside my hut. A flipbook of Rita peeling potatoes under the tree by the kitchen, humming around the spuds' curves.

I stayed supine for a few more minutes, savoring the remnants of my now routine lunchtime catnaps. Surrendering my impulse to rush back to the clinic after lunch, "in case something happened." I replaced it with a healthier "the national staff are incredibly competent and will call me when needed." It made me happier, and the staff were probably glad to have a break from me. Writing dry-eyed, joyful tales of Ric in my journal had become a part of each day, extending coffee hours with the expats and savoring the tranquil rhythms between tasks. These small, deliberate decisions were more effective in my survival than acting on impulsive, frantic energy.

I purchased the material for my doorway while on vacation, haggling with the vendor in Morocco because I knew it was customary, yet I likely ended up paying full price. Personalizing my space for at least another half a year was a tiny investment. Next to the ditch of the airstrip, I found a partially covered segment of a fifty-five-gallon drum with the bottom intact and the sides trimmed down to about two feet in height. I rescued it, placed it to the side of the entrance of my tukul, filled it with dirt, and planted the seeds I had brought but had never taken time to plant.

Before arriving at the mission, the organization advised me to bring personal items that could provide comfort amidst unfamiliar surroundings, such as a journal, flower seeds, a musical instrument, or some meaningful project. A touch of familiarity with an otherwise unknown environment. Something to do in our spare time. *Spare time.* I threw a couple of packs of seeds in my rucksack because they were lightweight, and for me, the thrill of nurturing growth, watering it, carefully inspecting it each day, and then applauding when it pops out of the hard soil and reaches toward the sky was magical. Ten months in, I never got around to planting them, so the packs of sunflower seeds sat on my shelves in my tukul, mostly enticing the hedgehog for the past year as he explored under the cover of most nights. There was something crucial for making what you have your own in any context, even for a short time. It made the awful days more bearable and the peaceful days more soothing. Flowers would eventually sprout in my recycled cutout drum, and the snazzy African-printed material flapping in the breeze clearly showed that I had spruced up my harbor.

My actions over time grew more deliberate. I carefully planted the seeds I brought from home to nurture new growth while deliberately strangling the vine of my childhood. Who would have known that ivy could still grow here in the fissures of this parched earth? Clutching me, coiled around my ankles, grabbing anything in its path, even in drought-like conditions. Still thriving. A relentless vise grip on my soul, but it took time for me to realize what fed, nurtured, and kept it alive.

It was me.

Now, I was unrestrained, free to move forward, ever since I set ablaze the haunting leaves of the false notion that I had lugged around on my shoulders.

I acknowledged that getting to this arid, sweltering place was a long journey, but worth it.

I sat on the edge of my mattress, returning a grin to the framed person, Ric, who beamed at me from my lopsided shelves. Securing the ties of my scrub pants, I slid into my clogs. In the distance, I heard the generator cough briefly before it roared to life. Perfect timing because I needed to charge my devices for an event in the maternity ward: movie night. The maternity staff was laboring tirelessly, and nearing the end of their reproductive health course I created when I arrived on the mission, a way to ramp up the national staff's medical competencies. It was a new training module that would provide a formal certificate to each member of the maternity staff who completed all the written and practical components. The national staff, without hesitation, engrossed themselves in the challenge. So, in return for their hard work, I pledged a celebration, a movie, and popcorn.

Eagerly anticipating our evening, I grabbed my computer and projector to harness the generator's energy.

A buzzing energy of excitement bounced around the walls of the maternity ward, partly from the novelty of the experience and partly from their achievements. As we finished our day, the staff returned to their homes to prepare for the event. Upon their return, clad in fresh attire, the women wore layers of vibrant-colored cloth, and the guys sported pressed pants, simple shoes defying mirrors, and short-sleeved button-up shirts made of similar traditional material. All in their flashiest best. I had only splashed some water on my face and combed my hair.

"Give it to me," Liz said as she reached to grab the overflowing bowl of popcorn from my arms.

"Thanks," I said as Moses approached me.

"I got this, Sheilee." And he gently relieved me of my computer and projector, and we all followed each other into the clinic.

"If we yank the tarp over the door, we could get it dark in here," I said.

Moses, Mayian, and Sarah rushed toward the door. Moses, the shorter of the two men, kiddingly shoved Mayian closer. He poked fun at his Nuer height, the human stilts for the task, and after a few minutes of tucking, twisting, and snickering at each other's advice, daylight and the promise of the outside cooler temperatures entering the room disappeared. My finger searched for the "Start" button on my computer. My battery-operated projector balanced on a wobbly plastic table connected to my finicky HP. *I hope this works.* The blocked door intensified the aroma of popcorn.

The usual gibberish of the staff dismantled into silence. Plastic chairs of all colors, most needing repair, all faced the makeshift screen. Because we never had enough, a few staff members wrestled the delivery table into the middle of the room, which became an ottoman for two hand-holding staff. What a conglomeration of unorganized goodness in this room. *I love these guys.*

Scrutinizing the group, I hoped nothing in this movie would upset or trigger them. Every person in this room had been touched by evil or the relentless struggles of life in this neglected part of the world. I found comfort in remembering that Ric and I adored *The Princess Bride*. It was a movie about true love between Buttercup and her farmhand, Westley, and their resolve to be together amidst the challenges of kidnappings, attempted assassinations, and Buttercup's forced marriage to an evil king. I had no idea then; I was worried about myself. *Would I fall to pieces watching one of our favorite movies?*

The opening scene began with a young boy lying in his bed. His bespectacled grandfather licked his thumb to turn a page. "It was the book my father used to read to me when I was sick, and I used to read it to your father, and today, I'm going to read it to you."

Every staff member transformed into a forward-leaning posture, as if gravitating to smell a bouquet of roses stuck to the scene on the wall. I tugged at the neck of my T-shirt to invite a cool breeze. No one else noticed because the entertainment trumped the stuffy room. Giggles of anticipation and popcorn chomping scampered around the perimeter of the earthen walls.

"Ah, this is good popcorn," Mayian bellowed, grinning while spitting flecks of popcorn and spittle on the floor.

Followed by a commanding, universal "shush!" from the group.

The staff giggled and shared amused nudges while they watched Westley and Buttercup exchange starry-eyed gestures.

Most female staff covered their mouths in disbelief when Buttercup was told the false news that Westley had died. Then, the staff's collective release of tension and excitement as the evil Vizzini drank the poison and fell over dead in the grass. I found delight in their myriad of expressions and gestures.

The group shrieked when the hooked-nosed, warty-faced Miracle Max opened his door's peephole. Standing outside, facing him, were the dark, curly-haired Inigo and the enormous Giant, with an unconscious Westley between them. The two men needed a miracle to bring Westley back to life. After convincing Max to help them, they carried the limp Westley into the house and plopped him on the table.

"It just so happens that your friend here is only mostly dead. There is a big difference between mostly dead and all dead," Miracle Max said. ". . . Mostly dead is slightly alive. All dead . . . well with all dead, there is usually only one thing you can do," he added.

"What's that?" asked Inigo

"Go through his clothes and look for loose change," said Max.

The national staff gasped. I laughed. Miracle Max positioned a bellow over Westley's mouth, instilled some puffs of air into his lungs, then made a miracle pill covered in chocolate. The humor in this wacky scene struck me in a way my earlier viewings never managed to. Because then it made sense.

When I arrived in Sudan, I was "mostly dead." Sudan has been my Miracle Max, and the staff my miracle pill. This unusual place had brought me back to life and forced life back into my soul.

At the film's end, Westley and his allies, Inigo and Fezzik, whom he gathered along the journey, stormed the castle. Fezzik embodied the pillar of strength, bridging their resolve between Inigo's vendetta against the man who murdered his father (who was in the castle) and Westley's desire to rescue his true love. Every national staff member was glued to the white screen, captivated by the sword fight between Inigo and his enemy. As their swords clinked from the strikes and parries coupled with the precise footwork of sidestepping, retreating, and circling their opponent, the clinic echoed with mumbled admiration and gulps of surprise.

Then, the staff blasted out of their seats, mimicking the brawl. They flicked their legs like a cross between judo precision and choreographed dance. Their extremities transformed into pretend swords. Moses, looking more like a lion tamer, clenched a broom in one hand and a plastic lawn chair in the other, pretending to fight with Mayian. I roared as I covered my mouth to curtail the sound, suppressing my urge to join in. Watching their smiles and shenanigans of joy was infectious. It was long overdue for me. Probably for them as well. The room was bustling with Sudanese Inigo Montoya, rooting for his cause.

The film finished with just a few burnt popcorn seeds left, stuck to the bottom of the pot. As the movie credits rolled, thunderous applause and united bodies hopped up and down, arms dancing above their heads in shared exhilaration. They all wished me goodnight, and I switched on my headlamp and trudged back to my tukul. On the first step outside the clinic, I felt a slippery crunch under my shoe. Probably another damn locust, but I did not look back.

That movie brought back so many memories, good and bad.

Early after Ric's diagnosis, we searched for a counselor to help us wade through the alligators of the little life he had left—someone to steer us. Heavy hearts had become an un-bearable, weary load. How could we enjoy our last moments watching the clock? Waiting for the chips to fall.

"You need to give yourself permission to take a day off from cancer," the counselor advised us.

"You can flush it, bury it, burn it, shit-can it, you choose," she added.

We looked at each other and cobbled together a smile. Cancer quashed momentarily. Going, going, gone. After watching this movie repeatedly, we traded in our agony for a spontaneous, brief adventure—a moment to retreat from the battle to erase the impending doom in our minds.

On the days we declared "cancer-free," we proudly donned our fleece PJs, refused to brush our teeth, and scoffed at the sunlight begging for permission to enter the living room. Two forty-something adults. One grinning, wafer-thin, jaundiced man and one average-looking, streaky-blond female snuggling up on the sofa. Popping in one DVD after another, both were taught at an early age to follow the rules.

We sidestepped the elephant in the room and downed pints of Chubby Hubby. We capitalized on this simple advice, a gift that allowed us to enjoy some tender last moments together. Humans often need years of repetition or a big event before we notice the fragrant flowers in all directions because we are usually too preoccupied with sparring with what we thought we could control: the weeds. It was reas-suring to be reminded of this lesson again and to sense eager anticipation while I waited for the flowers I planted next to my tukul to break free from the earth.

With some reluctance, I nearly decided against showing the film that evening, as I worried about the potential for the violent and disturbing content to trigger traumatic memories among the audience. However, I discovered that the national staff had already made significant progress in coming to terms with their histories, while I felt like I was still on the starting line, waiting for the gun to go off. They breathed only for today, the hands of their clocks never budging from "right now." My watch kept time with yesterday and tomorrow. They could drop whatever shit they had in their sack outside the clinic. I kept mine securely strapped to my leg. *Just in case.*

They were miles ahead of me, mastering mindfulness with ease. They savored the right now, the moment begging to be appreciated without judgment or interpretation. Free from the tangle of expectations about how things should unfold, they humbly adapted to their ever-changing and often unkind world. Control was not in their hands; they only held hope. The stories they shared with me solidified how civil wars, famine, and tribal clashes hampered their lives. Day in and day out, surviving so well. Their approach was not fatalistic but an authentic way to greet each day with presence and clarity.

I was the freak, the three-legged animal, still walking with a limp. I continued to lean into my failed expectations while hiding my pain. Each morning, after a quick two-step with my self-pity, I slipped into my Kevlar and headed to battle. No longer the child who imagined daffodils outside the window as the wooden spoon strummed her flesh, but an adult who replaced childhood dissociation with emotional armoring. Basically, it's the same. It's just labeled differently. *Don't let them see you sweat.* I needed to keep working on that.

Washing my hands at the compound's entrance, I headed straight toward my hut. The flicker of flashlights illuminated the rest of the tukuls. It was after ten, and the rest of the expats were in bed. I peeled my sweaty scrubs and wrapped myself in my lime-green sarong, knotting it at the center of my chest.

Almost like a magic act, I faced my nights with less dread because my insomnia was virtually nonexistent. My mind switched off on the nights I wasn't on call for the mission. I realized that sleep, though seemingly a small thing, had a profound impact: a well-rested mind, a clean slate, clarity, and the energy to greet a new day. Before entering my tukul, I left behind the what-ifs and could-have-beens. I smiled at the soothing calls of the owl and imagined the amusing tales it could tell about the comings and goings of the expats, allowing my mind to wander back to the place it once knew, cherishing the simple gift of rest.

The owl signed off for the night as I crawled beneath my net and tucked my torch under my pillow. He crooned a couple of singsongy *whoo-whoos*, and I smiled, rolling on my side. No doubt tomorrow morning's clinic will balloon into a repeat of tonight's judo dance moves, "You killed my father, prepare to die" speeches, imaginary sword fights, and hysterical laughing.

I can't wait.

CHAPTER 23: IF WE LISTEN

November 2010

A sudden clap of thunder in the early morning sent the expats scattering from their outside table into our office. The rain started slowly, and then the drops became heavier. The rainy season typically ran from May through November, but the locals told us it was drier than usual. I stepped outside the kitchen, my nose pointed toward the sky, sniffing like a retriever at the arrival of the rain. All I knew was I pined for a downpour, one I could witness standing out in the open, soaking me to the core. All the months of hot and hotter days, with no relief from the inferno, felt like my internal thermostat was being tampered with, cranked up bit by bit each day. It had occasionally rained, but I could not find cool since my arrival.

At first, the fat, widely spaced drops hit the loose dirt around my feet, flicking up the little puffs of dust. As the intensity increased, drops landed on my skull and coursed through my hair follicles, creating a tingling sensation from the runoff. I stood with my arms posed, resembling a figure on the cross. I shivered.

I have rarely allowed myself to stand in the rain and welcome each drop; my instinct has always been to seek shelter. While the months of oppressive heat may have played a role in my behavior, I failed to realize that the reason ran much deeper. It wasn't about the heat, defeatism, or hopeless negativity. It was about gratitude for the now.

I was changing.

I didn't bring this trait in my rucksack. It was one of the subtle yet profound gifts that gradually unfolded within me as I watched the ways of the Sudanese over the past several months. Despite repeated atrocities, they show remarkable strength as they live, smile, and dance. They stood tall, wiped sweat from their foreheads, lugged jerry cans of water on their heads, and clasped a free hand around the palm of a kid or two. No bitching about the weather; the food, or lack of it; their illness; their past horrors; or their lost loved ones from senseless wars. Why? Because they have listened to their past trauma. They refused to let their past hijack their now, understanding that the only thing they could wrangle was how they respond to it.

Watching them helped me stifle most of my expectations, allowing me to appreciate *most* of the clinic's chaos; savor the leisurely, unhurried tea breaks; and watch the grace unfold in this lively, off-the-beaten-path village. Recently, I have found myself more receptive than ever, yielding to the day's wild unfolding events. It felt so liberating to have stopped wrestling with many things that never needed taming.

The rain dwindled, and the sun dutifully continued warming the earth. I made my way to the clinic. The typical activity of the maternity ward was motionless, seeking respite from the humidity. Under the tree next to the clinic, Mayian and Sarah sat on chairs nestled in the shadow, sorting patient records and jotting essential data into our register book.

"Fifteen deliveries this week," said Mayian.

"And, they all lived," he added.

Heads down, they continued sorting through paper scraps to find reportable data. Rubbing my hands together, I nodded and strolled back into the clinic, thrilled for a moment of calm.

Then I heard an almighty screech. Close, but not close enough to see the cause. Then a gaggle of yelps grew in intensity. When I exited the clinic, the reason lay before me: a stretcher constructed of twigs tied with tan sisal rope and a woman on her left side. Her back to me, but as the stretcher entered the clinic, I glanced at her swollen abdomen. *At least thirty weeks pregnant.* Her splayed fingers covered her eyes. As I stooped down to touch her clammy skin, I instinctively recoiled at the overpowering, pungent odor. A combination of heat and disaster drenched her burgundy T-shirt dress. A dried ring of muck circled her lower legs, marking the height of her muddy trek. Shoeless and silent.

"Does anyone know what is going on?" I asked the three drenched men as they positioned the stretcher above the spattering of red below her.

"Can we find her family?" I asked the men.

"She came alone in a dugout canoe. Something was wrong with her baby," said one man. She shifted on the stretcher and uttered a gentle moan. "We found her at the river's edge." The guy who stood at the head of the stretcher said, "She left at sunrise."

The afternoon sun calculated her hours of paddling. Seven hours ago, her baby was still wiggling when she boarded her dugout. Without food, water, or assistance, she paddled and bled all the way here. Her family called her Nyachoal.

Shortly after her arrival, just before midday, I was washing my hands when Moses approached me, a half-worried smile across his typically cheerful demeanor.

"Sheilee, there is a new patient for you to see."

"Where is she?" I asked.

"Out front." He grabbed my elbow and tugged me toward the door.

When we arrived at the entrance, I looked around but saw no one. The subdued whimper below me caught my attention. I stepped back to see a woman on the ground *à quatre pattes*. She rested on her permanently flexed knees, hands on the ground before her, trying to keep her belly out of the red dirt. Two soil-stained, atrophied lower legs followed behind her. The definition of her deltoids highlighted the gravity of her bulbous abdomen. The lack of routine vaccines left her crippled with this horrible disease: polio. Tied to her kneecaps with tattered shoestrings were green, dust-covered flip-flops. Useless for her feet, but vital for her patella. Dirt-crusted lashes and her garments cloaked in a layer of days, she looked up at the staring group. Eyes still bright with optimism, but a metallic smell hinted at trouble.

In the preceding hours, her determination fired the thousands of elastic fibers in her biceps to lift her torso and propel herself across the desert. Two arms at a time, she made it to our feet. She left her tukul this morning because she sensed trouble in her pregnancy. Her uncooperative body did not stop her. The child was wiggling inside when she left—less than usual, but still moving. She crawled and bled all the way to us. That was six hours ago. Her family called her Nyatut.

Two women, one by land and one by water, had appeared from nowhere. They were not famous movie stars, authors, or sports figures, but two unknown women who were full of hope and determination. They were taking charge of what they could. Both of them were pregnant and bleeding, living in a tiny, distant village in Sudan.

The first came with the help of the Sobat River currents, a major Nile tributary. The second came with brute strength across the arid landscape.

Two indistinguishable stories: Two women, Sudanese, pregnant, bleeding, and their hardships causing a rise in infant mortality rates. Both recognized a warning sign in pregnancy and took measures to get to the clinic. Both arrived alone, dehydrated, exhausted, covered with dirt and dried blood. Both with strength beyond my imagination. Neither blaming nor angry with the world or the outcome.

A couple of days after they stabilized, these two women sat with the other women in the ward, shared sorghum, laughed, and held the other women's babies.

Five days later, their resting heart rates returned to baseline, and their abdomens were no longer taut; the visible wet marks on the front of their dresses revealed the wasted nutrition. When it was time for them to go home, they hugged the staff and returned home as they came, alone— Nyachoal in her beautiful dug-out boat, and Nyatut in her flip-flop-covered knees. My two new heroes.

I thought about the lack of parity in the world.

Witnessing this brought me to tears—big, heavy tears— linked to observing raw, uncensored suffering. Staring into the eyes of gut-wrenching determination. The in-your-face kind. The unfairness of the world. The shitty part of being conceived in Sudan. Despite that, these two women demonstrated living in the moment, accepting what life gave them, being content with any outcome, and cherishing even fleeting moments of joy.

This event caused lots of noise in my head.

We are products of where we were conceived. What would I have done, lie there kicking and screaming, begging for help? Would I have had the power and fortitude to do what they did? Why not just lie down and die? *Where do they get their hope?* Maybe they thought life awaited one more beautiful moment, so screw the self-loathing and take a chance. Or it was more about not expecting anything today and accepting what the universe threw at them. So just jump on the magic carpet and see where it takes you. It was a delicate balancing act between expectations and hope.

Did I believe I could sidestep all the suffering, including mine, by coming here? I didn't think about it when I joined this mission, but I wonder now if I naively thought witnessing others suffering would take my mind off my sorry self. Somehow, whipping me back into shape. Put my head back on straight. I was unprepared for the magnitude of suffering I would observe during this mission. But what made me stand up and pay attention was how the Sudanese responded with grace, hope, and acceptance of their fate. They were so much more than their trauma; they were courageous allies with their fear. *So courageous.*

I laughed at myself, thinking about my impulsive button that landed me in Sudan. It wasn't courageous; it was an ego-soothing move, a way to prove distance would cure me. I didn't trust myself with the past or the future. Without a solution, distance was my only way out. Yet it wasn't an escape; it was merely a detour, leading me back to the same old miserable emotions. Just on a different continent. A hot one at that. Driven by pure fear.

Over the eleven months, I learned the actual "fuck-it" button should be about acceptance and steadily moving forward. It stems from encounters with various unassuming yet profound silent souls in Sudan, those who carried incredible messages and wielded hidden powers—

Like Nyachoal and Nyatut.

And the four men who grabbed destiny by the horns and carried the ill woman to the clinic.

And the joyful women who waited daily on the bench for medical care.

And the accepting women who gave birth yet left the clinic without the precious babies they delivered.

And the TBAs who walked miles, in all conditions, to our monthly meetings, asking for nothing in return.

And the national staff who burst into an explosive dance for no real reason, just because.

Trauma teaches us something if we listen.

Now, I was finally listening.

CHAPTER 24: TWO OUT OF THREE

January 2011

Despite how far I felt I had come, most days in the clinic still tested my resolve. Little things of little importance still grated on my nerves. It was probably normal, but I couldn't find the pulse point then. I could not see Sudan as an honest mirror, reflecting my resilience and exposing my frailties. I was only paying attention to the latter because I still had the overpowering tendency to fixate on what lay ahead, often neglecting to celebrate the victories I had already achieved.

The issue I struggled with was the cultural differences between myself and everything around me. Most days, drastic dissimilarities between the staff and me made my uptight Western habits glaring in the clinic. Since my arrival, I noticed everyone in the clinic throwing rubbish on the floor: gauze wrappers, boxes holding IV tubing, empty medicine bottles, and scribbled notes. Patients followed suit. I placed various buckets around the clinic to serve as waste cans.

"Liz, could you throw the paper you have in your hands in the trash bucket?" I asked.

"Where is it?" she asked as I noticed it was only a foot from her foot.

"Right there," I said as I pointed to the bucket.

She grinned. "Okay, Sheilee."

Then she dropped what she held, half landing in the bucket and the rest bouncing off the rim onto the floor. Occupied by her current task, she continued without looking back. I bent forward and picked it up. It felt so important at the time and so ridiculous now.

Sarah asked me if she could take the buckets home "because they don't get used." When I reminded her they were for trash, she snickered and said, "Sheilee, you are so funny."

And the crowds that blossomed out of nowhere made me take a deep breath and strive for a Zen-like presence. Everything drew a crowd in Sudan: A medical procedure, a birth, a dog fight, a dead snake killed by the guard, or even a private conversation between patients, caregivers, and medical staff all equaled action, and action equaled a crowd. With my head down, concentrating on a delivery, I might look up to find a slow trickle of people slowly filtering into the room and lowering themselves into a crouch, as if to minimize their presence.

When I requested my translator to dismiss everyone except the patient's caregiver, he often replied, "I won't be able to see what you are doing if I translate for you."

But the positive thing about the crowds was that they brought the frequently missing cleaning lady back to the ward, and she now desired to sweep the floor directly under my feet.

Anonymous community members often interrupted private conversations with patients and families. An innocent passerby would join the discussions, offer their two cents, and attempt to help the group decide about medical care. I always felt like it was an intrusion, but the rest of the group always welcomed the advice. Why should I be offended? Again, I wasted energy trying to control a process that worked. Two heads, as they say. It was beneficial for me to maneuver from time to time in the gray zone because it stretched my limits and forced me to release what didn't matter.

Yet, on another sweltering day in January, a year in the mission, with a cloudless blue sky, the ominous gray zone reappeared. I stood in the clinic doorway with Liz, watching a group of kids giving the local donkey a towel snap with a piece of cloth they carried, trying to convince him to move from the footpath leading to town. When the twisted material thwacked his hindquarters, the donkey delivered a startled bray and turned his head in surprise toward the laughing group of boys. *Boys are universally the same.*

Liz saw her first, and then I did—a walking gray zone.

As she got closer, I noticed her right arm supporting the rectangular basket on her head, alive with the sounds of an older infant wrapped inside. Her other arm swung to balance her stride. The cadence of her breathing grew louder as she grew nearer. Her enormous abdomen stretched the fibers of her dress and caused her to keep her weight on her heels, as if trying not to topple over. She pulled in gulps of air when she reached us as she tried to catch her breath. Liz scurried across the room to grab a chair.

"Holy cow. That is the biggest belly I have ever seen," I said.

"Sit here," Liz said softly, taking the woman's basket from her head and guiding her to the chair.

"Why is half of her index finger black?" I asked as I touched her discolored index finger.

Focusing on her finger gave me more time to think about her situation. *What should I do first?*

"The election," Liz said. The woman now dabbed the sweat beads from her forehead and swatted the flies from her forearms.

The referendum. I had almost forgotten. The black-tipped finger was a way to verify their participation in the vote. After casting their vote, I learned they had to dip their pointer finger in a jar of indelible black ink. The South eagerly anticipated the election, their long-awaited independence. Breaking away from the North meant they could liberate themselves from decades of being unable to control their natural resources.

I stared at my diagnostic tools on the table beside me: a plastic tape measure partially torn at the three-centimeter mark, and a metal fetoscope. On days like this, I couldn't wait to return to a medical facility with better diagnostics, a lab down the hall, an obstetrician on call, and brilliant colleagues in the next exam room eager to offer advice. A French obstetrician invented the fetoscope in the nineteenth century to eavesdrop on fetal heart tones. It resembles an aluminum ice cream cone—the brown sugar-cone variety. To use it, the operator balances the wide end of the cone facing the passenger. Then, you place your ear on the pointy end that holds a small flange and count the thumps. Antiquated, but still useful. The only way to get an ultrasound was to wait a week for our supply plane, transport the patient on it, and have the scan conducted where the aircraft picked up our supplies. Sometimes you get what you get, so I moved on, grabbed the fetoscope, and walked toward the patient.

Liz pulled the stepstool close to the exam table. The patient placed her right foot on the first step, paused, inhaled deeply, and gave us a look like "give me a minute." With our help, she got the other foot on the stool and twisted her body around to sit. *This belly is mammoth.* I traversed her taut protuberance with the fetoscope, from north to south, east to west, and back again—an explorer of sorts. I heard heartbeats and felt vibrations and kicks, but could not tell who the travelers were. Her abdomen was so taut and firm from the pregnancy that it felt like a stretched balloon, ready to burst with the slightest touch.

"Her last period?" I asked Liz.

They exchanged their language, and Liz gave me a pleading glance that said, "Stop asking that question." It was my habit, my training. Something that made no sense in a place where women were uncertain of the start but assured of the conclusion, and spot on at predicting the arrival. I emitted a long, deep breath and let it go. I had more pressing matters to attend to.

Stumped again, flung back into my unsettling, out-of-control zone. *This place is a control freak's nightmare.*

"Can you ask her if she will spend the night with us?" was all I could think of.

Liz and the patient engaged in a ten-minute conversation, and then she turned to me and said, "Yes."

Liz wrapped her hands around the patient's upper arm, and I did the same on the other side. We then pulled her back into a sitting position.

"Tell her I hear two strong heartbeats," I said. *Maybe a third, too, but I was not sure.* I kept that to myself.

We walked her into the patient-filled ward to settle her for the night. When we entered, the chatter of the inpatient women ceased. In one bed, a new mom bundled her four-hour-old baby, her overfilled baskets, and gourds with fermented sorghum. She hurried to the mat she placed on the floor alongside the bed, relinquishing her spot to our needier patient.

Days passed, and we repeated the same routine, measuring tape too short and the fetoscope around and around—the dance of the little ones, tricking me at every turn. A crackling radio interrupted my lunch at the expat compound on day three after her arrival. Moses.

All he said was, "Come."

Oh boy, here we go. I dropped my spoon and sprinted to the clinic, sucking the lunch rice from the crevices of my teeth. My body sprinted while my head ran through this conundrum's obstetrical dos and don'ts. And there it was, the crowd. Over twenty people stood around the entrance of the maternity ward. *Gathered for what?* As I ran past, I gave them a slight bow of my head and a "maale" and continued toward the entrance of the delivery room. I kicked off my clogs and tugged on the knee-high green gum boots from the collection in the corner. They were a first come, first served joint property for our team. The delivery room had a cement floor with a poorly functioning drain, so the boots ensured dry feet.

Moses expertly set up our delivery kit and helped the woman with her ginormous abdomen onto the table. He spoke calmly to her in their language. Tiny beads of sweat gathered on his forehead, hers and mine.

At the far end of the delivery room, I noticed three crouched, weathered-faced women with their backs to the wall.

I stopped momentarily and asked Moses, "Who are they?"

"Her three mothers," he replied.

I regarded them with a quick smiling nod and refocused.

And then, like an imaginary starter pistol, the patient let out a deep guttural groan. My gloved fingers searched internally for a firm presenting part, but what felt like an overfilled party balloon stood in the way: the amniotic sac. *Shit. Shit. Shit.* Her urge to push gave me the desire to run. A rapid rupture of her membranes could cause the first passenger in line to crash in an improper exiting position. *Or worse yet, the umbilical cord.*

"Moses, please tell her we want her on her left side." I knew this would increase blood flow to the uterus and babies and take the pressure off of her other internal organs.

We both struggled to help her, our hands trying to grip her sweaty arms.

"Let's also lower her head," I said, hoping to take advantage of gravity and prevent the membranes from rupturing rapidly.

Clear amber fluid dripped on the floor, and then, as expected, an unwelcome gush spilled out into the tops of my boots. *So much for dry feet.* The impatient first newborn slid out with ease, tiny but spitting and sputtering like a lawnmower on the first pass of the grass-cutting season after a long, cold winter in the barn. I handed her to Moses, and he dried her and handed her to Mother #1.

Why are there three mothers? Do they know something?

Waiting for her turn, the second infant followed, feet first, trying to outshine her sister's earlier arrival. After we dried and stimulated her, her squeal told us not to worry. I handed her to Mother #2.

Now just the placentas, and we are home free.

I glanced at Mother #3, hoping she did not feel left out. Expressionless, ready to accept whatever came her way. I inserted my hand again and felt another tense balloon. *Now I get it.* Too nervous to laugh at the irony, I felt a tap dance on my fingers, as if the movement reminded me not to forget the youngest still inside. And with the next contraction, her membranes burst and sent the last of the waters rushing along with the last sister. And she, like the one before her, entered soles first.

Once her two little legs extended, the momentum of her birth ceased.

"Hands off the breech until you see the nape of the neck," I told Moses, the mantra hammered into my head in training.

Then, after you see that tuft of hair and the head remains inside, you place your fingers in the mouth of the baby to gently flex the chin on their chest to aid in the delivery. The beauty of a solid education brought forth effortlessly when the moment called for it. I fumbled for the infant's mouth, unable to find it, and then she just popped out. As I wiped off her face, it revealed her anomaly: pursed lips like she was whistling. She was alive then, but could not beat the anomaly fate had bestowed upon her. I handed her to Mother #3. All three mothers were equally happy, equally blessed, peering at their gifts.

Each infant barely tipped the scales at one thousand grams. Two strong and wailing. One still. Here, death was accepted, albeit ruthless and painful; it was just part of their reality. Not welcomed, just received. The mighty mother, pale but stable, who had just birthed triplets without a peep, was resting in her space, one baby on each breast. Removing my gloves, I chuckled, noticing a collection of sweat at the tips of each finger. I washed up.

Still, in daylight, I noticed a trail of more family members gathering as I peeked outside to escape the oppressive heat of the delivery room. The wise attendants of earlier spotted me, the three mothers. They ran toward me, grabbed my hands, and pulled me into a forming circle of women—the dance. I thought back on all the dances I've joined in, celebrating significant and insignificant, simple moments.

I wanted to remember the ululation, the cry of African women, representing a soul-cleansing ritual of joy or sorrow. That rolling, high-pitched "lililililililili" allowed us to fully immerse ourselves in the moment and release the deep-seated emotions within. I know now that sound will forever echo in the corridors of my memory.

Women, young and old, surrounded me again. They grabbed hands, sweaty arms around each other, and moved in unison. A circle moved clockwise with rhythmic hopping and singing. We celebrated all three infants and the moment's magic and abandoned the bitterness of loss.

Because it was like that here.

I glanced at myself: a T-shirt stained with my profession and a sagging elastic waistband on the African skirt I bought in the market in Morocco. *What a sight.* But the best part, when I looked down at my green rubber boots, was that they were not a pair, but a pair of lefts. They pointed in the same freakish direction. With a flick of my head, I shook my head of sweaty, unruly hair. I stomped my two left feet and mimicked the howling of the older women as I followed their dance strides.

So many things out of my control.

So many things in my control.

I thanked my listeners for this unbelievable experience, yet I most deeply thanked my resilience for guiding me back to this mission.

CHAPTER 25: SCRUBBING THE AFRICAN DUST

May 2011

What a glorious morning, still cool and silent. The two tiny treasures I now held sacred. Felix, the cat, was weaving in and out of my legs, purring to beat the band as I drank my next-to-last cup of instant coffee with the stinky powdered milk. Homeward bound in twenty-four hours. As I reached down to pet him, I felt the rough scabs on his head, a testament to his past skirmishes with the village cats, probably striving to maintain his solitary dominion in the expats' compound. The word home stirred a curious sensation in the pit of my stomach, not a punch-in-the-gut kind, but more like the flutter of moths. Somehow, most of that fear had evaporated, and now I knew my "home" had extraordinary possibilities. Any place where I kicked off my shoes and left them by the door, where my blood pulsed through my veins, and where my soul found peace could now be called home—a new chapter. I turned and glanced at my mud tukul, fondly reminiscing about what a harbor it had been.

A memory nudged me back to grad school when that hippy dude came to a class and gave an impromptu lecture about humanitarian work. How that short fifteen minutes spoke to me. It felt so untouchable then, but here I was, about to finish my first mission. A year and a half ago, I had landed on what felt like an unknown planet. But as I adapted to this strange new world—except for the heat and throwing rubbish on the floor—I realized I was an anomaly. Laid bare, stripped to the bone, and vulnerable. Seeking a path through the rawness and somehow succeeding. *It took a village to shape this woman.* I intended to savor my final twenty-four hours in Sudan by soaking up intangible treasures, moments unencumbered by ribbons or fancy trimmings yet rich with memories and beautiful humans. All lightweight and easy to carry wherever I ended up.

I gently pushed Felix out of the way and walked to the area of the compound where the mamas did the laundry. *I need to wash my clogs.* Until that moment, I had never taken the time to scrub my shoes. Yet there I was, feeling the need to do this. I let out a soft, amused breath, thinking it was my maternal "nesting," an instinct to ready myself for the impending, eagerly anticipated moment. Dumping a generous amount of the overpowering flower-scented Omo into the water of the community basin, I watched it swirl, the saturated flakes pulling the dry ones under. I immersed each clog. *So worth their money. I have walked miles in these things.*

I began to scrub my shoes with the overused scrub brush; its bristles splayed out in all directions from the base. Bubbles drifted, and the stronger ones grabbed the puffs of wind and went in their direction. White suds replaced with oxidized red color of the soil, leaving a rusty-colored scum ring adhering to the inside of the basin. After I finished, I dumped the water onto the dry dirt, and the cascade of tiny bubbles meandered away from the spill, trailing each other, then merged into the tributaries formed from the mama's morning laundry rinse water.

This was it. I was really leaving.

I was so ready and so not.

Fifty percent of my brain desperately wanted to leave. That half wished for a break from the heat, dust, hard work, and crappy food. *I am officially underweight.* In a few days, I will return to my take-it-for-granted life: washing machines, icy drinks, going to an actual movie theater, and talking on the phone with Lisa. A break in the craziness, an ability to be completely anonymous, a place where no one could track my movements. But the other half of my gray matter dreaded the goodbyes. The connections I had forged with both expats and national staff were invaluable. Yet the wisdom gleaned from the national staff, through countless hours spent together, would be the most difficult to part with. The ones that effortlessly jumped over the bar of my constantly raised expectations. The ones that now stood tall at the foot of the exam table, asking one of their colleagues to hand them supplies as they proficiently birthed a baby. The ones who hacked together a wooden sign and placed it at the entry of our new clinic with the painted words NYAKIMBLE VILLAGE. The ones I trust will continue to learn and find a better life in their new country. But unfortunately, the ones I will probably never see again.

I put the community bucket back in its place so the mamas could find it at the end of their day. Because each day, after they finished their afternoon shift in the kitchen, they headed to once-bright-colored plastic wash basins, now faded from the sun, to wash up. They lifted a jerry can, one they brought each morning when we were still sleeping, and poured water into the containers, mindful of using only the smallest amount. Then they carried the containers to a shady spot big enough to accommodate both of them and plunged their toes into the bath with a smirk. When they finished, they gathered the vibrant cloth that hung from the tree branches, which they had set aside earlier to shield them from the grease splatters while frying our food. Draping the fabric over their heads, knotted at one shoulder, transforming back into something more festive, like my going-to-town clothes. At the end of their routine, they sat, opposite shoulders touching, chatting softly, rubbing vegetable oil on their overworked soles—another poignant reminder of embracing the moment.

I had little to take home. I gave my trainers to Moses; we had the same size feet. I gifted my stethoscope to Mayian, a present for his steadfast commitment to the women we cared for. Most of my daily clothes were worn, faded, and stained, so I put them in the giveaway pile. I planned to leave with the clothes on my back and a few essentials in my rucksack: my journal, a picture of Ric, and a handful of gifts from the staff. My rucksack bore a much lighter burden. It would carry out less than the permitted fifteen kilograms allowed to bring in, but my heart was brimming with far more than I arrived with.

This afternoon, I got to say a proper goodbye to the national staff; there was no shame in sneaking out the back door. Hanna and Amy had already left the mission and had been replaced with newbies. Since Rupert was on holiday, nobody had to suffer through an awkward goodbye.

I passed Tut on my way to the clinic, sitting at the guard station.

"Tomorrow?" he yelled with his bunched-up eyebrows.

"Yes," I said as I put my arms out like the wings of a plane and made an engine noise with my lips. Giving me a one-sided frown, he shook his head and looked at the ground.

The morning clinic went smoothly, as if choreographed. There were just a few patients, and all the deliveries and babies were doing well in the ward. Afterward, we gathered our chairs outside the clinic in the tree's shadow. We passed around a cylindrical pack of cookies, each person taking a couple. Each member, even timid Liz, took a moment to speak.

Moses began. Pushing back from his chair, he stood and asked, "Guess who I am?"

He pulled forcefully on the neck of his shirt, blew out a puff of air, and said in a high-pitched voice, "Oh my God, I'm so hot."

The group exploded with laughter. *He nailed that.*

When the laughter settled, Moses went to his serious side. "You were like another comother to us. Encouraging, loving, strict, and always funny," he said.

Everyone clapped.

I was happy with the notes of humor.

Then, it was Mayian's turn. He stood with a wide gait and brushed the front of his shirt free from wrinkles before beginning to speak. "Sheilee, you treated us all as equals. No one can take what you gave us." I heard agreeing mumbles from the rest of the group.

As I thought I might break down, he added, "Plus, now I am a good detective." The group roared.

I wondered if this is what it felt like to be a mother, proud of my team, of their confidence, and of the newly gained obstetric skills—skills and techniques they worked daily to master, even in foreign languages. And Mayian was right: Education was an indelible gift, now wholly theirs and untouchable. Their circumstances, no matter what, could not take this away.

Then Sarah stood and added, "When you are gone, we will help the babies kick their way out."

Stay strong, Sheila, don't cry. But a few tears snuck out, bounced over the contours of my uplifted cheeks, swiftly eclipsed by the uproarious laughter that bubbled up from within me.

As I've come to know and cherish, I was confident there would be a dance. It was just like that. Someone always had a mobile phone. I saw Moses reach into his pocket and pull out his phone. He placed it on the arm of his chair, and then, with a click, the music played the last beats of our last dance together.

The morning of my departure arrived.

I felt less like a weasel; stronger now, knowing I came back and finished what I set out to do. As I gathered my things in my tukul, I looked around, noting it looked identical to my arrival. Empty, my old mosquito net removed, shelves dusty but bare, and the mattress with an even bigger butt indent in the middle. The only difference was the material hanging in the doorway, a welcome gift for the next expat. For the last time, I ducked under the door frame. I was skilled at this, knowing how far to dip my head to avoid hitting it on the low-hanging grass roof. I admired the two sunflowers poking out of the dirt in the cut-off metal barrel beside my door, doing a shimmy dance in the morning breeze. Kind of a send-off.

With each step toward the airstrip, I felt short of breath, as if an invisible hand was squeezing the air out of my lungs, wringing the life out of me, or at least the life I had grown comfortable with over the past year and a half. And I knew this was the final adieu to the national staff. Expats staff used the expression, "See you someplace else in the world," as a goodbye, meaning meeting up on another mission. But the national staff did not have this luxury of coming or going. They got the next expat who arrived on the next plane, and eighteen months ago, they got me.

The maternity staff stood cheering. It was a strange farewell to hear a cheer, yet one that kept my tears at bay. After we exchanged hugs, shoulder slaps, handshakes, and words, it was time to board.

I walked up the three steps of the plane, which had felt so wrong months ago.

I didn't know what I was going back to, but I knew it would be okay because that was tomorrow, and at this moment, it was about the now. Of course, I would do more missions, but I had no definitive details, just that I would. I was confident I needed to leave. It was time for another expat to come in and refresh my oldness—new energy, as they say. The organization had asked me to extend the mission, but I had already extended it once, and there came a time. The maternity staff huddled in a group, flapping and showing off their new reproductive health certificates. Now, they were a team that functioned with flawless precision. Liz stood next to Sarah, arm in arm. Moses was next to Mayian, holding hands, and the rest of the team was beaming and bidding me goodbye.

Adieu, my flock of goodness.

"Are you ready to leave?" Jason, the pilot, asked as I sat and buckled my seatbelt.

I was relieved it was him and that there would not be any pretakeoff religious gestures.

"Yes." My voice cracked like a preadolescent boy.

The engine whirled as Jason turned the plane toward the end of the runway. I waved, squinting through the sunlight and the scratched plane window, watching the world I knew become a blurry, indiscernible haze.

Ci locda teeth. Thank you. Thank you.

Two days later, when I took my window seat on my flight from Amsterdam to the US, I did a silent happy dance, knowing the plane doors were about to close and the aisle seat next to me was empty. Hours before, I sat waiting for my flight at the drafty airport. My mouth was wide open, and I felt like an anthropologist conducting fieldwork, trying to understand humans' rituals, traditions, and dynamics in a developed country. Observing the flashy clothes, the stores with their fluorescent spotlights shining down on the latest perfumes, people carrying overloaded meals in the food courts, the overpowering scents of cleanliness, and the clicking of high-heeled shoes in the corridors. I was an interloper in the world I once knew.

Just before the plane door closed, one last passenger, a dark-haired man, thick around the middle, wearing a shiny navy suit, bolted into the plane and took the seat I had hoped would remain empty. *Shit!* He stashed his briefcase overhead and flopped next to me with a huff. It was like an invitation to ask him why he was exhausted; instead, I gave him a polite nod in exchange. After take-off, he began to chatter. I did not feel like talking and had not yet adjusted to a world with all this *stuff.* Plus, how would I ever explain the past year and a half?

"You on vacation?" he asked, his voice tinged with a typical US Southern accent.

Oh boy.

"Nope," I said, looking straight ahead.

I shifted in my seat and pulled out the emergency exit card from the seatback in front of me, feigning interest, hoping he would stop asking questions.

I wondered if exiting the mission was as drastic as returning to the privileged world after living in a mud hut. My life's contents were in one rucksack, and the rest of the world seemed overloaded. This world felt unbalanced.

"Going home?" he asked.

I am going home.

"Uh, yes," I answered in a quippy way, hoping he would get the hint.

"Where were you?" he continued.

"Sudan," I said sarcastically, wondering if he knew where it was.

I pulled the paperback I purchased at Schiphol Airport from its plastic sack. I flicked the empty peanut butter cup wrappers stuck to the cover into the bag. *They were so good.* I opened the book to the first page.

"Was it hot there?" he asked.

I burst into an uncontrollable fit of laughter. He shot me a few sideways glances mixed with a scowl, trying to figure out the reason behind my outburst. That word, *heat*, had a different meaning since my time in Sudan.

As my giggling petered out, I collected my wits and replied, "Very."

I reached over my head, cranked the air on full blast, leaned against the seatback, and closed my eyes. For the rest of the flight, he alternated between sleeping, taking frequent bathroom breaks, and shuffling papers in his briefcase, occasionally interspersed by bouts of snoring.

Thank God he never asked me any more questions.

CHAPTER 26: LATER

July 2011

Hello again, you beautiful Black Hills.

I sat in a sagging-bottom canvas lawn chair smack-dab in the middle of a weathered deck perched on the mountainside of my property. Thirty months have passed since I slept beside Ric's warm body, heard him slurp his tea and laugh, or wondered if he was still breathing. My usual neighbors surrounded me: Ponderosa pines, elk, coyotes, and a welcoming nighttime sky peppered with stars made me feel content. I couldn't wait to watch the light wither, decolorizing the pines into a charcoal sketch. Returning allowed me to see and feel this once more. The refreshing summer night air hissed through the pines, turning chilly, and I needed to add some warmer clothes. The relentless heat in Sudan and shedding seven kilos left my body unable to withstand the cold.

I stepped inside the Rambler and walked down the hall to the closet. I flipped open the mirrored closet door, where my overalls hung. *The ones Ric bought me to keep me warm when we built the fence.* Kicking off my shoes, I slid my body inside, pulling the industrial-size zipper up to my neck. My familiar ill-fitting beanie rested atop a pile of T-shirts, so I seized it and pulled it snugly over my ears. Hanging on the inside of the opposite door was Ric's red unitard. I inhaled suddenly and sharply because it was the first personal object of Ric's I had seen in almost two years. And then, just like before, I grasped the soft cotton and buried my face, trying to smell him.

But his scent was gone—that citrusy cologne he used to wear called "Happy." *It was so appropriate.*

Oh no, I can't do this.

And then I waited, feeling a slight jiggle of the camper from the wind outside.

I waited for that familiar sensation, like a tooth being pulled without Novocain.

And I waited.

For the first time, I still felt pressure and tugging, along with the metallic taste in the back of my throat. I could hear the unsettling crunching and cracking as the tooth of my past was twisted from the socket, but it didn't hurt as much. Grief was still there, tracking me to Africa and back. Yet I felt transformed; somehow, it had softened, having witnessed the rewards of embracing life's curveballs through the lens of Sudanese culture.

I cleared my throat and moved back down the hall toward the door. I unzipped the top pocket of my rucksack, removed Ric's picture, and set him on the table, looking outward. His nighttime words, "I love you, always have, always will," made me smile.

I turned the metal latch on the RV door and went outside on the deck. As the sun sank from its stage, the air became cooler. I reached into my left pocket and immediately felt the gritty remnants of a leftover cigarette, glad the urge was gone. I placed my other hand in the opposite pocket.

What is that?

My fingers walked around a smooth object, and my brain tried to identify it.

I knew what it was when I felt the outcropping of the childproof lid. The empty medicine bottle was still there. I swallowed.

Thank goodness I was still on this earth. What would I have missed if I had taken my life? Thoughts of what I would have missed suddenly overwhelmed me.

I wouldn't have scaled the highest African mountain or met Moses, Liz, Mayian, Ahmed, Ed, Ahieu, Sarah, Tut, James, Kate, Rupert, Hanna, and even Amy.

I would neither have experienced the African women's cry nor witnessed its meaning.

I wouldn't have understood Barb's words were never about me.

I wouldn't have dived to the bottom, stayed submerged, and eventually floated to the top, laughing.

I wouldn't have realized grief would pursue me to the farthest corners of the earth.

I wouldn't have grasped the uniqueness of my journey, the paths I treaded, the obstacles I leaped over, and the moments I closed my eyes. At last, I was where I wanted to be, on my terms, eager to take on the world's adventures and obstacles. All these experiences, including the pain, molded my essence, intertwined, and gathered into a complex orb that now defined my soul.

The yipping coyotes in the distance mirrored the high-pitched notes of my memories—the ululation. The Nuer women's long, wavering, high-pitched sound conveyed profound emotions. I've learned that expression was a means to channel life's light and shadows, enabling them to let go of joy and sorrow and reconnect with the present moment. And all the dancing . . . well, just because it was like that there.

Looking at the silhouette of the mountains and the moon, which was spreading a thin layer of light on the field below, I inhaled the frigid, minty air.

That's when it hit me: I possessed a strength I had never known.

Ric had been right all along.

~~THE END~~

THE BEGINNING

AUTHOR'S NOTE

This book is my version of my memory.

Memory is an intensely individual experience. Everyone remembers the same story differently. I've poured my heart into recounting my experiences, drawing from the journals that shaped my journey. Some names, locations, and details have been changed to maintain privacy and create a smoother narrative. The conversations are not verbatim, but my reflection of my past. I invite readers to connect with the essence of the story through my remembrances that have deeply transformed me.

ACKNOWLEDGMENTS

This story began not at a desk, but in a closet. While unpacking volumes of journals, hundreds of pages scribbled in faded ink, stained with tears and smudged with sweat, a narrative emerged.

But I did not arrive here alone. Not even close.

To Ally Berthiaume, my content and development editor at The Write Place Right Time—thank you for gently nudging me beyond my comfort zone and teaching me to excavate the soul of this story. Your insight, humor, and steady encouragement shaped this book in ways I could not have imagined.

To my beta readers—Stephanie Tudyk, Heidi Beguin, Jennifer Capler, Minerva Rivera, and Heidi Wess—thank you for stepping into these early pages with open hearts and thoughtful eyes.

Special gratitude to Lisa Lucca, high-level manuscript editor and human extraordinaire—your sharp eye, candor, and encouragement helped me refine this work with precision and grace.

Heartfelt thanks to Stephanie King and Dr. Chris Mills. Thank you for always believing in my words and voice. Always.

Endless gratitude to my American bestie, Lisa Milburn, my soul sister—you quieted my doubts before they had a chance to grow.

To my dear dog-loving, desert-hiking partner, Denise Emery—thank you for listening, every step of the way.

To the Montana Fat Bastards—Dr. Jeff Perotti, Maria Sievers, Dr. Greg Holzman, and Donna Shull—thank you for loving Ric and standing by me over the years. Your loyalty means everything.

An immense thank you to Dr. Jacquie Pinard, my French bestie, for those beautifully tangled philosophical conversations that helped me rediscover the quiet things that live beneath the surface.

To Tim Brinker—dreamer, colleague, bringer of joy—thank you for reminding me to stay true to myself and to find light even in the hard places.

To my father—joyful, brilliant, endlessly curious—you taught me to question the world and love it all the more for its mystery.

To my favorite cousin, Kelly Broughton—your unwavering encouragement and humor carried me these past few years.

To my beloved Aunt Mary, now ninety-two. Your constant check-ins, your determination to stay well until this book is in your hands, touched me beyond words.

And to every family member who wrapped me in love after Ric's death—thank you.

To Médecins Sans Frontières (MSF)—thank you for your courage, compassion, and commitment. To the national and expatriate staff who became my teachers and family, especially Rupert and Hanna—thank you for allowing me to walk beside you. The proceeds of this book will help fund the education of Sudanese national staff children—my humble offering in return for all you gave me.

To She Writes Press, Brooke Warner, and the entire SWP team—thank you for your vision, support, and belief in women's voices.

To Laure Conklin Kamp, my counselor, thank you for helping me find the trail out of the woods.

To the readers, thank you for picking up this book. I hope, somewhere in these pages, you feel seen. I hope it lingers.

And to Ric—my partner, my love—wherever you've flown to, I imagine you scouting out a perfect feeder, chirping with joy at the beauty below. You are in every chapter. You always will be.

Thank you. Merci. Asante. Shukran. Ci Locda Teeth.

ABOUT THE AUTHOR

Sheila Kimble-Haas, a nurse practitioner and midwife who graduated from the University of Pennsylvania, dedicated her career to caring for marginalized communities. She practiced in Native American reservations, remote Arctic villages, and various African nations through humanitarian groups.

After more than ten years in France, she returned to the Southwest. In Las Cruces, New Mexico, she found what she needed: the stark beauty of the desert, a community of friends, and enough solitude to put her stories on paper.

But those itchy feet never rest for long. They're drawing her back across the Atlantic to France, carrying with her the desert's lessons and an unquenchable thirst for the road ahead.

Author photo © Lisa Mayhew-Ortiz

Looking for your next great read?

We can help!

Visit www.shewritespress.com/next-read
or scan the QR code below for a list
of our recommended titles.

She Writes Press is an award-winning
independent publishing company founded to
serve women writers everywhere.